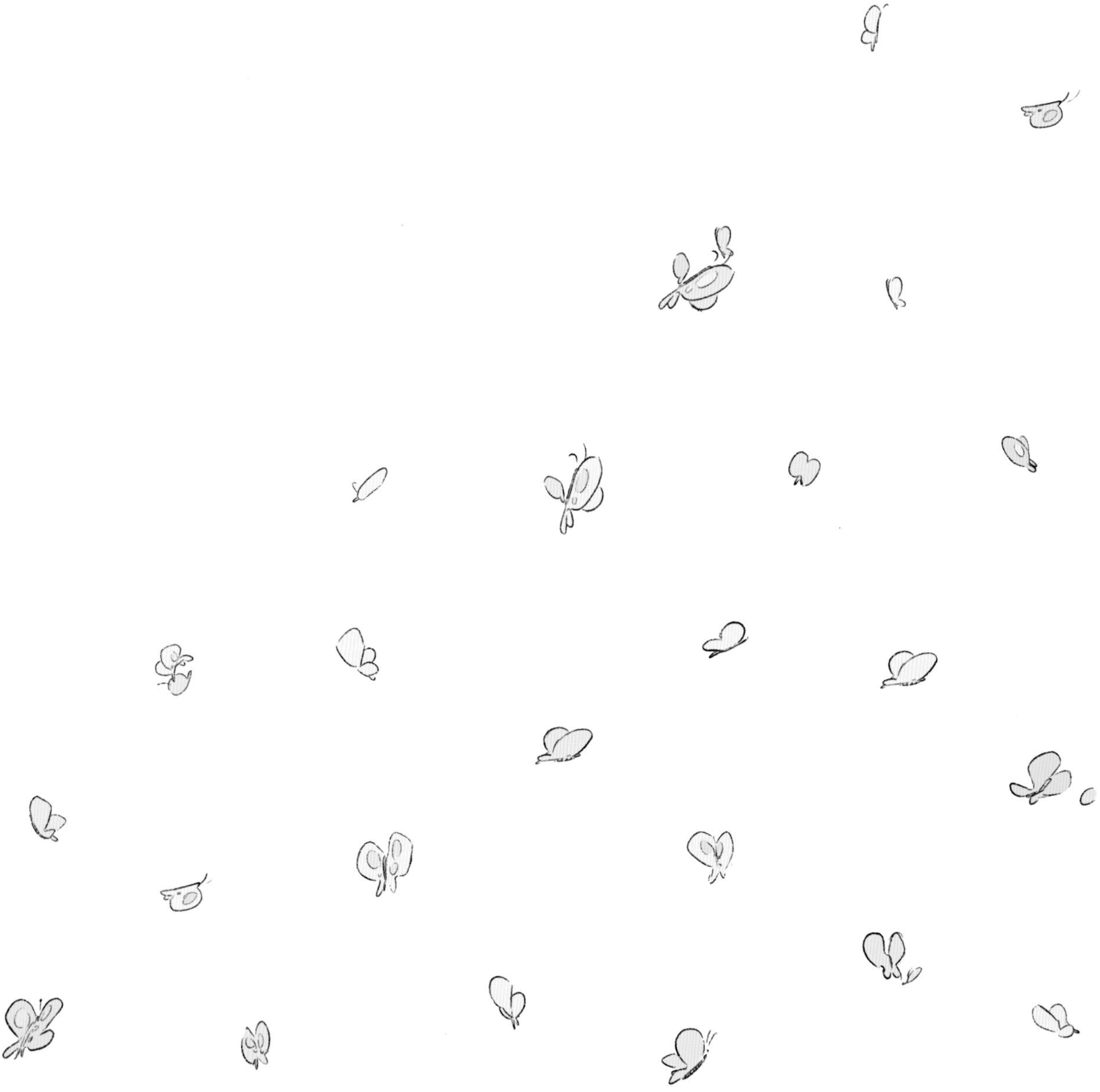

Always Never ™

Writer and artist
Jordi Lafebre

Colorists
Clémence Sapin
Jordi Lafebre

English Translation by
Montana Kane

Lettering by
Cromatik Ltd.

Dark Horse Books

President and Publisher

Mike Richardson

Editor

Konner Knudsen

Collection designer

May Hijikuro

Digital art technician

Samantha Hummer

Neil Hankerson **Executive Vice President** Tom Weddle **Chief Financial Officer** Dale LaFountain **Chief Information Officer** Tim Wiesch **Vice President of Licensing** Vanessa Todd-Holmes **Vice President of Production and Scheduling** Mark Bernardi **Vice President of Book Trade and Digital Sales** Randy Lahrman **Vice President of Product Development and Sales** Cara O'Neil **Vice President of Marketing** Ken Lizzi **General Counsel** Dave Marshall **Editor in Chief** Davey Estrada **Editorial Director** Chris Warner **Senior Books Editor** Cary Grazzini **Director of Specialty Projects** Lia Ribacchi **Creative Director** Michael Gombos **Senior Director of Licensed Publications** Kari Yadro **Director of Custom Programs** Kari Torson **Director of International Licensing** Christina Niece **Director of Scheduling**

Published by Dark Horse Books
A division of Dark Horse Comics LLC
10956 SE Main Street, Milwaukie, OR 97222

ads@darkhorse.com | ComicShopLocator.com

Originally published as "Malgré Tout" by Europe Comics
Edited by Anna Howell
Translated by Montana Kane
Graphic design and artistic direction by Philippe Ravon

©2020 DARGAUD BENELUX (DARGAUD-LOMBARD S.A.)
www.dargaud.com | www.europecomics.com

First edition: August 2022
Ebook ISBN 978-1-50673-138-4 | Hardcover ISBN 978-1-50673-137-7

3 5 7 9 10 8 6 4 2
Printed in China

Library of Congress Cataloging-in-Publication Data

Names: Lafebre, Jordi, 1979- author, artist. | Sapin, Clémence, colourist. | Kane, Montana, translator.
Title: Always never / created, written, and drawn by Jordi Lafebre ; colorists, Clémence Sapin and Jordi Lafebre ; English translation by Montana Kane.
Other titles: Malgré tout. English
Description: First edition. | Milwaukie, OR : Dark Horse Books, 2022. | Summary: "After forty years of being madly in love, Ana and Zeno are finally retiring and giving their romance a chance to bloom while they both still have time left. A unique but relatable love story told in reverse, with each chapter stepping further back through the decades of touch and go courting, showing both the heartbreaking moments that kept the two lovers apart and the beautiful moments that kept their flame alive"– Provided by publisher.
Identifiers: LCCN 2022000683 (print) | LCCN 2022000684 (ebook) | ISBN 9781506731377 (hardcover) | ISBN 9781506731384 (ebook)
Subjects: LCGFT: Romance comics. | Graphic novels.
Classification: LCC PN6747.L336 M3513 2022 (print) | LCC PN6747.L336 (ebook) | DDC 741.5/944–dc23/eng/20220204
LC record available at https://lccn.loc.gov/2022000683
LC ebook record available at https://lccn.loc.gov/2022000684

Love, that exempts no one beloved from loving.
DANTE
The Divine Comedy
Inferno, Canto V, verse 103

We are human after all.
DAFT PUNK

A big thank you to Ryun Reuchamps, Javi Rey, Andrea Jofre, and Mar Català for reading over my script dozens of times.

Thank you to Matteo Alemanno for his advice on Venice, and to Maria Nicolau for the menu in Chapter 4.

Thank you to all those—credited or not—who supported and helped me during the making of this book.

Thank you, Mar, for your support, love, and patience.

Jordi

CHAPTER
20

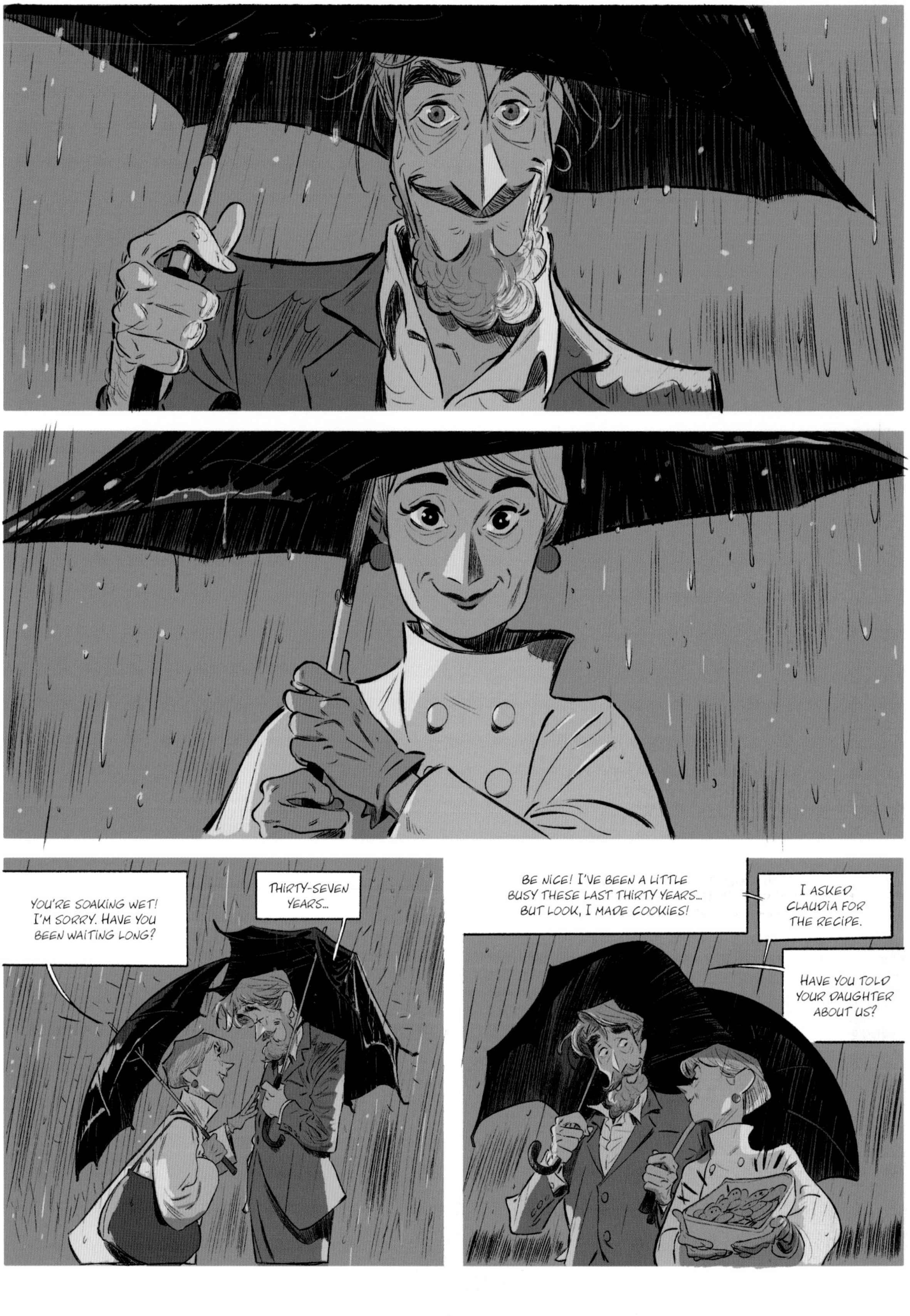
YOU'RE SOAKING WET! I'M SORRY. HAVE YOU BEEN WAITING LONG?
THIRTY-SEVEN YEARS...
BE NICE! I'VE BEEN A LITTLE BUSY THESE LAST THIRTY YEARS... BUT LOOK, I MADE COOKIES!
I ASKED CLAUDIA FOR THE RECIPE.
HAVE YOU TOLD YOUR DAUGHTER ABOUT US?

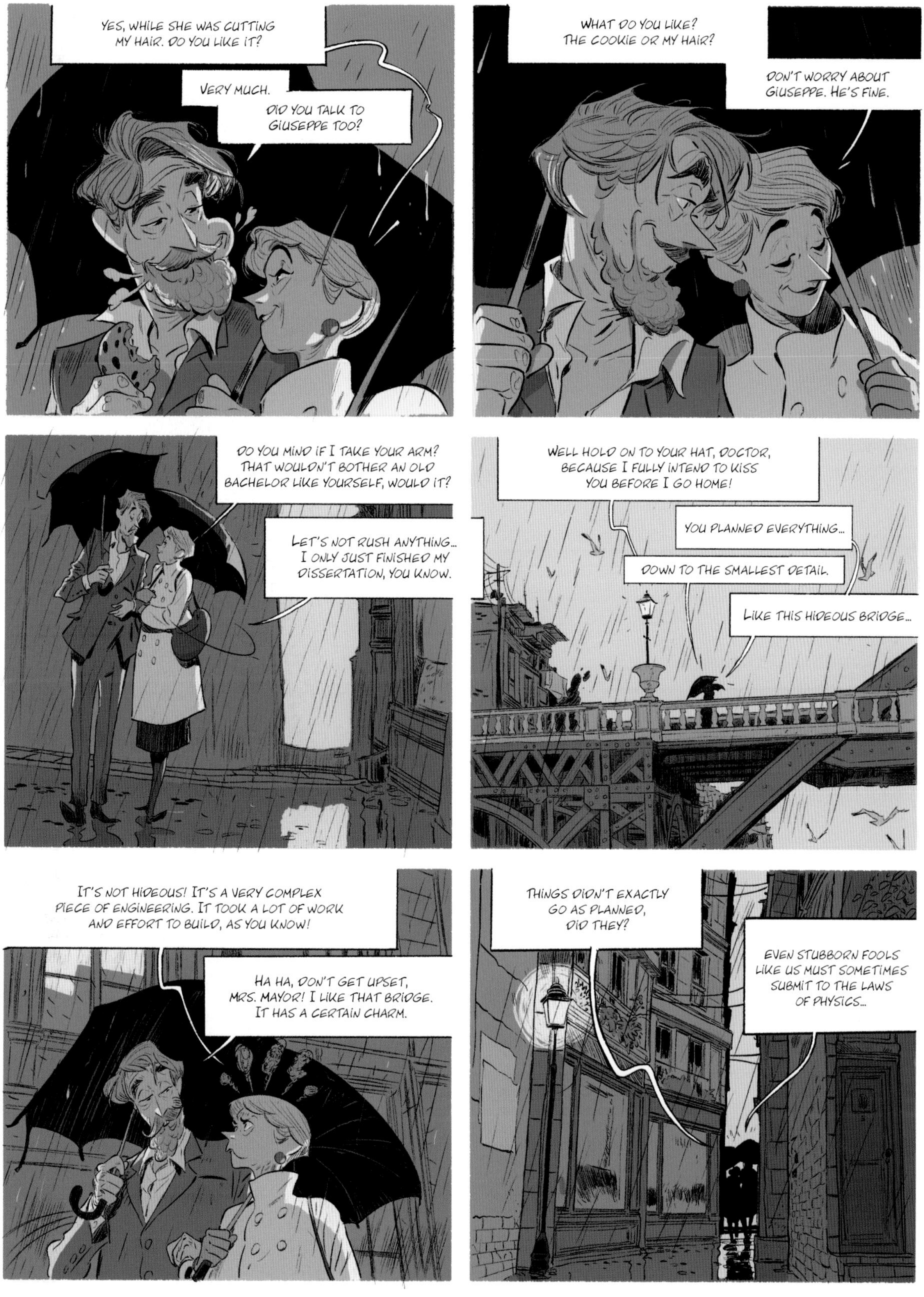
YES, WHILE SHE WAS CUTTING MY HAIR. DO YOU LIKE IT?
VERY MUCH.
DID YOU TALK TO GIUSEPPE TOO?
WHAT DO YOU LIKE? THE COOKIE OR MY HAIR?
DON'T WORRY ABOUT GIUSEPPE. HE'S FINE.
DO YOU MIND IF I TAKE YOUR ARM? THAT WOULDN'T BOTHER AN OLD BACHELOR LIKE YOURSELF, WOULD IT?
LET'S NOT RUSH ANYTHING... I ONLY JUST FINISHED MY DISSERTATION, YOU KNOW.
WELL HOLD ON TO YOUR HAT, DOCTOR, BECAUSE I FULLY INTEND TO KISS YOU BEFORE I GO HOME!
YOU PLANNED EVERYTHING...
DOWN TO THE SMALLEST DETAIL.
LIKE THIS HIDEOUS BRIDGE...
IT'S NOT HIDEOUS! IT'S A VERY COMPLEX PIECE OF ENGINEERING. IT TOOK A LOT OF WORK AND EFFORT TO BUILD, AS YOU KNOW!
HA HA, DON'T GET UPSET, MRS. MAYOR! I LIKE THAT BRIDGE. IT HAS A CERTAIN CHARM.
THINGS DIDN'T EXACTLY GO AS PLANNED, DID THEY?
EVEN STUBBORN FOOLS LIKE US MUST SOMETIMES SUBMIT TO THE LAWS OF PHYSICS...

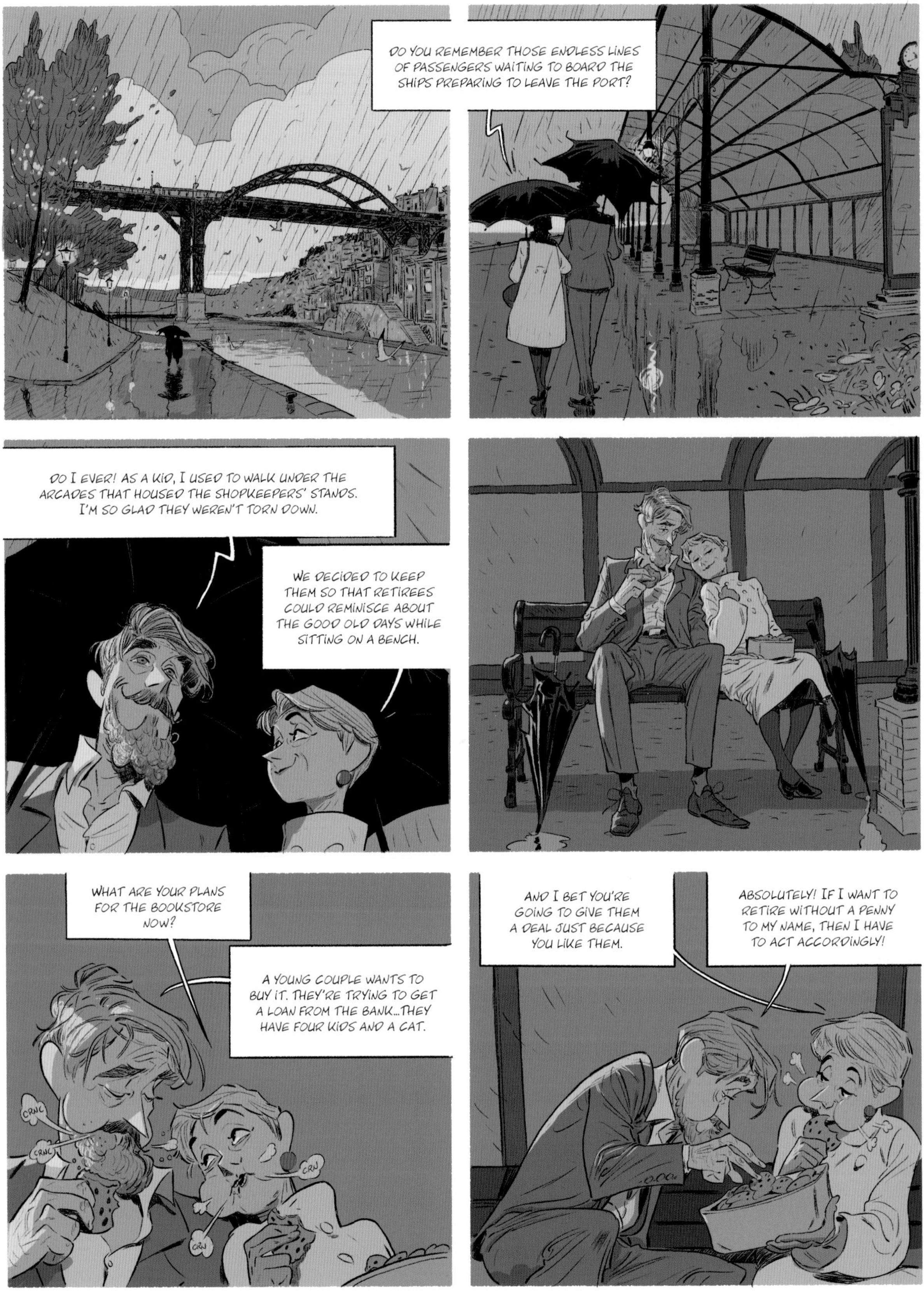
DO YOU REMEMBER THOSE ENDLESS LINES OF PASSENGERS WAITING TO BOARD THE SHIPS PREPARING TO LEAVE THE PORT?
DO I EVER! AS A KID, I USED TO WALK UNDER THE ARCADES THAT HOUSED THE SHOPKEEPERS' STANDS. I'M SO GLAD THEY WEREN'T TORN DOWN.
WE DECIDED TO KEEP THEM SO THAT RETIREES COULD REMINISCE ABOUT THE GOOD OLD DAYS WHILE SITTING ON A BENCH.
WHAT ARE YOUR PLANS FOR THE BOOKSTORE NOW?
A YOUNG COUPLE WANTS TO BUY IT. THEY'RE TRYING TO GET A LOAN FROM THE BANK...THEY HAVE FOUR KIDS AND A CAT.
AND I BET YOU'RE GOING TO GIVE THEM A DEAL JUST BECAUSE YOU LIKE THEM.
ABSOLUTELY! IF I WANT TO RETIRE WITHOUT A PENNY TO MY NAME, THEN I HAVE TO ACT ACCORDINGLY!

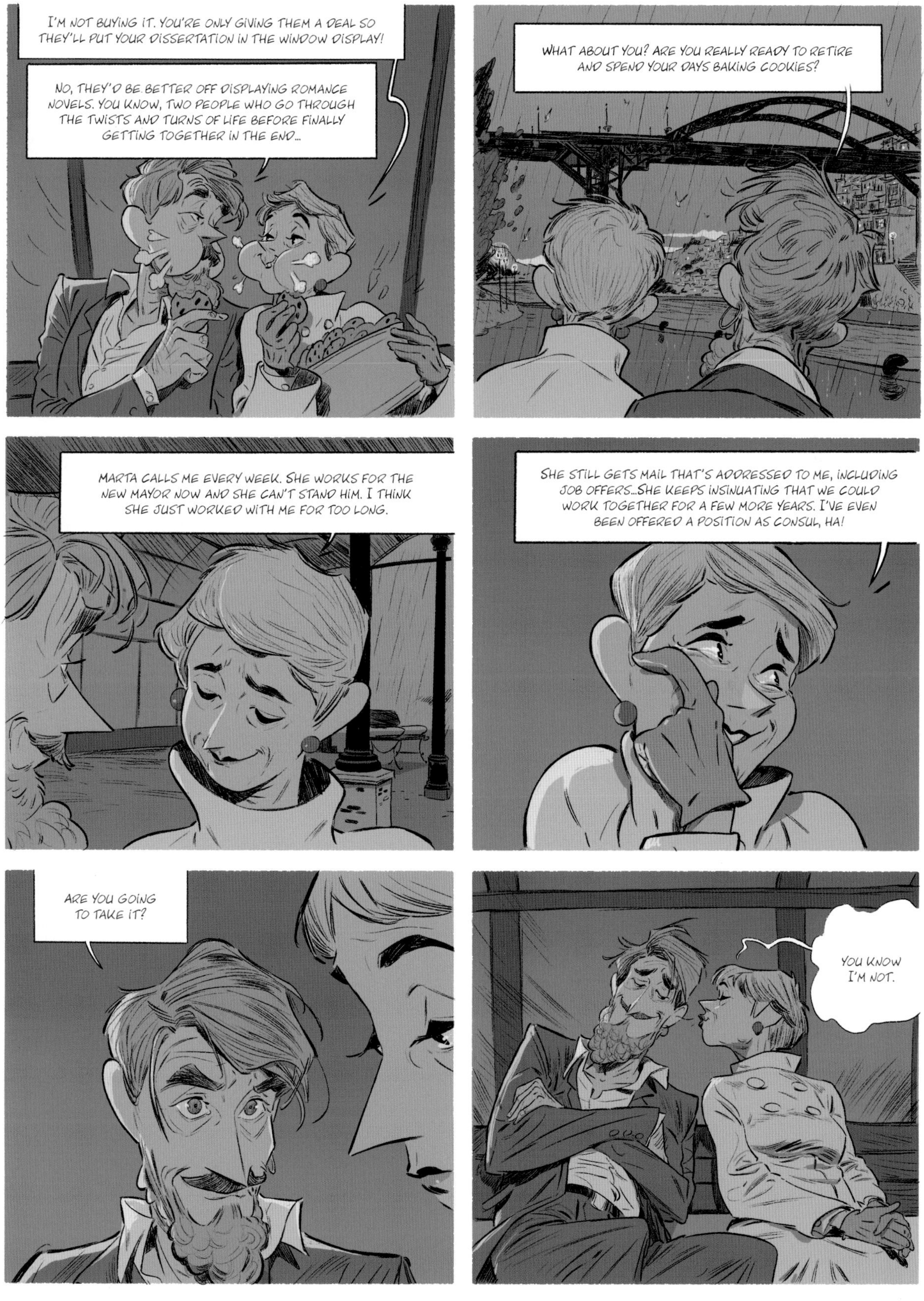
I'M NOT BUYING IT. YOU'RE ONLY GIVING THEM A DEAL SO THEY'LL PUT YOUR DISSERTATION IN THE WINDOW DISPLAY!
NO, THEY'D BE BETTER OFF DISPLAYING ROMANCE NOVELS. YOU KNOW, TWO PEOPLE WHO GO THROUGH THE TWISTS AND TURNS OF LIFE BEFORE FINALLY GETTING TOGETHER IN THE END...
WHAT ABOUT YOU? ARE YOU REALLY READY TO RETIRE AND SPEND YOUR DAYS BAKING COOKIES?
MARTA CALLS ME EVERY WEEK. SHE WORKS FOR THE NEW MAYOR NOW AND SHE CAN'T STAND HIM. I THINK SHE JUST WORKED WITH ME FOR TOO LONG.
SHE STILL GETS MAIL THAT'S ADDRESSED TO ME, INCLUDING JOB OFFERS...SHE KEEPS INSINUATING THAT WE COULD WORK TOGETHER FOR A FEW MORE YEARS. I'VE EVEN BEEN OFFERED A POSITION AS CONSUL, HA!
ARE YOU GOING TO TAKE IT?
YOU KNOW I'M NOT.

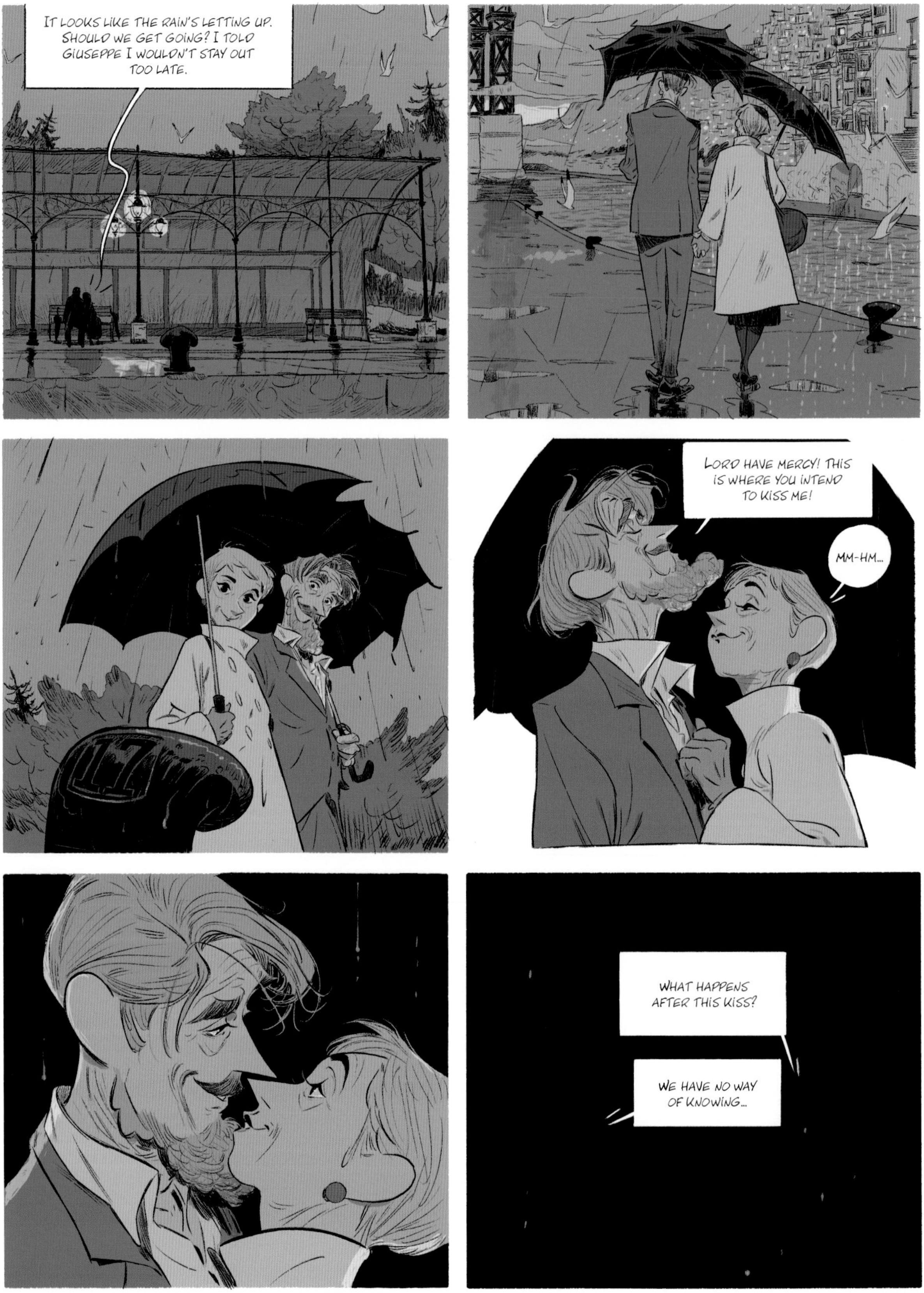
IT LOOKS LIKE THE RAIN'S LETTING UP. SHOULD WE GET GOING? I TOLD GIUSEPPE I WOULDN'T STAY OUT TOO LATE.
LORD HAVE MERCY! THIS IS WHERE YOU INTEND TO KISS ME!
MM-HM...
WHAT HAPPENS AFTER THIS KISS?
WE HAVE NO WAY OF KNOWING...

CHAPTER
19

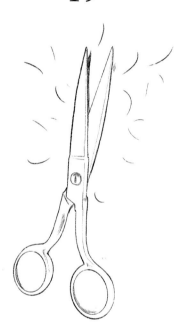

YOU HAVE TO REALLY KNEAD THE DOUGH TO GET RID OF THE LUMPS, AND LET IT REST SO THE SPICES CAN RELEASE THEIR FLAVORS.

BAKING REQUIRES PATIENCE, WHICH WE BOTH KNOW ISN'T ALWAYS YOUR STRONG SUIT...

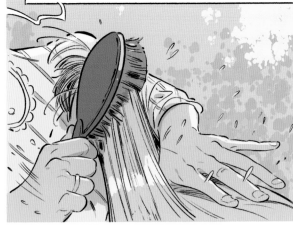

TAKE YOUR HAIR, FOR EXAMPLE! SURE, IT TAKES TIME, BUT IT'S GORGEOUS. IT'S REALLY A SHAME TO CUT IT.

BUT SO BE IT. THEN YOU ROLL THE DOUGH INTO SMALL BALLS AND STICK THEM IN THE OVEN...

NOT TOO HOT, MIND YOU! COOKIES DON'T LIKE IT ROUGH!

CHAK

ARE YOU SURE YOU WANT TO CHOP IT ALL OFF?

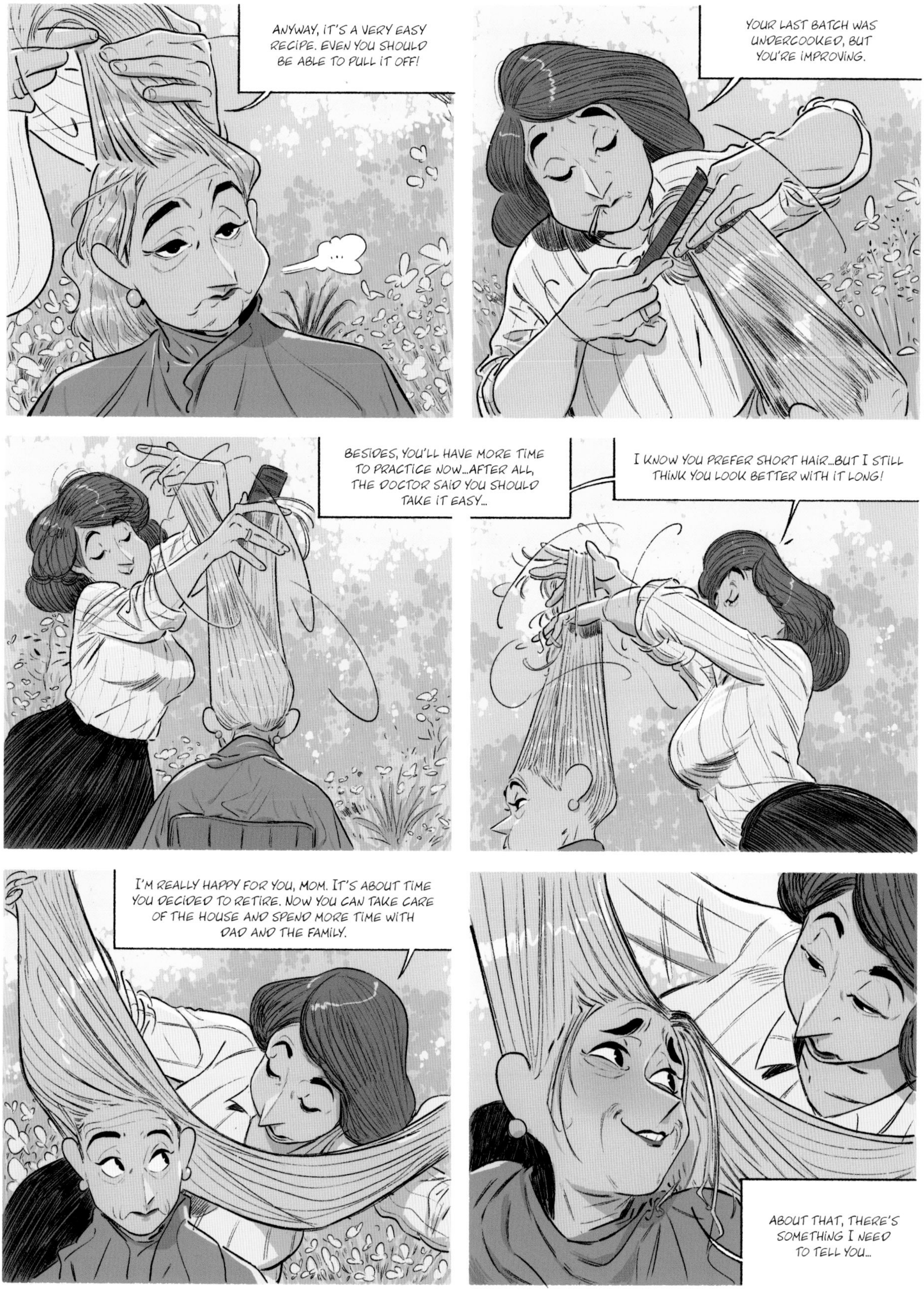
ANYWAY, IT'S A VERY EASY RECIPE. EVEN YOU SHOULD BE ABLE TO PULL IT OFF!
...
YOUR LAST BATCH WAS UNDERCOOKED, BUT YOU'RE IMPROVING.
BESIDES, YOU'LL HAVE MORE TIME TO PRACTICE NOW...AFTER ALL, THE DOCTOR SAID YOU SHOULD TAKE IT EASY...
I KNOW YOU PREFER SHORT HAIR...BUT I STILL THINK YOU LOOK BETTER WITH IT LONG!
I'M REALLY HAPPY FOR YOU, MOM. IT'S ABOUT TIME YOU DECIDED TO RETIRE. NOW YOU CAN TAKE CARE OF THE HOUSE AND SPEND MORE TIME WITH DAD AND THE FAMILY.
ABOUT THAT, THERE'S SOMETHING I NEED TO TELL YOU...

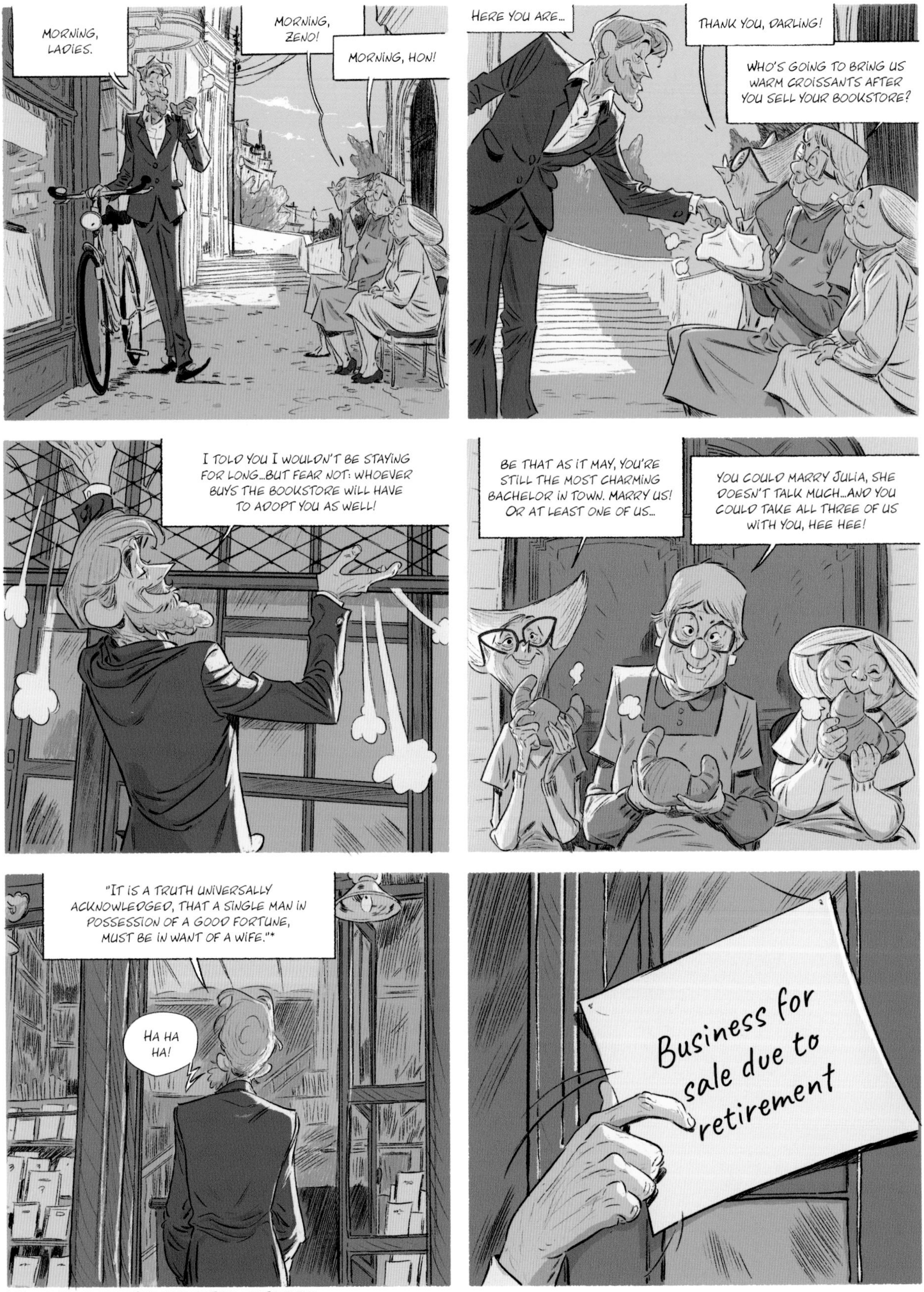
MORNING, LADIES.
MORNING, ZENO!
MORNING, HON!
HERE YOU ARE...
THANK YOU, DARLING!
WHO'S GOING TO BRING US WARM CROISSANTS AFTER YOU SELL YOUR BOOKSTORE?
I TOLD YOU I WOULDN'T BE STAYING FOR LONG...BUT FEAR NOT: WHOEVER BUYS THE BOOKSTORE WILL HAVE TO ADOPT YOU AS WELL!
BE THAT AS IT MAY, YOU'RE STILL THE MOST CHARMING BACHELOR IN TOWN. MARRY US! OR AT LEAST ONE OF US...
YOU COULD MARRY JULIA, SHE DOESN'T TALK MUCH...AND YOU COULD TAKE ALL THREE OF US WITH YOU, HEE HEE!
"IT IS A TRUTH UNIVERSALLY ACKNOWLEDGED, THAT A SINGLE MAN IN POSSESSION OF A GOOD FORTUNE, MUST BE IN WANT OF A WIFE."*
HA HA HA!
Business for sale due to retirement

* THE OPENING WORDS OF JANE AUSTEN'S *PRIDE AND PREJUDICE*.

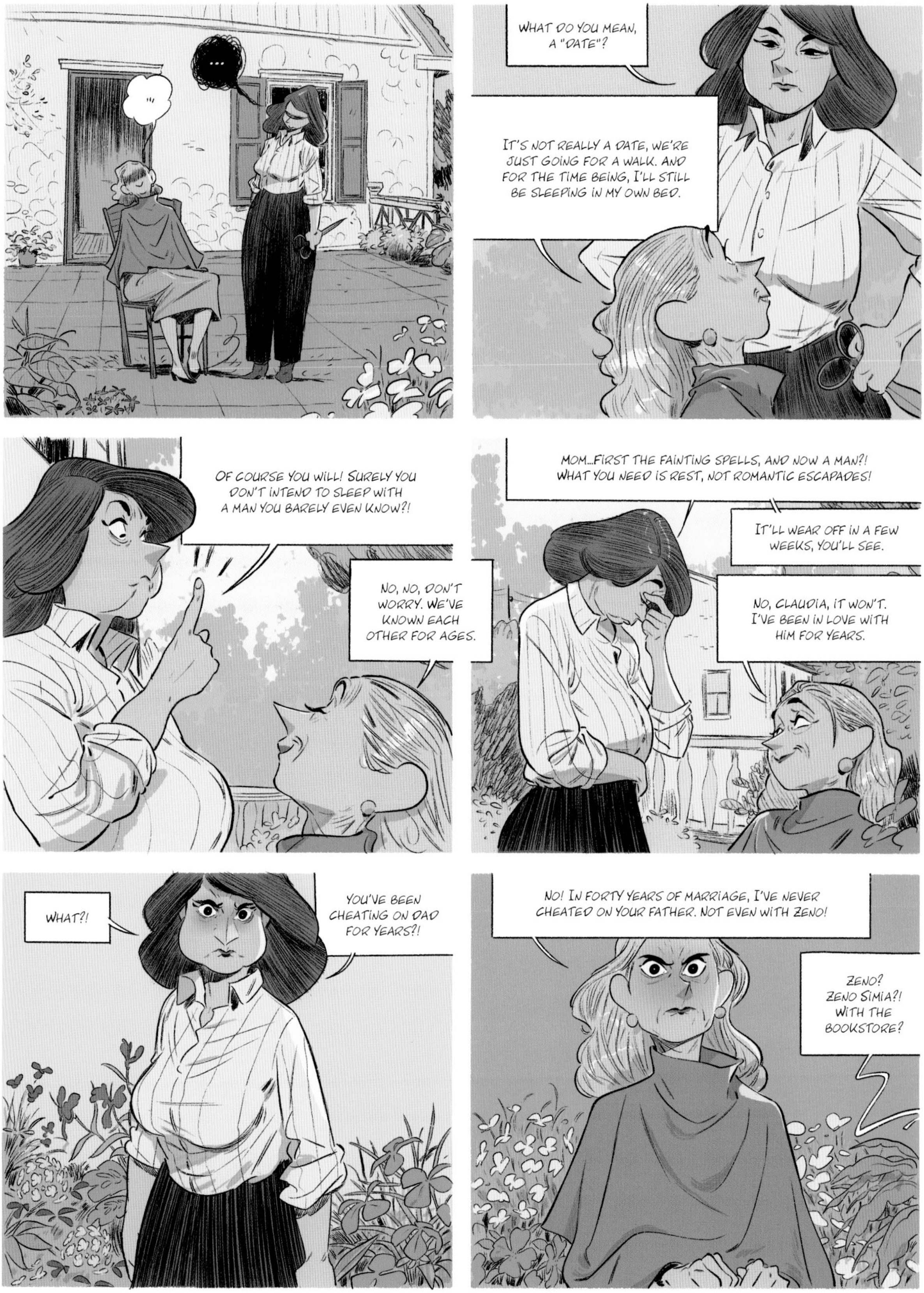
...
...
WHAT DO YOU MEAN, A "DATE"?
IT'S NOT REALLY A DATE, WE'RE JUST GOING FOR A WALK. AND FOR THE TIME BEING, I'LL STILL BE SLEEPING IN MY OWN BED.
OF COURSE YOU WILL! SURELY YOU DON'T INTEND TO SLEEP WITH A MAN YOU BARELY EVEN KNOW?!
NO, NO, DON'T WORRY. WE'VE KNOWN EACH OTHER FOR AGES.
MOM...FIRST THE FAINTING SPELLS, AND NOW A MAN?! WHAT YOU NEED IS REST, NOT ROMANTIC ESCAPADES!
IT'LL WEAR OFF IN A FEW WEEKS, YOU'LL SEE.
NO, CLAUDIA, IT WON'T. I'VE BEEN IN LOVE WITH HIM FOR YEARS.
WHAT?!
YOU'VE BEEN CHEATING ON DAD FOR YEARS?!
NO! IN FORTY YEARS OF MARRIAGE, I'VE NEVER CHEATED ON YOUR FATHER. NOT EVEN WITH ZENO!
ZENO? ZENO SIMIA?! WITH THE BOOKSTORE?

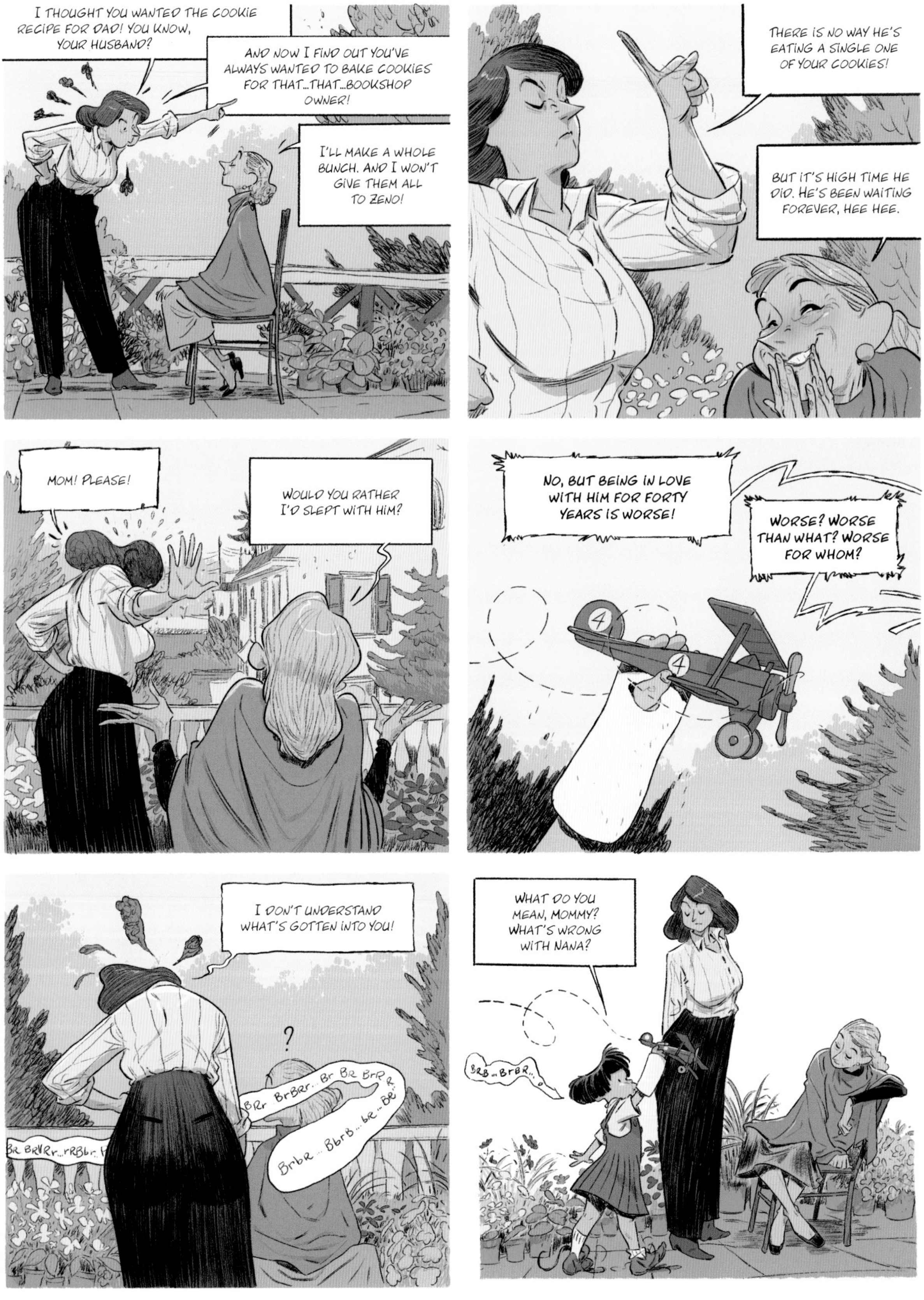
I THOUGHT YOU WANTED THE COOKIE RECIPE FOR DAD! YOU KNOW, YOUR HUSBAND?
AND NOW I FIND OUT YOU'VE ALWAYS WANTED TO BAKE COOKIES FOR THAT...THAT...BOOKSHOP OWNER!
I'LL MAKE A WHOLE BUNCH. AND I WON'T GIVE THEM ALL TO ZENO!
THERE IS NO WAY HE'S EATING A SINGLE ONE OF YOUR COOKIES!
BUT IT'S HIGH TIME HE DID. HE'S BEEN WAITING FOREVER, HEE HEE.
MOM! PLEASE!
WOULD YOU RATHER I'D SLEPT WITH HIM?
NO, BUT BEING IN LOVE WITH HIM FOR FORTY YEARS IS WORSE!
WORSE? WORSE THAN WHAT? WORSE FOR WHOM?
I DON'T UNDERSTAND WHAT'S GOTTEN INTO YOU!
?
BRr BrBRr... Br BR BrR R
BrbR... BbrB... bR... BR
WHAT DO YOU MEAN, MOMMY? WHAT'S WRONG WITH NANA?
BRB... BrBR...

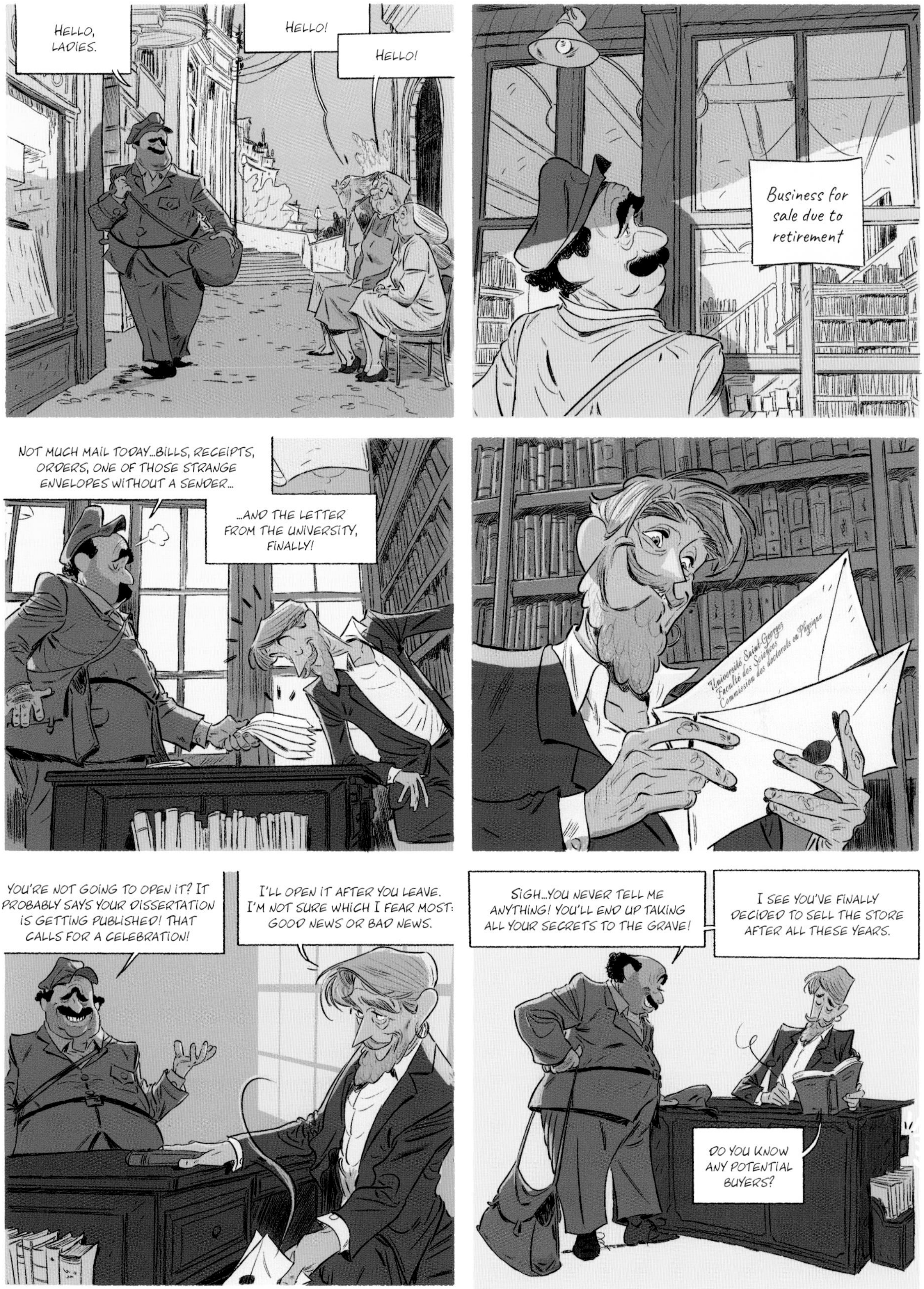
HELLO, LADIES.
HELLO!
HELLO!
Business for sale due to retirement
NOT MUCH MAIL TODAY...BILLS, RECEIPTS, ORDERS, ONE OF THOSE STRANGE ENVELOPES WITHOUT A SENDER...
...AND THE LETTER FROM THE UNIVERSITY, FINALLY!
Université Saint-Georges
Faculté des Sciences
Commission des doctorats en Physique
YOU'RE NOT GOING TO OPEN IT? IT PROBABLY SAYS YOUR DISSERTATION IS GETTING PUBLISHED! THAT CALLS FOR A CELEBRATION!
I'LL OPEN IT AFTER YOU LEAVE. I'M NOT SURE WHICH I FEAR MOST: GOOD NEWS OR BAD NEWS.
SIGH...YOU NEVER TELL ME ANYTHING! YOU'LL END UP TAKING ALL YOUR SECRETS TO THE GRAVE!
I SEE YOU'VE FINALLY DECIDED TO SELL THE STORE AFTER ALL THESE YEARS.
DO YOU KNOW ANY POTENTIAL BUYERS?

ACTUALLY, ONE OF MY COUSINS IS MOVING TO THE NEIGHBORHOOD. LOOKING TO TAKE OVER A BUSINESS. HE AND HIS WIFE HAVE FOUR KIDS AND A CAT. SO LOTS OF MOUTHS TO FEED. MAYBE YOU COULD GIVE THEM A GOOD DEAL?

TELL THEM TO STOP BY, I'D LOVE TO MEET THEM!

LET'S BE HONEST, THIS PLACE COULD USE A LITTLE FAMILY-RUN ATMOSPHERE...

SO NOW THAT YOU HAVE YOUR DOCTORATE, YOU'RE LEAVING AGAIN?

I NEVER STAY FOR VERY LONG...AND I DOUBT ANYBODY WILL MISS ME.

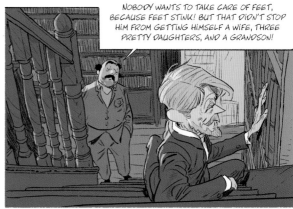

ONE OF MY BROTHERS IS A DOCTOR. A PODIATRIST, AND A GOOD ONE! MY FEET TAKE A BEATING WITH ALL THE WALKING I DO EVERY DAY, BUT HE ALWAYS MAKES THEM GOOD AS NEW!

NOBODY WANTS TO TAKE CARE OF FEET, BECAUSE FEET STINK! BUT THAT DIDN'T STOP HIM FROM GETTING HIMSELF A WIFE, THREE PRETTY DAUGHTERS, AND A GRANDSON!

I'M NOT A PHYSICIAN, I HAVE A DOCTORATE IN PHYSICS.

PHYSICIST, PHYSICIAN...SAME DIFFERENCE! EITHER WAY, DOCTOR OR NOT, IT'S NOT GOOD FOR A MAN TO BE ALONE! TRAVELING AROUND THE WORLD LIKE A VAGABOND, GROWING OLD ALONE...

DON'T WORRY ABOUT ME, I'VE RECEIVED PLENTY OF MARRIAGE PROPOSALS.

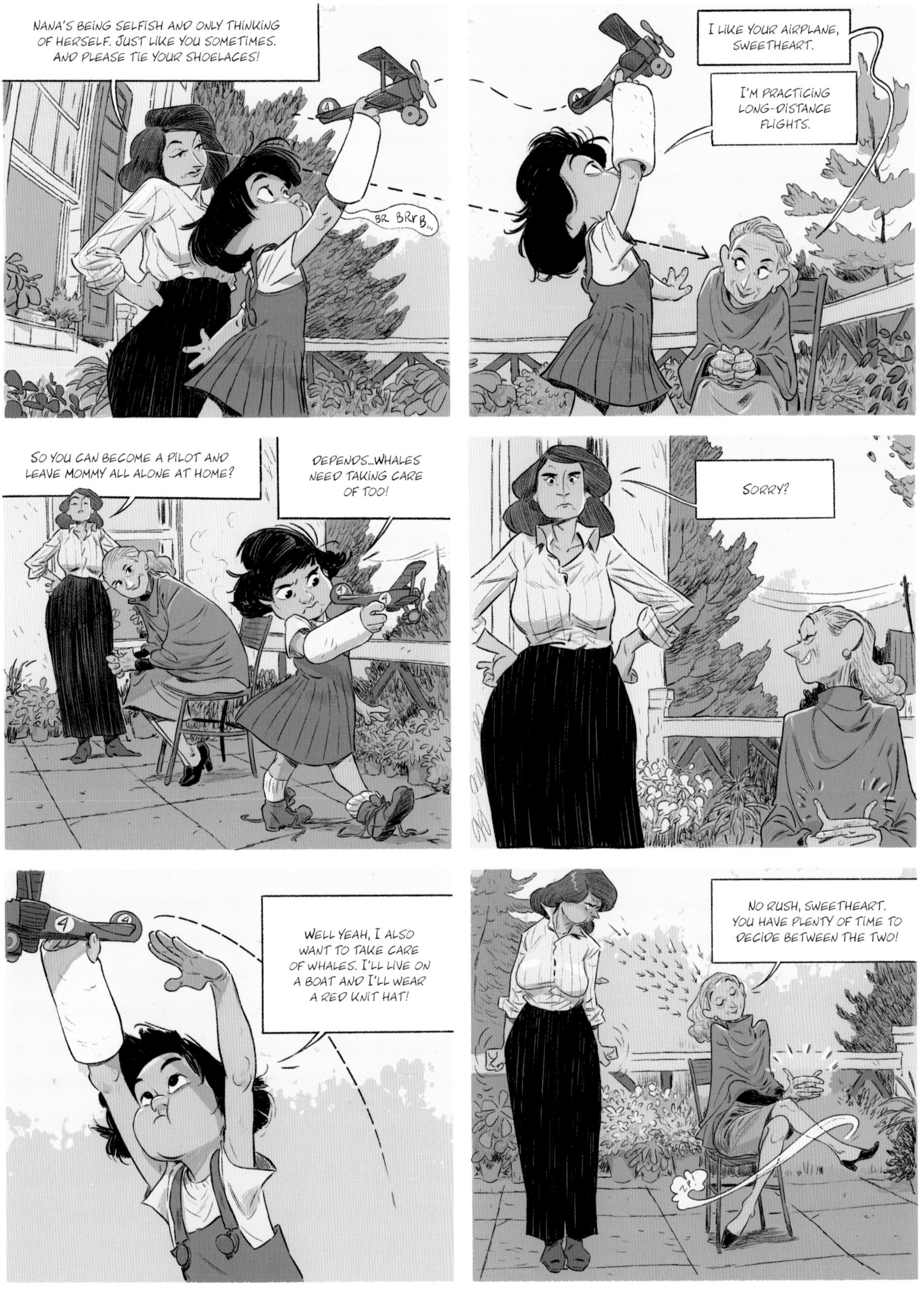

NANA'S BEING SELFISH AND ONLY THINKING OF HERSELF. JUST LIKE YOU SOMETIMES. AND PLEASE TIE YOUR SHOELACES!
BR BRrB...
I LIKE YOUR AIRPLANE, SWEETHEART.
I'M PRACTICING LONG-DISTANCE FLIGHTS.
SO YOU CAN BECOME A PILOT AND LEAVE MOMMY ALL ALONE AT HOME?
DEPENDS...WHALES NEED TAKING CARE OF TOO!
SORRY?
WELL YEAH, I ALSO WANT TO TAKE CARE OF WHALES. I'LL LIVE ON A BOAT AND I'LL WEAR A RED KNIT HAT!
NO RUSH, SWEETHEART. YOU HAVE PLENTY OF TIME TO DECIDE BETWEEN THE TWO!

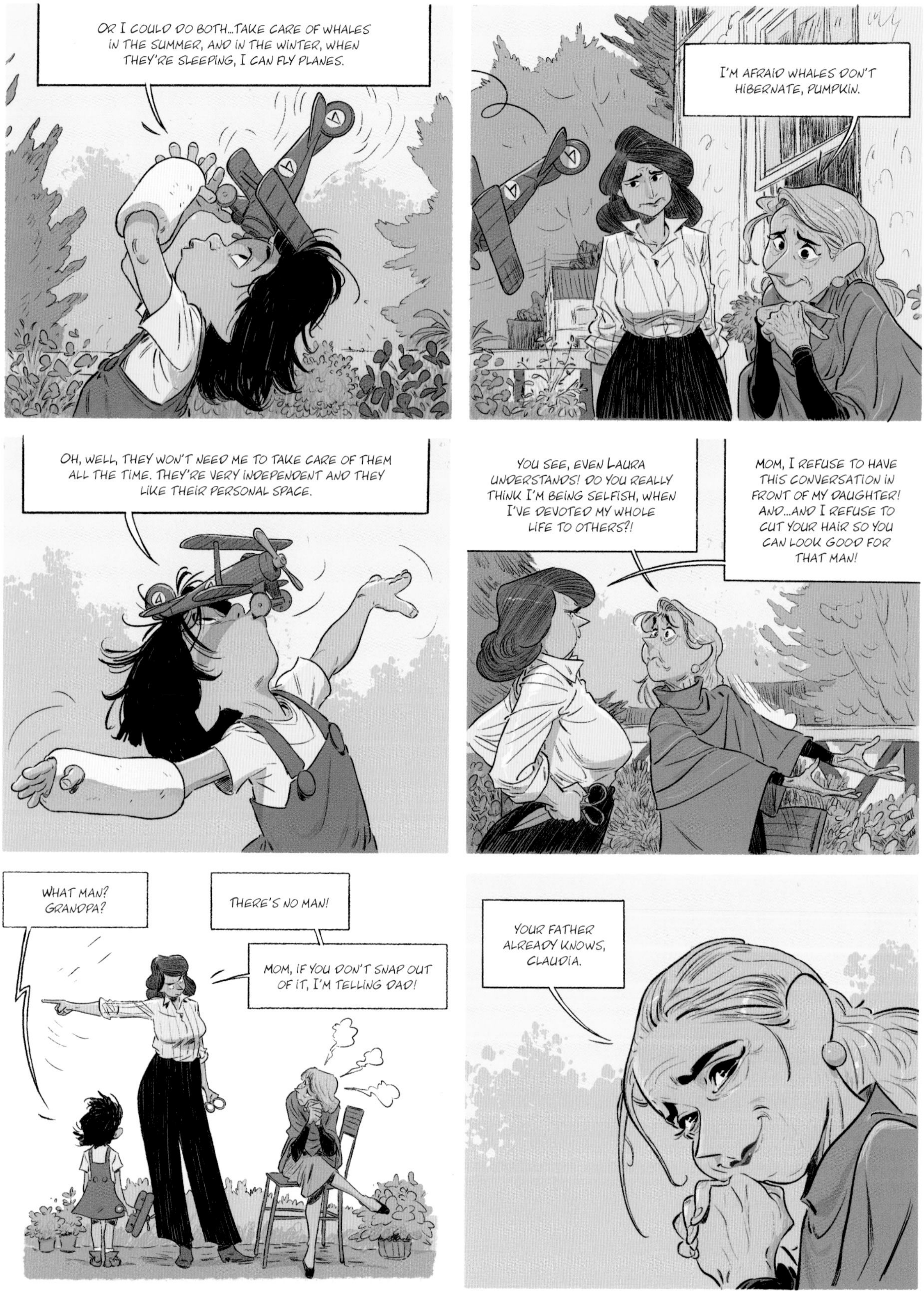
OR I COULD DO BOTH...TAKE CARE OF WHALES IN THE SUMMER, AND IN THE WINTER, WHEN THEY'RE SLEEPING, I CAN FLY PLANES.
I'M AFRAID WHALES DON'T HIBERNATE, PUMPKIN.
OH, WELL, THEY WON'T NEED ME TO TAKE CARE OF THEM ALL THE TIME. THEY'RE VERY INDEPENDENT AND THEY LIKE THEIR PERSONAL SPACE.
YOU SEE, EVEN LAURA UNDERSTANDS! DO YOU REALLY THINK I'M BEING SELFISH, WHEN I'VE DEVOTED MY WHOLE LIFE TO OTHERS?!
MOM, I REFUSE TO HAVE THIS CONVERSATION IN FRONT OF MY DAUGHTER! AND...AND I REFUSE TO CUT YOUR HAIR SO YOU CAN LOOK GOOD FOR THAT MAN!
WHAT MAN? GRANDPA?
THERE'S NO MAN!
MOM, IF YOU DON'T SNAP OUT OF IT, I'M TELLING DAD!
YOUR FATHER ALREADY KNOWS, CLAUDIA.

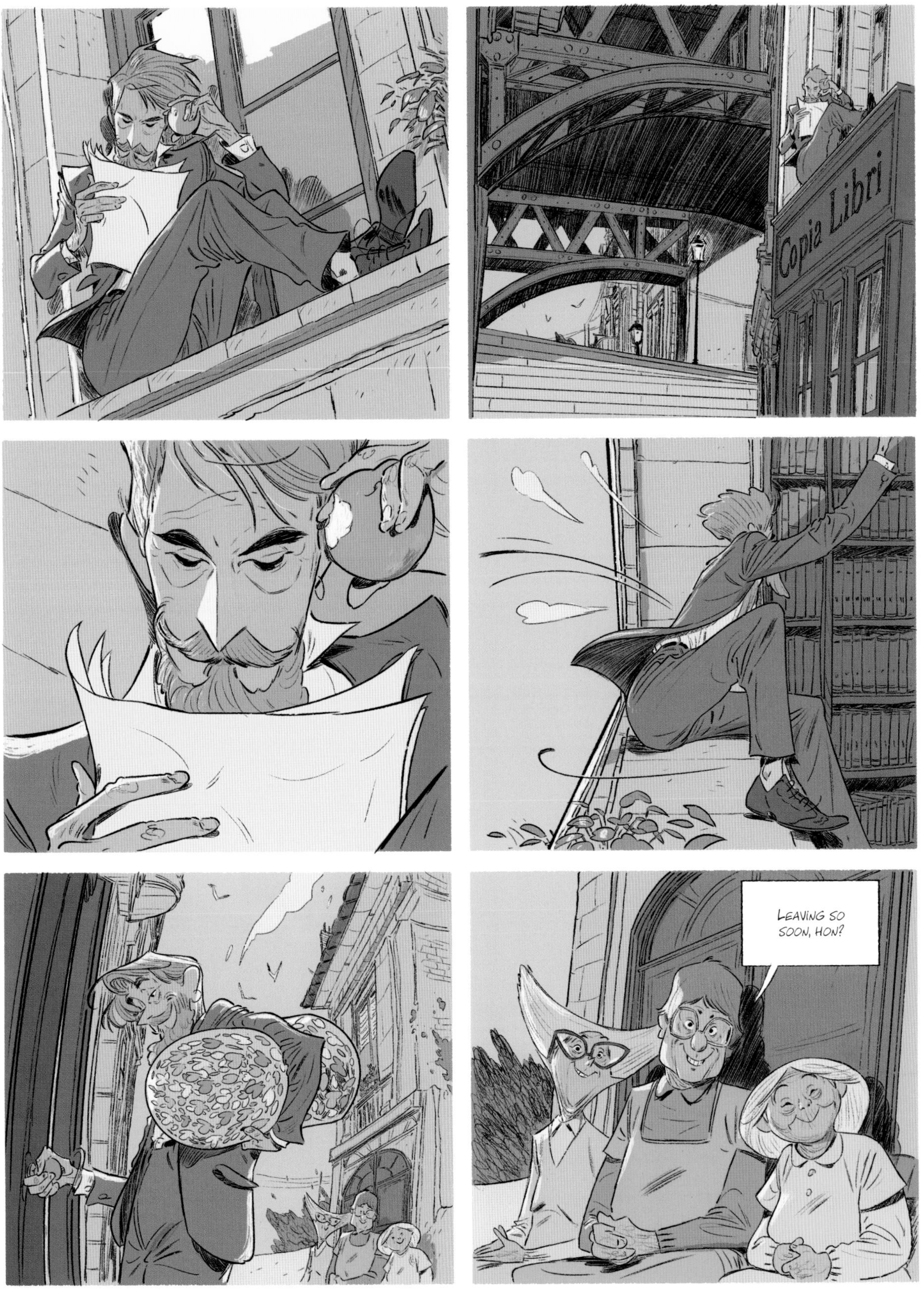
Copia Libri
Leaving so soon, hon?

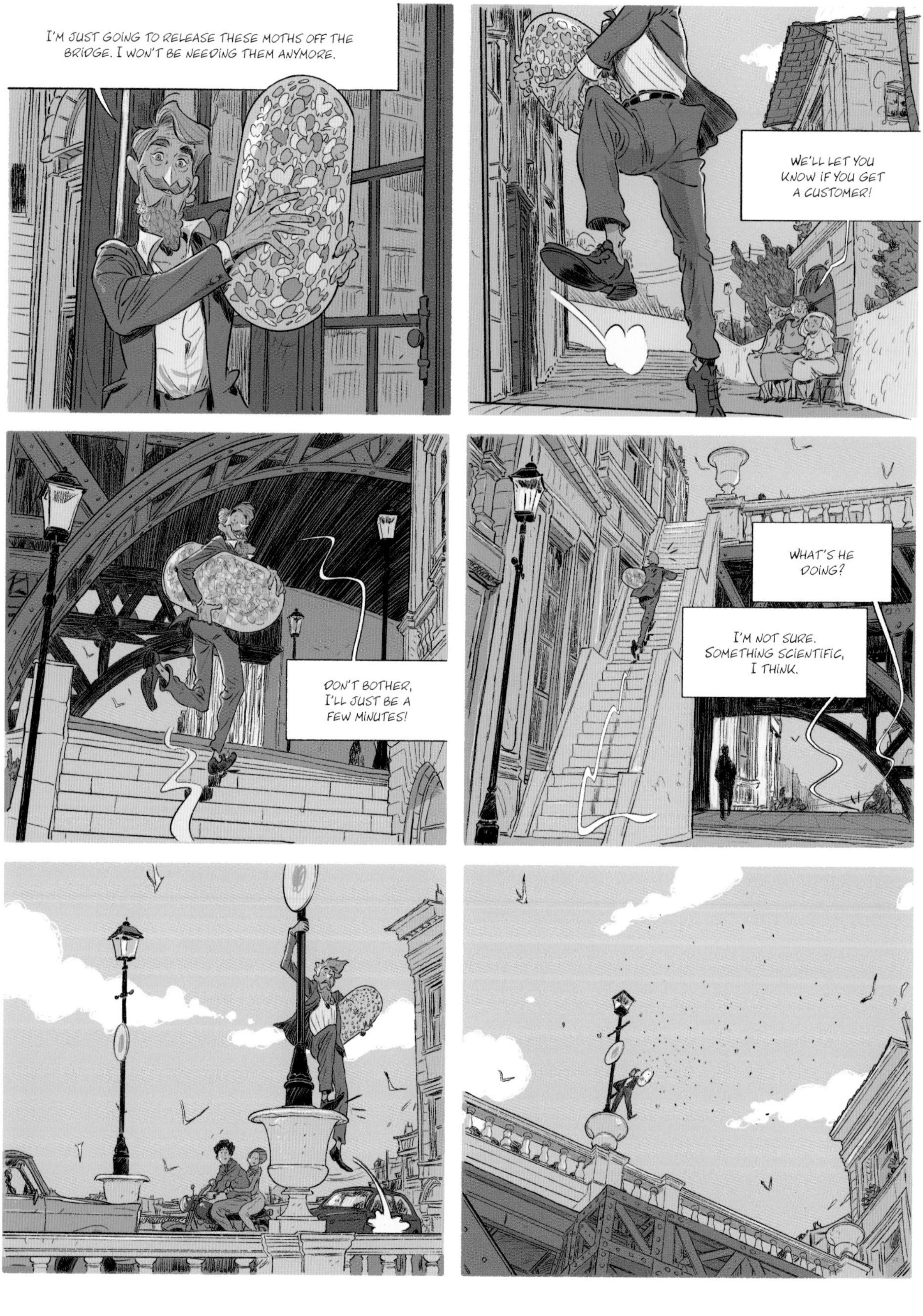
I'M JUST GOING TO RELEASE THESE MOTHS OFF THE BRIDGE. I WON'T BE NEEDING THEM ANYMORE.
WE'LL LET YOU KNOW IF YOU GET A CUSTOMER!
DON'T BOTHER, I'LL JUST BE A FEW MINUTES!
WHAT'S HE DOING?
I'M NOT SURE. SOMETHING SCIENTIFIC, I THINK.

CHAPTER 18

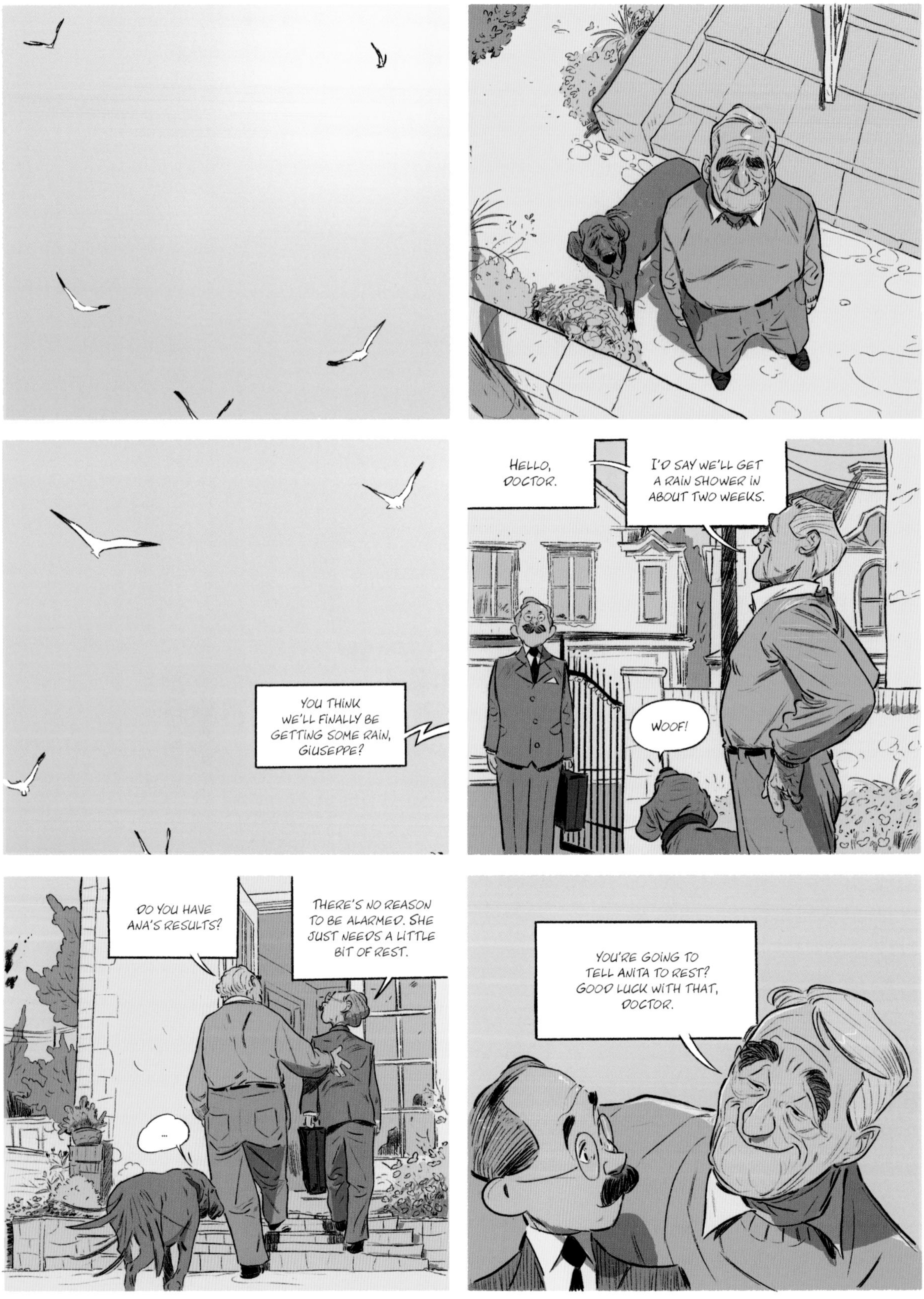

YOU THINK WE'LL FINALLY BE GETTING SOME RAIN, GIUSEPPE?
HELLO, DOCTOR.
I'D SAY WE'LL GET A RAIN SHOWER IN ABOUT TWO WEEKS.
WOOF!
DO YOU HAVE ANA'S RESULTS?
THERE'S NO REASON TO BE ALARMED. SHE JUST NEEDS A LITTLE BIT OF REST.
...
YOU'RE GOING TO TELL ANITA TO REST? GOOD LUCK WITH THAT, DOCTOR.

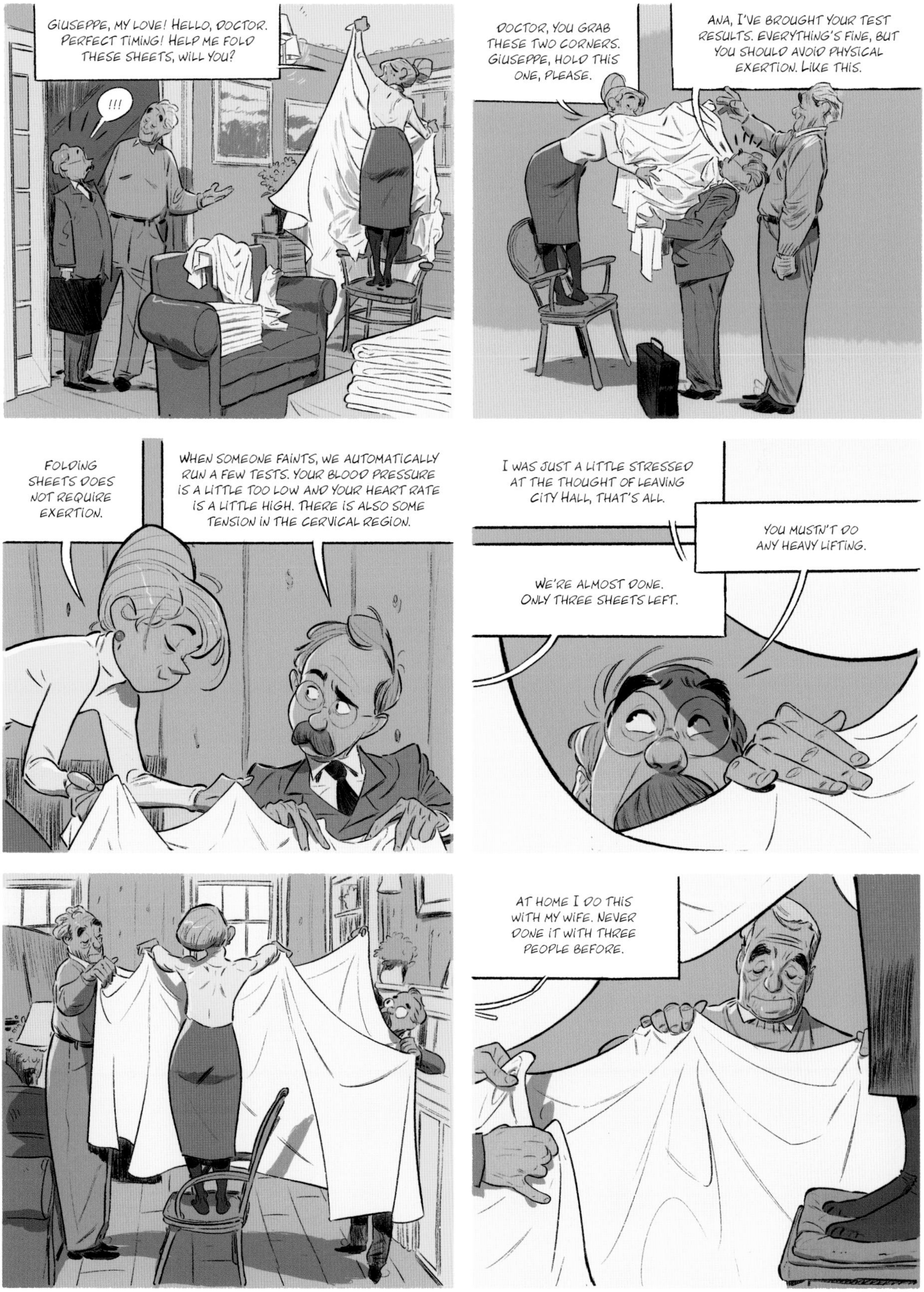
GIUSEPPE, MY LOVE! HELLO, DOCTOR. PERFECT TIMING! HELP ME FOLD THESE SHEETS, WILL YOU?
!!!
DOCTOR, YOU GRAB THESE TWO CORNERS. GIUSEPPE, HOLD THIS ONE, PLEASE.
ANA, I'VE BROUGHT YOUR TEST RESULTS. EVERYTHING'S FINE, BUT YOU SHOULD AVOID PHYSICAL EXERTION. LIKE THIS.
FOLDING SHEETS DOES NOT REQUIRE EXERTION.
WHEN SOMEONE FAINTS, WE AUTOMATICALLY RUN A FEW TESTS. YOUR BLOOD PRESSURE IS A LITTLE TOO LOW AND YOUR HEART RATE IS A LITTLE HIGH. THERE IS ALSO SOME TENSION IN THE CERVICAL REGION.
I WAS JUST A LITTLE STRESSED AT THE THOUGHT OF LEAVING CITY HALL, THAT'S ALL.
YOU MUSTN'T DO ANY HEAVY LIFTING.
WE'RE ALMOST DONE. ONLY THREE SHEETS LEFT.
AT HOME I DO THIS WITH MY WIFE. NEVER DONE IT WITH THREE PEOPLE BEFORE.

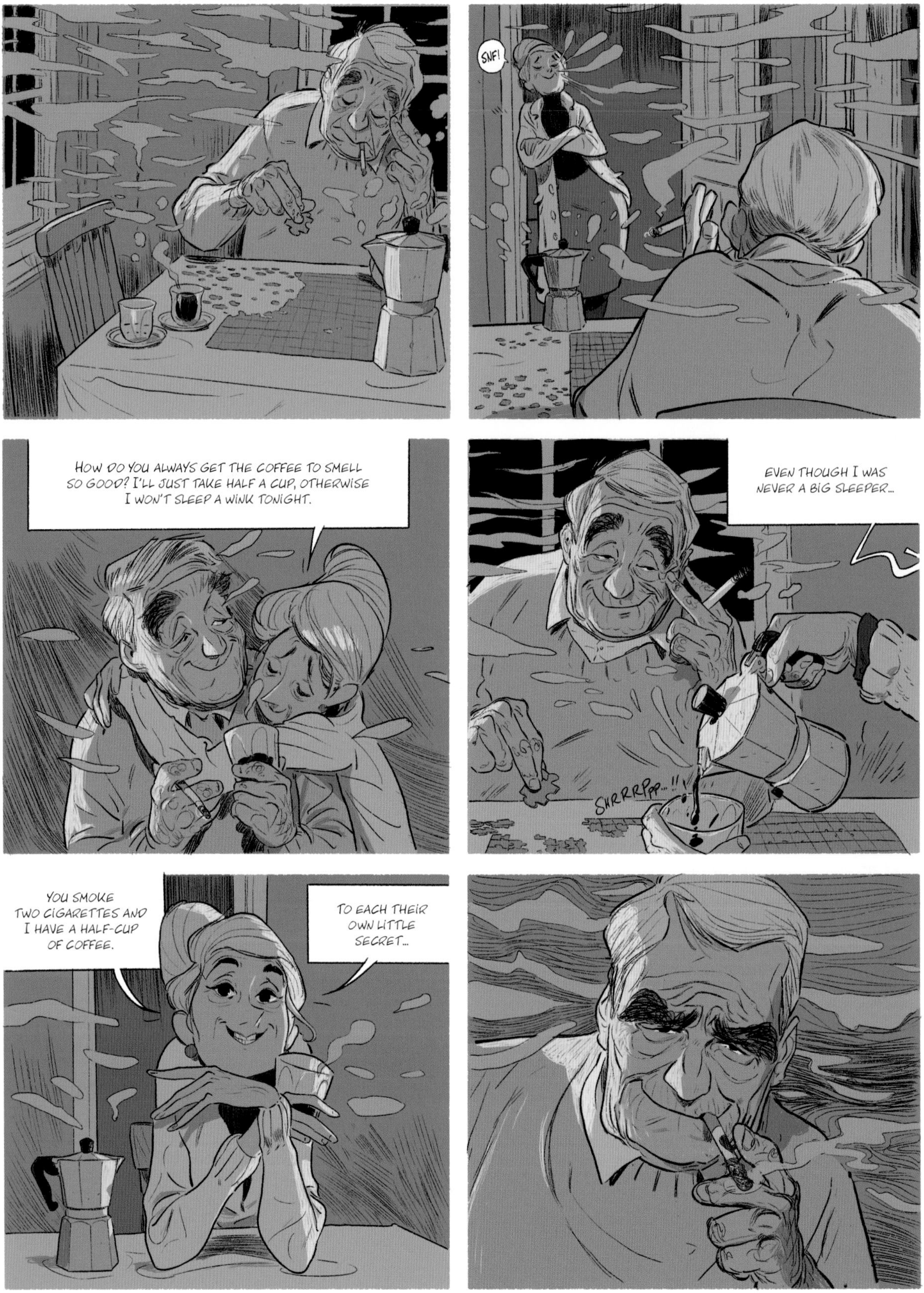
SNF!
HOW DO YOU ALWAYS GET THE COFFEE TO SMELL SO GOOD? I'LL JUST TAKE HALF A CUP, OTHERWISE I WON'T SLEEP A WINK TONIGHT.
EVEN THOUGH I WAS NEVER A BIG SLEEPER...
SHRRRPPP...!!
YOU SMOKE TWO CIGARETTES AND I HAVE A HALF-CUP OF COFFEE.
TO EACH THEIR OWN LITTLE SECRET...

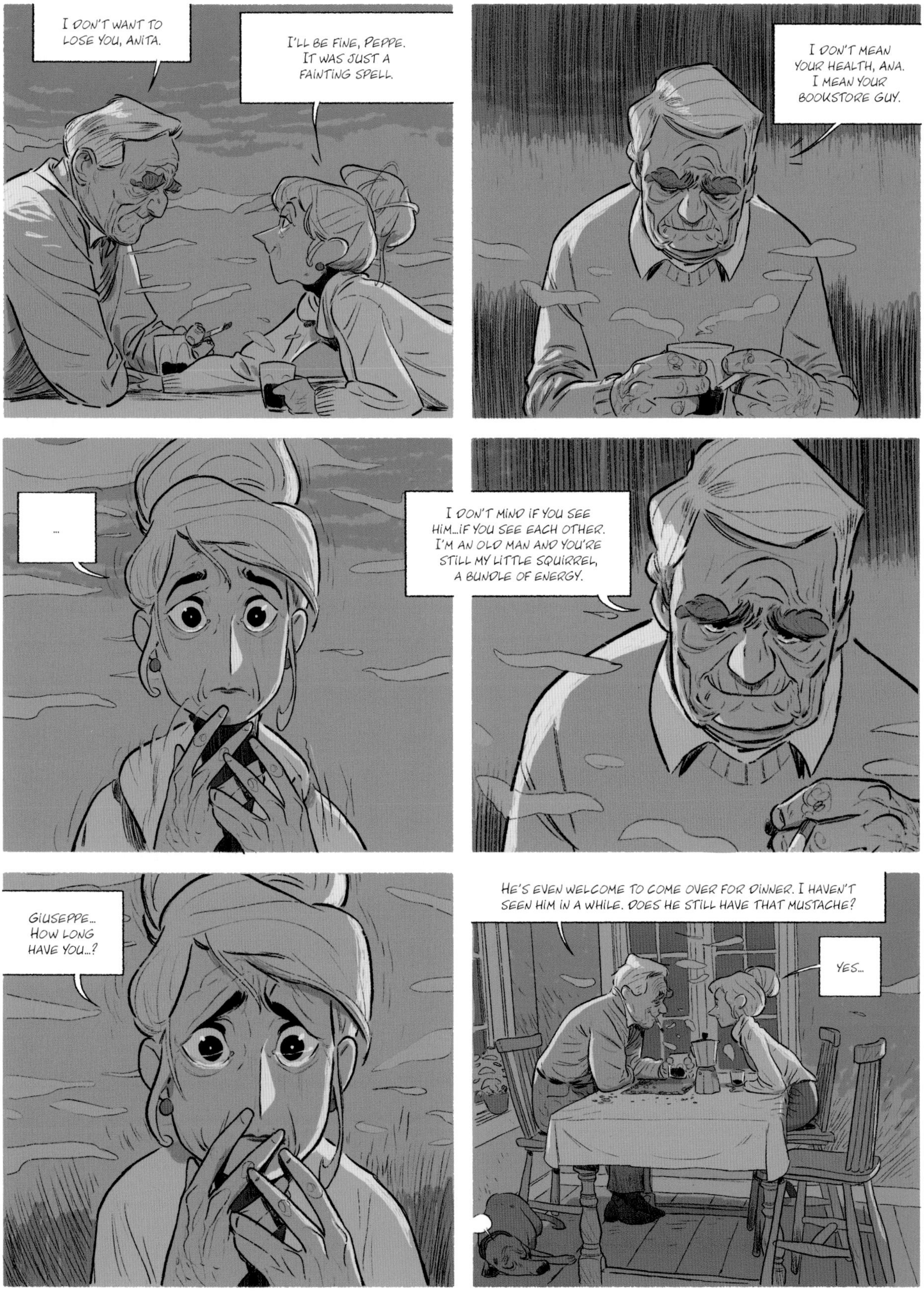
I DON'T WANT TO LOSE YOU, ANITA.
I'LL BE FINE, PEPPE. IT WAS JUST A FAINTING SPELL.
I DON'T MEAN YOUR HEALTH, ANA. I MEAN YOUR BOOKSTORE GUY.
...
I DON'T MIND IF YOU SEE HIM...IF YOU SEE EACH OTHER. I'M AN OLD MAN AND YOU'RE STILL MY LITTLE SQUIRREL, A BUNDLE OF ENERGY.
GIUSEPPE... HOW LONG HAVE YOU...?
HE'S EVEN WELCOME TO COME OVER FOR DINNER. I HAVEN'T SEEN HIM IN A WHILE. DOES HE STILL HAVE THAT MUSTACHE?
YES...

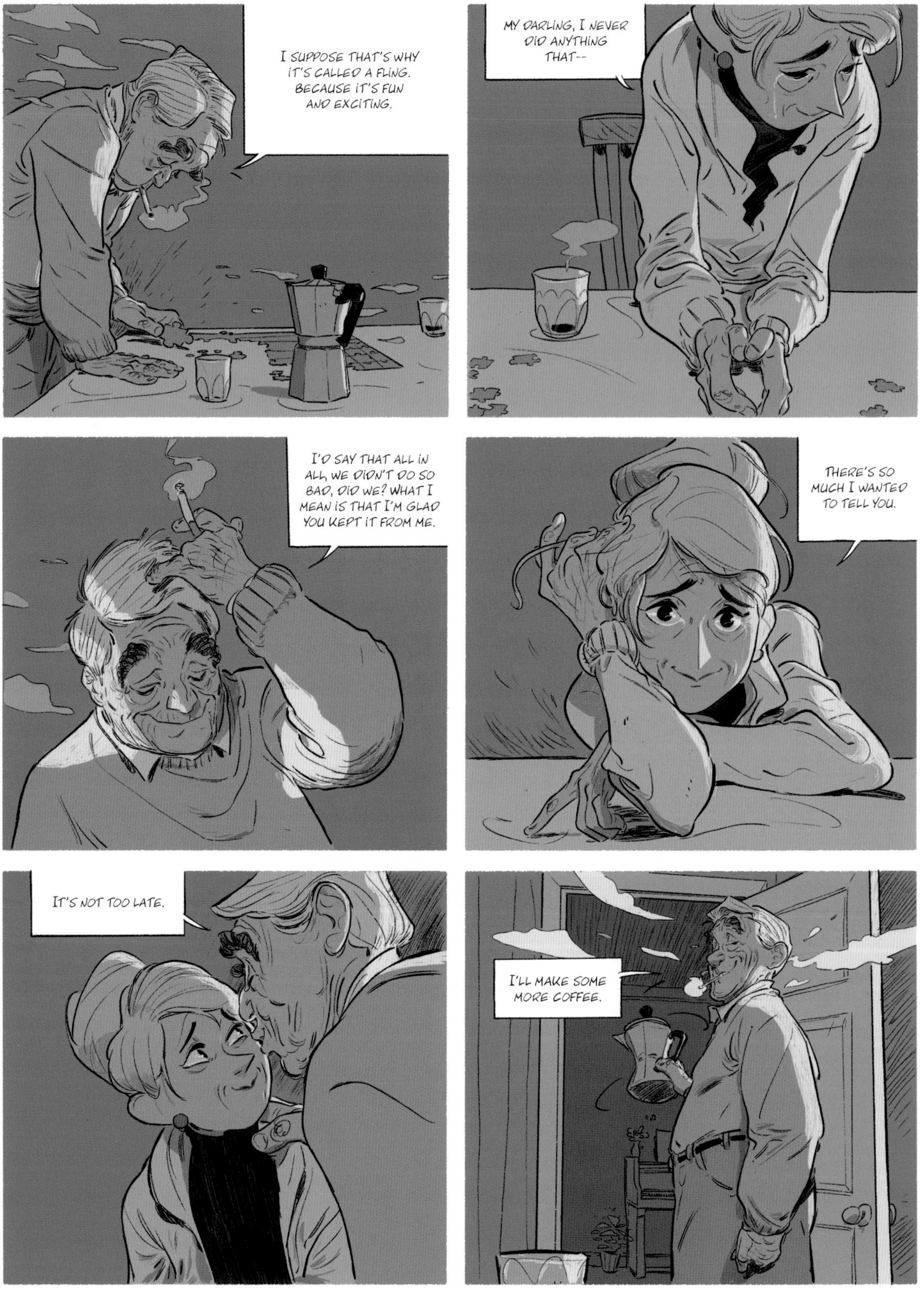
I SUPPOSE THAT'S WHY IT'S CALLED A FLING. BECAUSE IT'S FUN AND EXCITING.
MY DARLING, I NEVER DID ANYTHING THAT--
I'D SAY THAT ALL IN ALL, WE DIDN'T DO SO BAD, DID WE? WHAT I MEAN IS THAT I'M GLAD YOU KEPT IT FROM ME.
THERE'S SO MUCH I WANTED TO TELL YOU.
IT'S NOT TOO LATE.
I'LL MAKE SOME MORE COFFEE.

CHAPTER
17

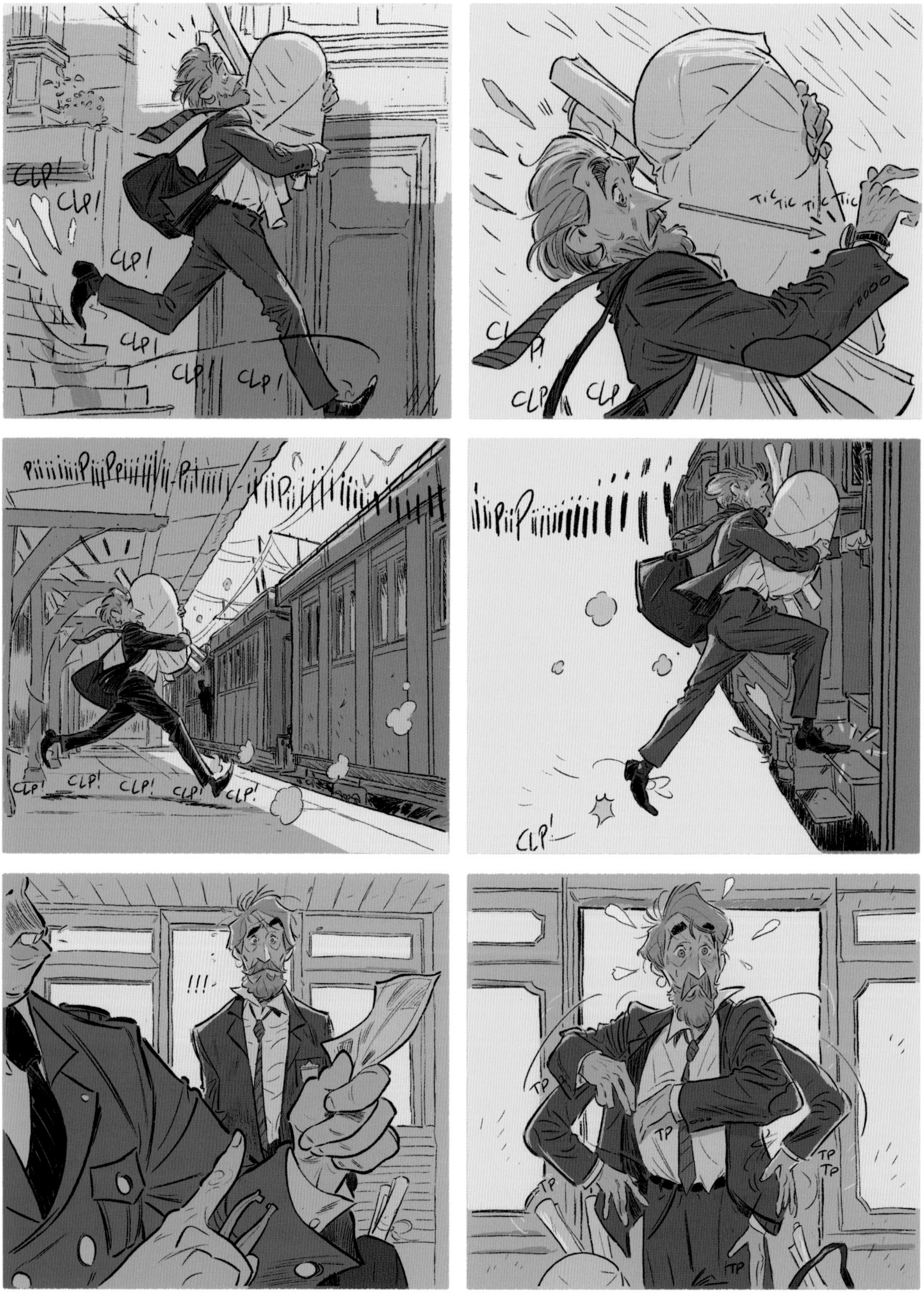
CLP!
CLP!
CLP!
CLP!
CLP!
CLP!
TIC TIC TIC TIC
CLP!
CLP
CLP
CLP! CLP! CLP! CLP! CLP!
CLP!
!!!
TP
TP
TP
TP TP
TP

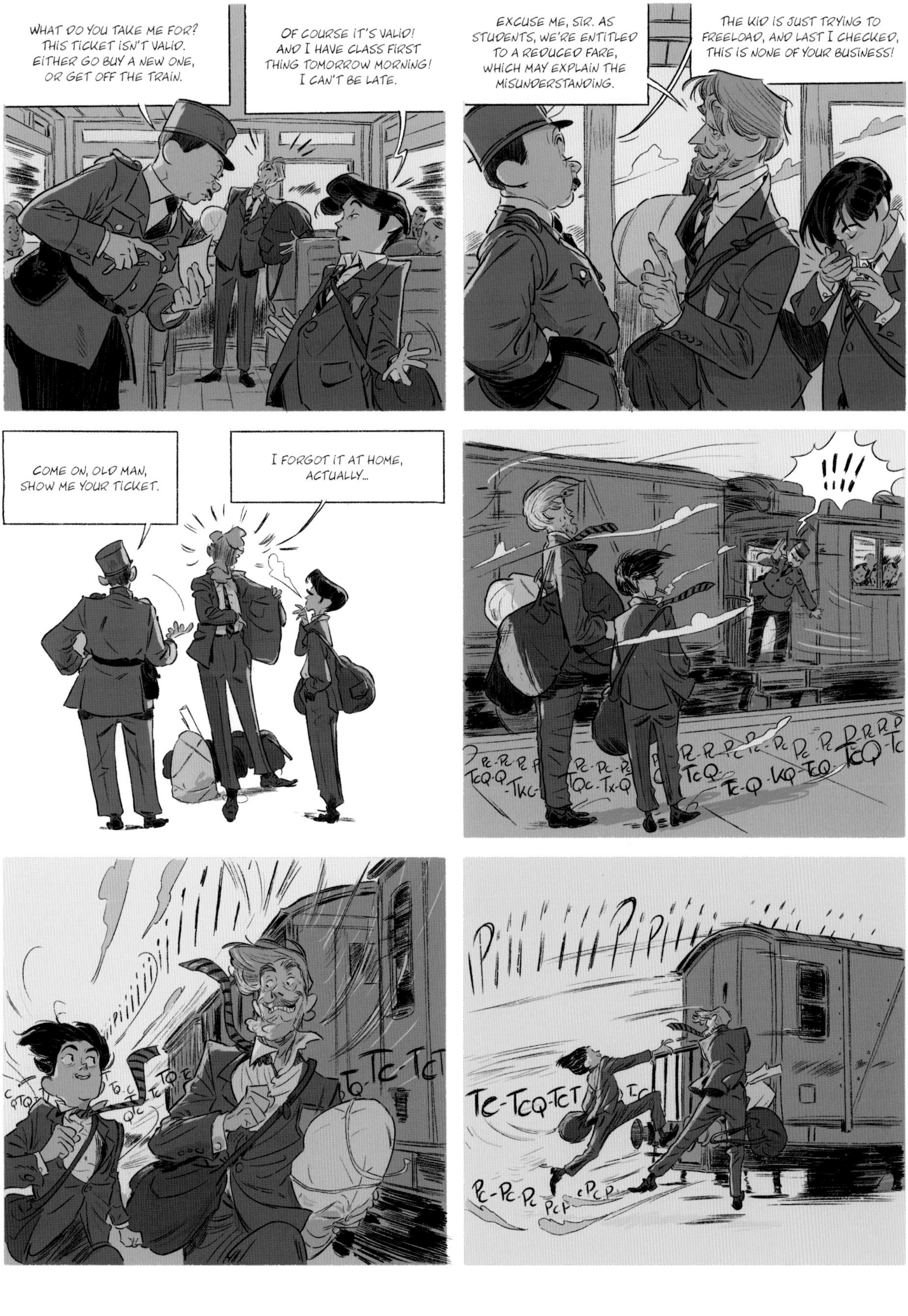
WHAT DO YOU TAKE ME FOR? THIS TICKET ISN'T VALID. EITHER GO BUY A NEW ONE, OR GET OFF THE TRAIN.
OF COURSE IT'S VALID! AND I HAVE CLASS FIRST THING TOMORROW MORNING! I CAN'T BE LATE.
EXCUSE ME, SIR. AS STUDENTS, WE'RE ENTITLED TO A REDUCED FARE, WHICH MAY EXPLAIN THE MISUNDERSTANDING.
THE KID IS JUST TRYING TO FREELOAD, AND LAST I CHECKED, THIS IS NONE OF YOUR BUSINESS!
COME ON, OLD MAN, SHOW ME YOUR TICKET.
I FORGOT IT AT HOME, ACTUALLY...
!!!!
Tc-Tcq-Tct
Pc-Pc-Pc

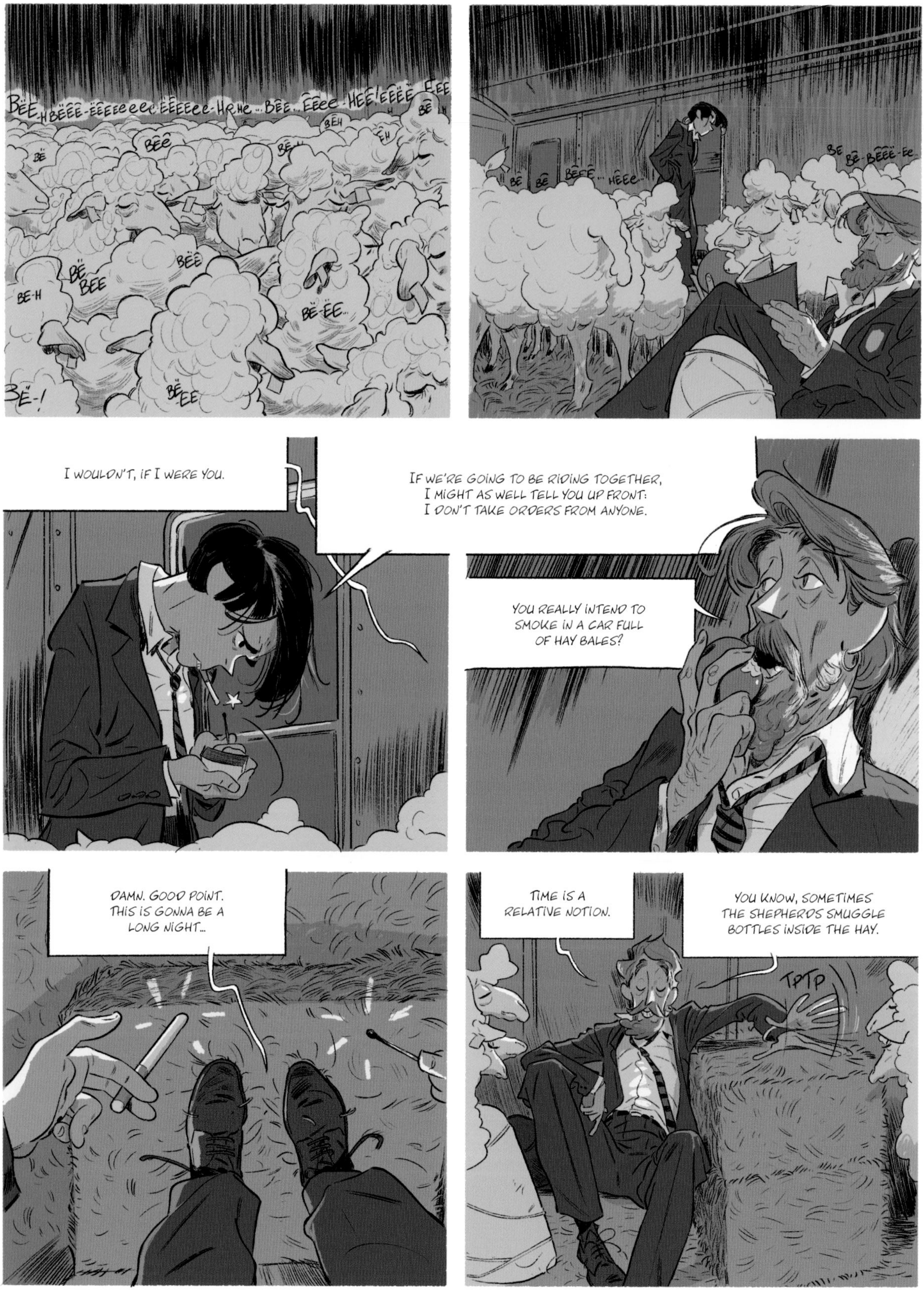
BE BE-BEËË-EE
I WOULDN'T, IF I WERE YOU.
IF WE'RE GOING TO BE RIDING TOGETHER, I MIGHT AS WELL TELL YOU UP FRONT: I DON'T TAKE ORDERS FROM ANYONE.
YOU REALLY INTEND TO SMOKE IN A CAR FULL OF HAY BALES?
DAMN. GOOD POINT. THIS IS GONNA BE A LONG NIGHT...
TIME IS A RELATIVE NOTION.
YOU KNOW, SOMETIMES THE SHEPHERDS SMUGGLE BOTTLES INSIDE THE HAY.
TPTP

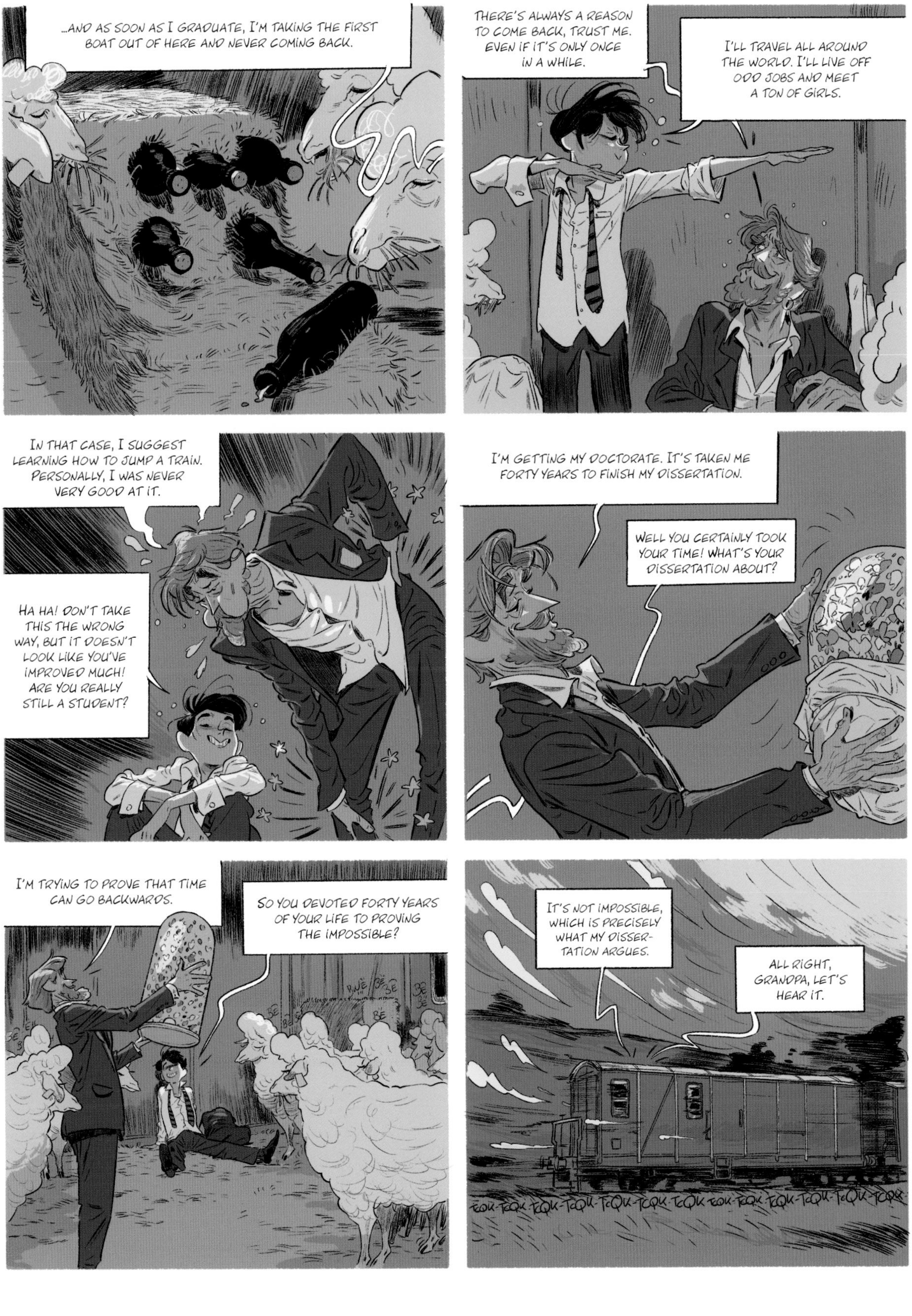
...AND AS SOON AS I GRADUATE, I'M TAKING THE FIRST BOAT OUT OF HERE AND NEVER COMING BACK.
THERE'S ALWAYS A REASON TO COME BACK, TRUST ME. EVEN IF IT'S ONLY ONCE IN A WHILE.
I'LL TRAVEL ALL AROUND THE WORLD. I'LL LIVE OFF ODD JOBS AND MEET A TON OF GIRLS.
IN THAT CASE, I SUGGEST LEARNING HOW TO JUMP A TRAIN. PERSONALLY, I WAS NEVER VERY GOOD AT IT.
HA HA! DON'T TAKE THIS THE WRONG WAY, BUT IT DOESN'T LOOK LIKE YOU'VE IMPROVED MUCH! ARE YOU REALLY STILL A STUDENT?
I'M GETTING MY DOCTORATE. IT'S TAKEN ME FORTY YEARS TO FINISH MY DISSERTATION.
WELL YOU CERTAINLY TOOK YOUR TIME! WHAT'S YOUR DISSERTATION ABOUT?
I'M TRYING TO PROVE THAT TIME CAN GO BACKWARDS.
SO YOU DEVOTED FORTY YEARS OF YOUR LIFE TO PROVING THE IMPOSSIBLE?
IT'S NOT IMPOSSIBLE, WHICH IS PRECISELY WHAT MY DISSER-TATION ARGUES.
ALL RIGHT, GRANDPA, LET'S HEAR IT.

THE UNIVERSE AS WE KNOW IT WAS THE CONSEQUENCE OF AN ENORMOUS EXPLOSION CALLED THE BIG BANG.

THIS BIG BANG, THE EXPLOSION OF A TINY BALL OF ENERGY, NOT ONLY SPREAD THE UNIVERSE'S MATTER, BUT IT ALSO PROPELLED TIME FORWARD.

HOWEVER, NO LAW OF PHYSICS PREVENTS TIME FROM MOVING BACKWARD.

IT IS NEVERTHELESS VIRTUALLY IMPOSSIBLE FOR ANY SUCH PHENOMENON TO EVER OCCUR. YOU SEE, EVERYTHING TENDS TO EXPAND AND BECOME INCREASINGLY DISORGANIZED AND DISORDERLY.

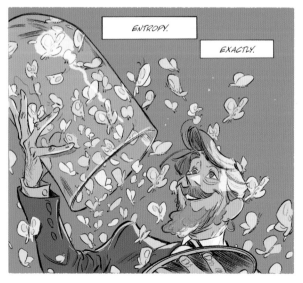

ENTROPY.

EXACTLY.

AS SOON AS IT IS SUBJECTED TO DISORDER, MATTER NEVER REORGANIZES ITSELF SPONTANEOUSLY. AND TIME, WHEN PROPELLED FORWARD, DOESN'T STOP.

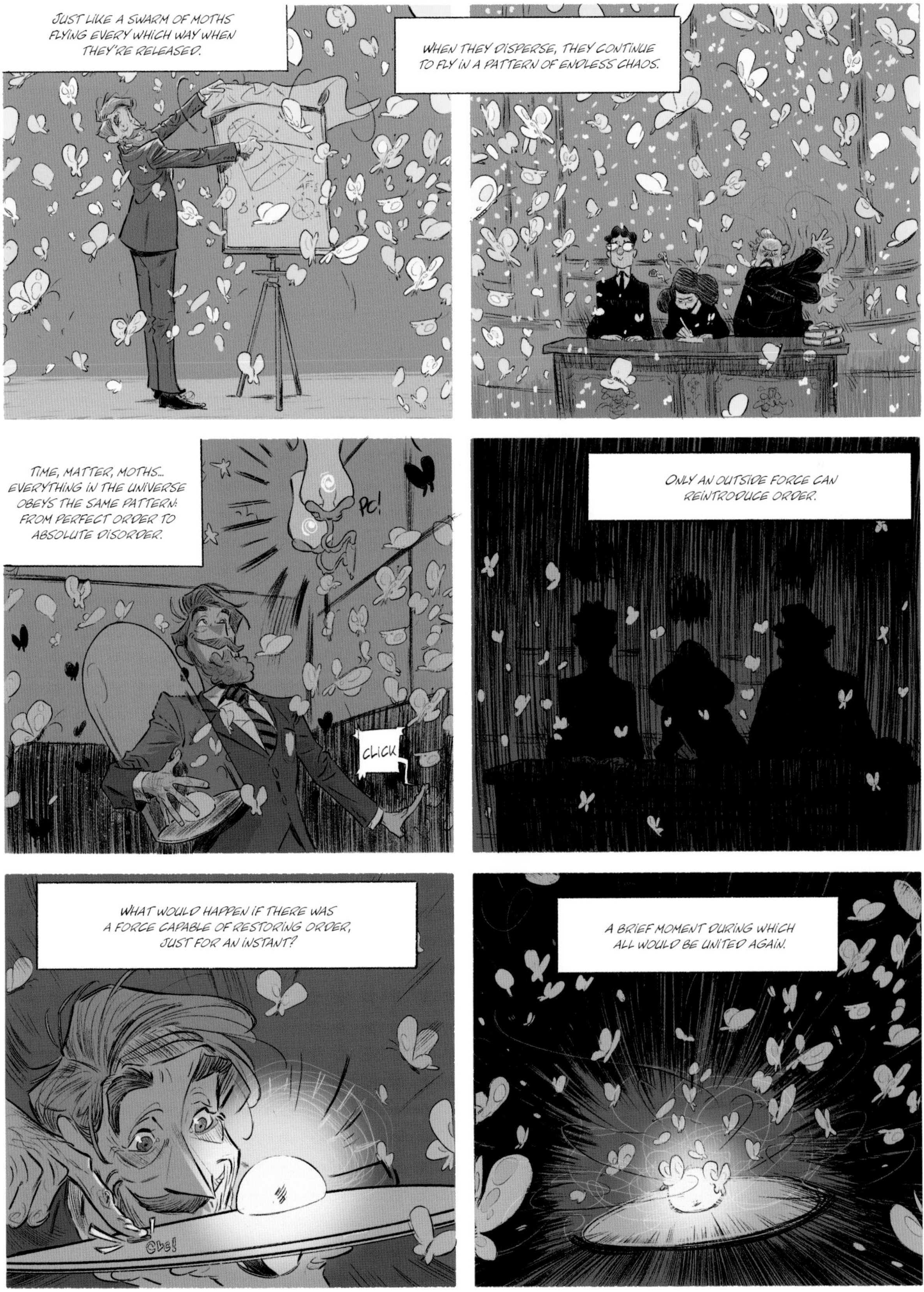
JUST LIKE A SWARM OF MOTHS FLYING EVERY WHICH WAY WHEN THEY'RE RELEASED.
WHEN THEY DISPERSE, THEY CONTINUE TO FLY IN A PATTERN OF ENDLESS CHAOS.
TIME, MATTER, MOTHS... EVERYTHING IN THE UNIVERSE OBEYS THE SAME PATTERN: FROM PERFECT ORDER TO ABSOLUTE DISORDER.
PC!
CLICK
ONLY AN OUTSIDE FORCE CAN REINTRODUCE ORDER.
WHAT WOULD HAPPEN IF THERE WAS A FORCE CAPABLE OF RESTORING ORDER, JUST FOR AN INSTANT?
A BRIEF MOMENT DURING WHICH ALL WOULD BE UNITED AGAIN.

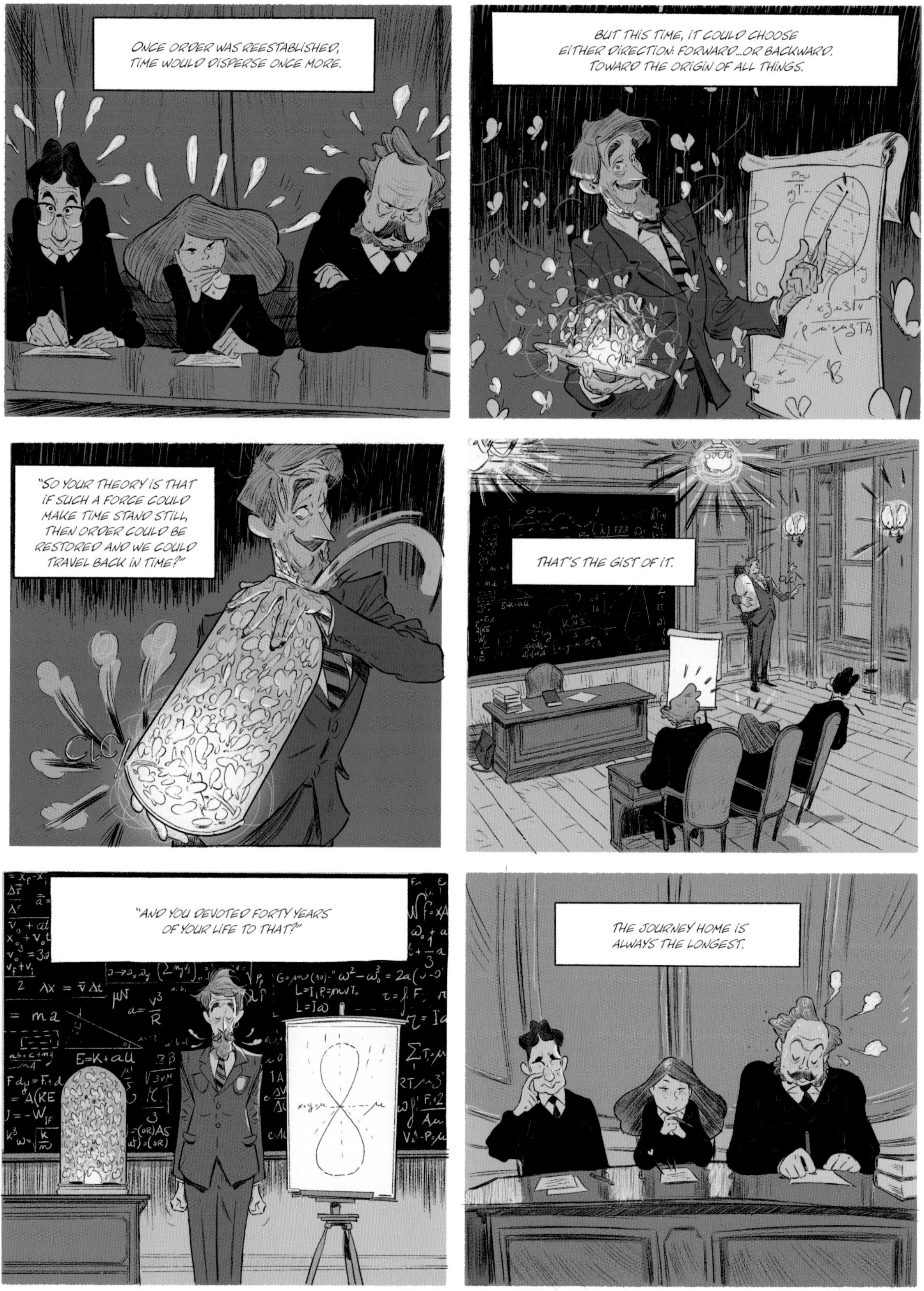
ONCE ORDER WAS REESTABLISHED, TIME WOULD DISPERSE ONCE MORE.
BUT THIS TIME, IT COULD CHOOSE EITHER DIRECTION: FORWARD...OR BACKWARD. TOWARD THE ORIGIN OF ALL THINGS.
"SO YOUR THEORY IS THAT IF SUCH A FORCE COULD MAKE TIME STAND STILL, THEN ORDER COULD BE RESTORED AND WE COULD TRAVEL BACK IN TIME?"
CLIC!
THAT'S THE GIST OF IT.
"AND YOU DEVOTED FORTY YEARS OF YOUR LIFE TO THAT?"
THE JOURNEY HOME IS ALWAYS THE LONGEST.

CHAPTER
16

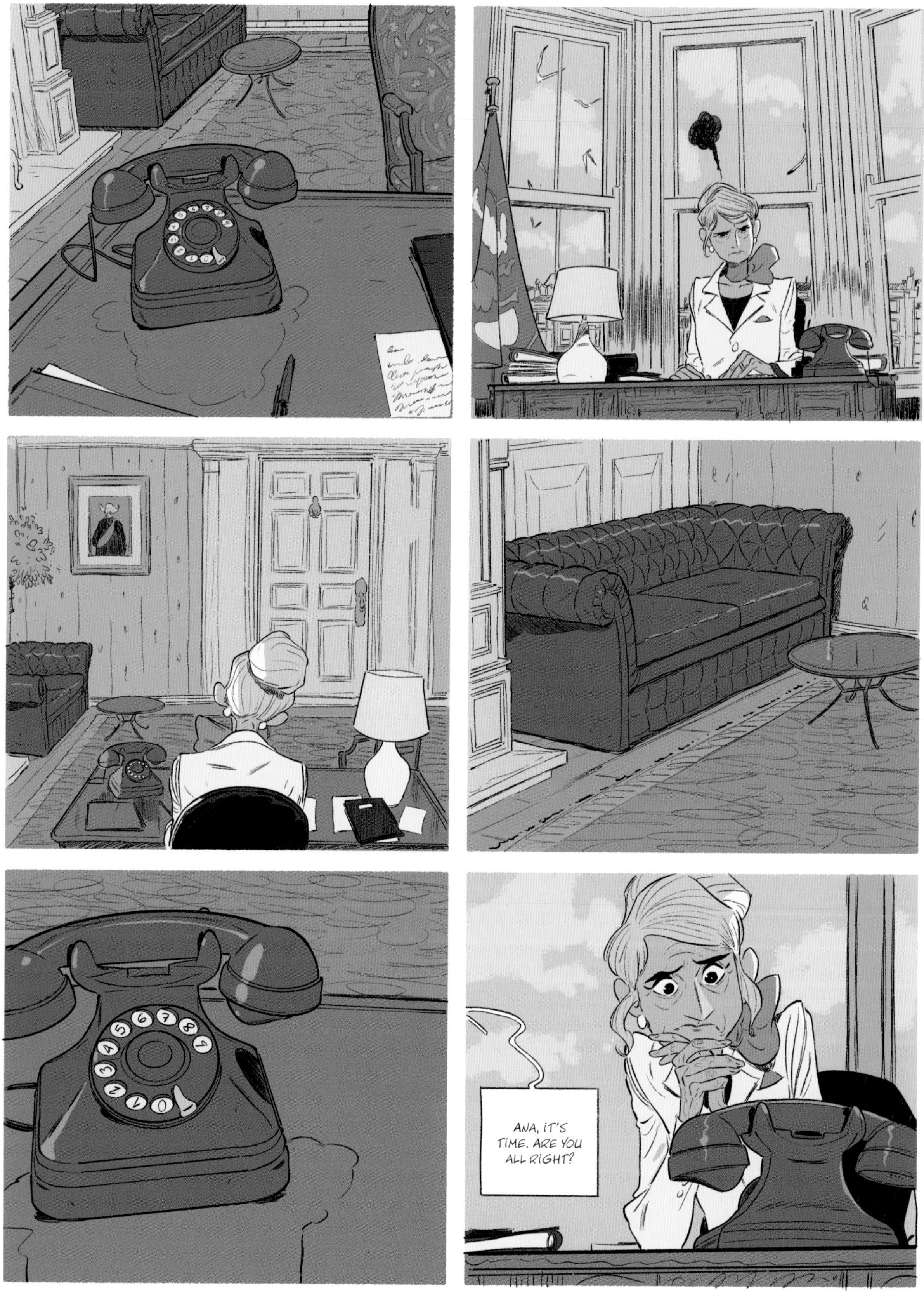
ANA, IT'S TIME. ARE YOU ALL RIGHT?

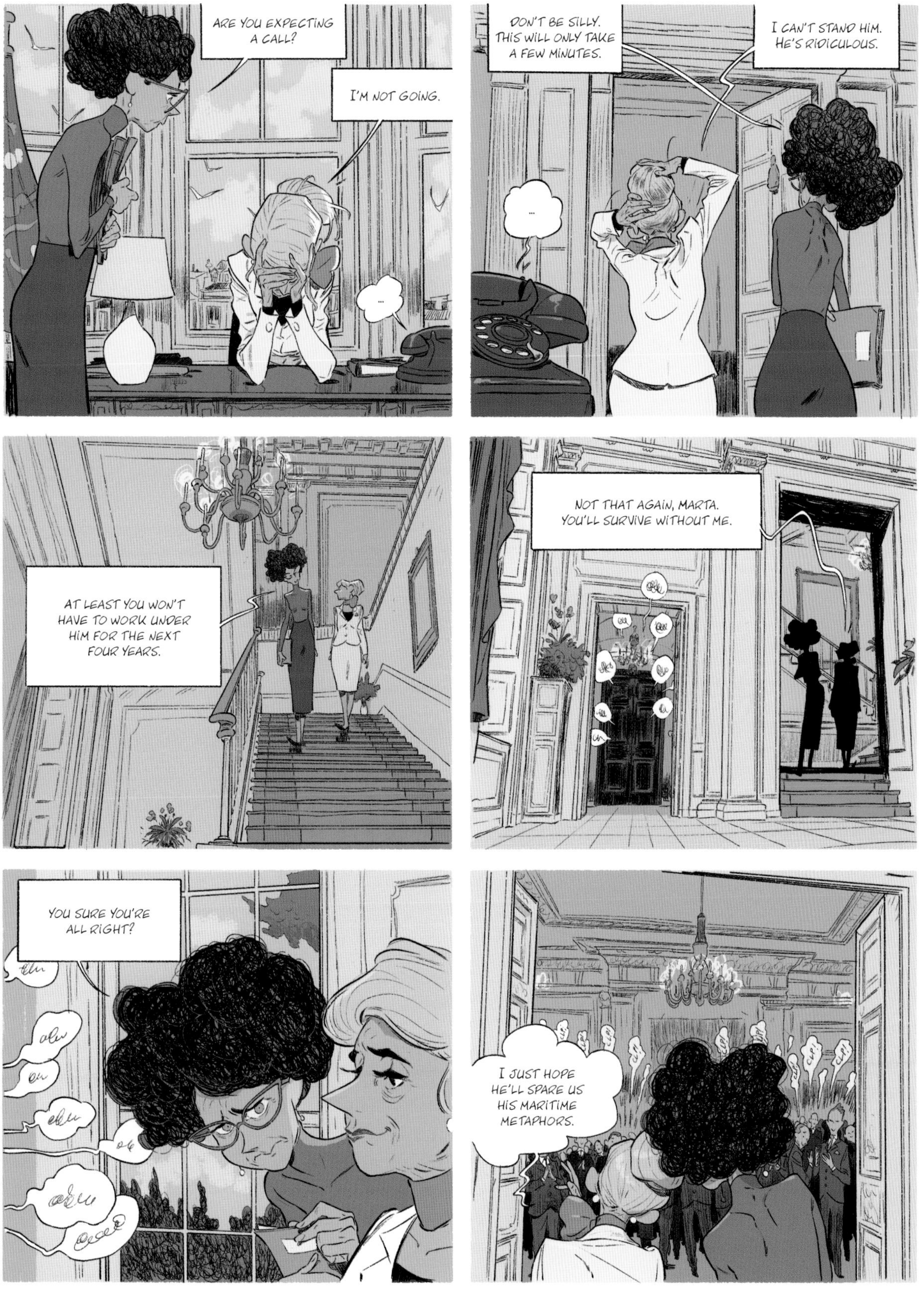
ARE YOU EXPECTING A CALL?
I'M NOT GOING.
...
DON'T BE SILLY. THIS WILL ONLY TAKE A FEW MINUTES.
I CAN'T STAND HIM. HE'S RIDICULOUS.
...
AT LEAST YOU WON'T HAVE TO WORK UNDER HIM FOR THE NEXT FOUR YEARS.
NOT THAT AGAIN, MARTA. YOU'LL SURVIVE WITHOUT ME.
YOU SURE YOU'RE ALL RIGHT?
I JUST HOPE HE'LL SPARE US HIS MARITIME METAPHORS.

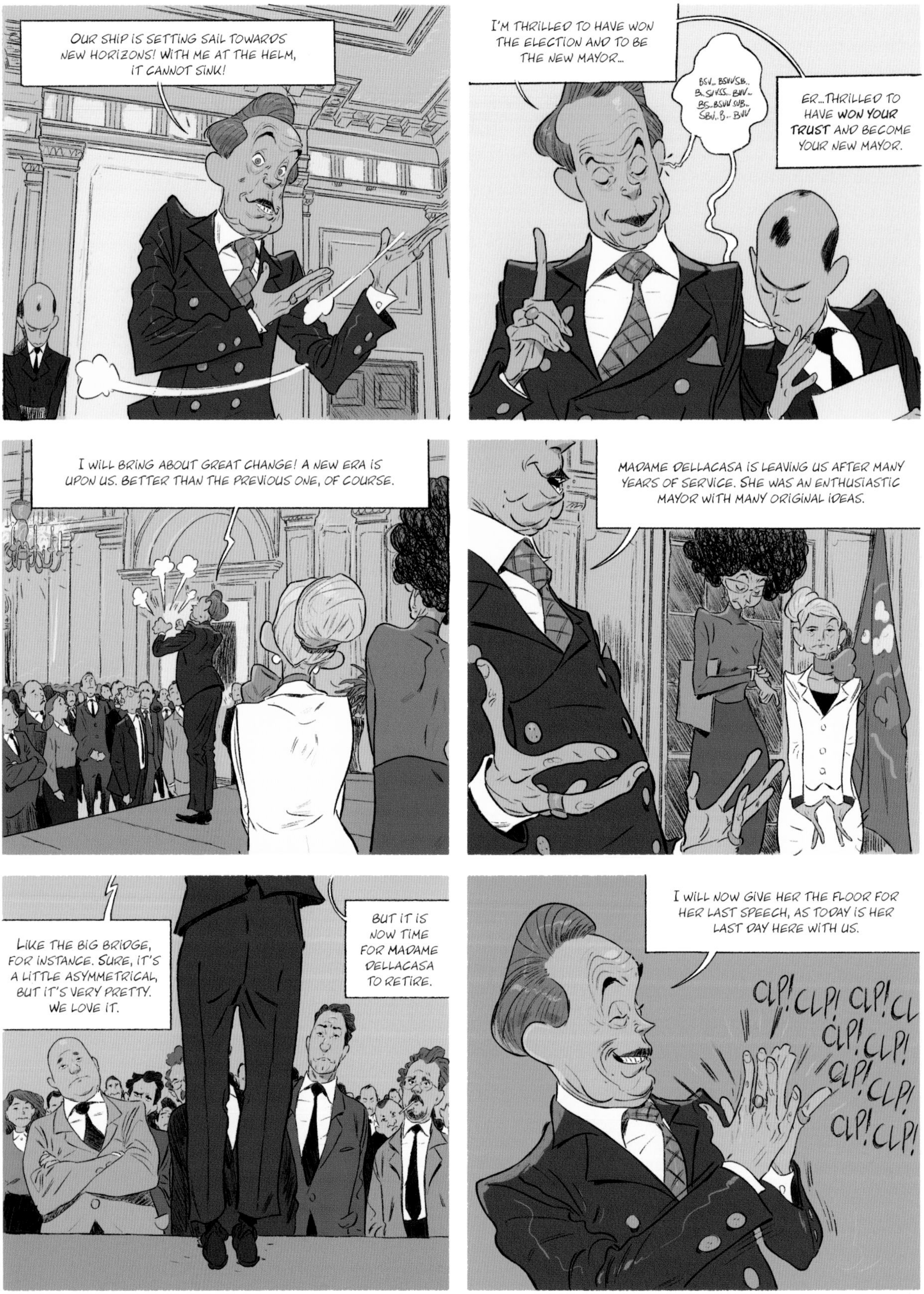
OUR SHIP IS SETTING SAIL TOWARDS NEW HORIZONS! WITH ME AT THE HELM, IT CANNOT SINK!
I'M THRILLED TO HAVE WON THE ELECTION AND TO BE THE NEW MAYOR...
BSV... BSVVSB.. B..SVVSS... BVV... BS..BSVV SUB.. SBV..B... BVV
ER...THRILLED TO HAVE **WON YOUR TRUST** AND BECOME YOUR NEW MAYOR.
I WILL BRING ABOUT GREAT CHANGE! A NEW ERA IS UPON US. BETTER THAN THE PREVIOUS ONE, OF COURSE.
MADAME DELLACASA IS LEAVING US AFTER MANY YEARS OF SERVICE. SHE WAS AN ENTHUSIASTIC MAYOR WITH MANY ORIGINAL IDEAS.
LIKE THE BIG BRIDGE, FOR INSTANCE. SURE, IT'S A LITTLE ASYMMETRICAL, BUT IT'S VERY PRETTY. WE LOVE IT.
BUT IT IS NOW TIME FOR MADAME DELLACASA TO RETIRE.
I WILL NOW GIVE HER THE FLOOR FOR HER LAST SPEECH, AS TODAY IS HER LAST DAY HERE WITH US.
CLP! CLP! CLP! CL CLP! CLP! CLP! CLP! CLP! CLP!

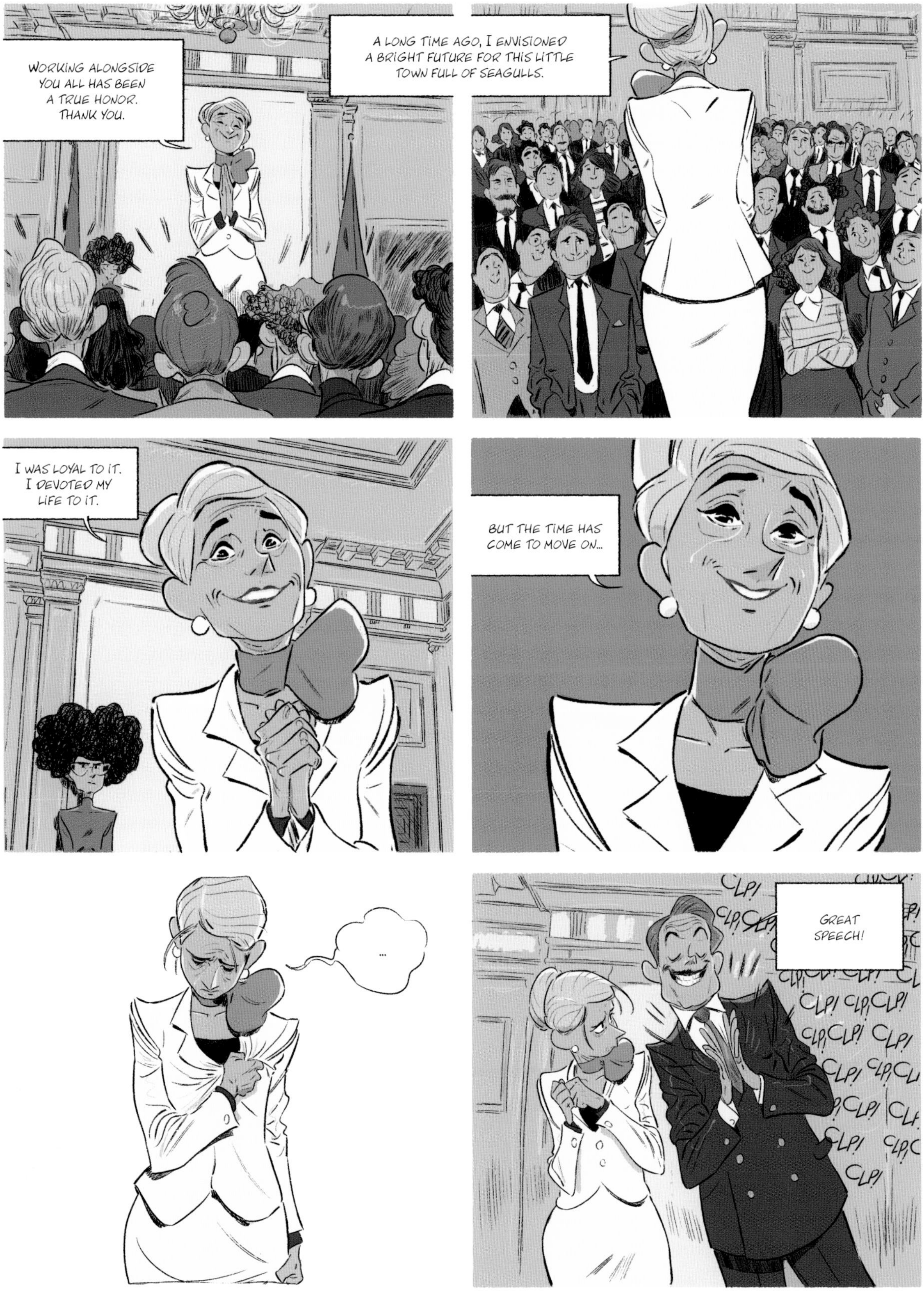
WORKING ALONGSIDE YOU ALL HAS BEEN A TRUE HONOR. THANK YOU.
A LONG TIME AGO, I ENVISIONED A BRIGHT FUTURE FOR THIS LITTLE TOWN FULL OF SEAGULLS.
I WAS LOYAL TO IT. I DEVOTED MY LIFE TO IT.
BUT THE TIME HAS COME TO MOVE ON...
...
GREAT SPEECH!
CLP! CLP! CLP! CLP! CLP! CLP! CLP! CLP! CLP!

...AND DON'T FORGET TO SIGN YOUR LETTER OF RESIGNATION BEFORE YOU LEAVE.

STARTING TODAY, I AM THE HIGHEST RANKING OFFICIAL. THIS NEEDS TO BE MADE VERY CLEAR TO EVERYONE.

WHAT ARE THESE PEOPLE DOING?

OUT WITH THE OLD, IN WITH THE NEW, MADAME DELLACASA. THIS IS MY OFFICE NOW, AFTER ALL.

THEY CAN'T JUST THROW IT ALL OUT!

THIS FURNITURE UNDOUBTEDLY HAS SENTIMENTAL VALUE FOR YOU AND HOLDS MANY MEMORIES, WE ARE VERY MUCH AWARE OF THAT. BUT I WANT TO PROJECT AN IMAGE OF CHANGE!

YOU CAN BUY IT BACK FROM THE TOWN, IF YOU WISH.

RiiiiiiiiiiiiiiiiNG!!!

44

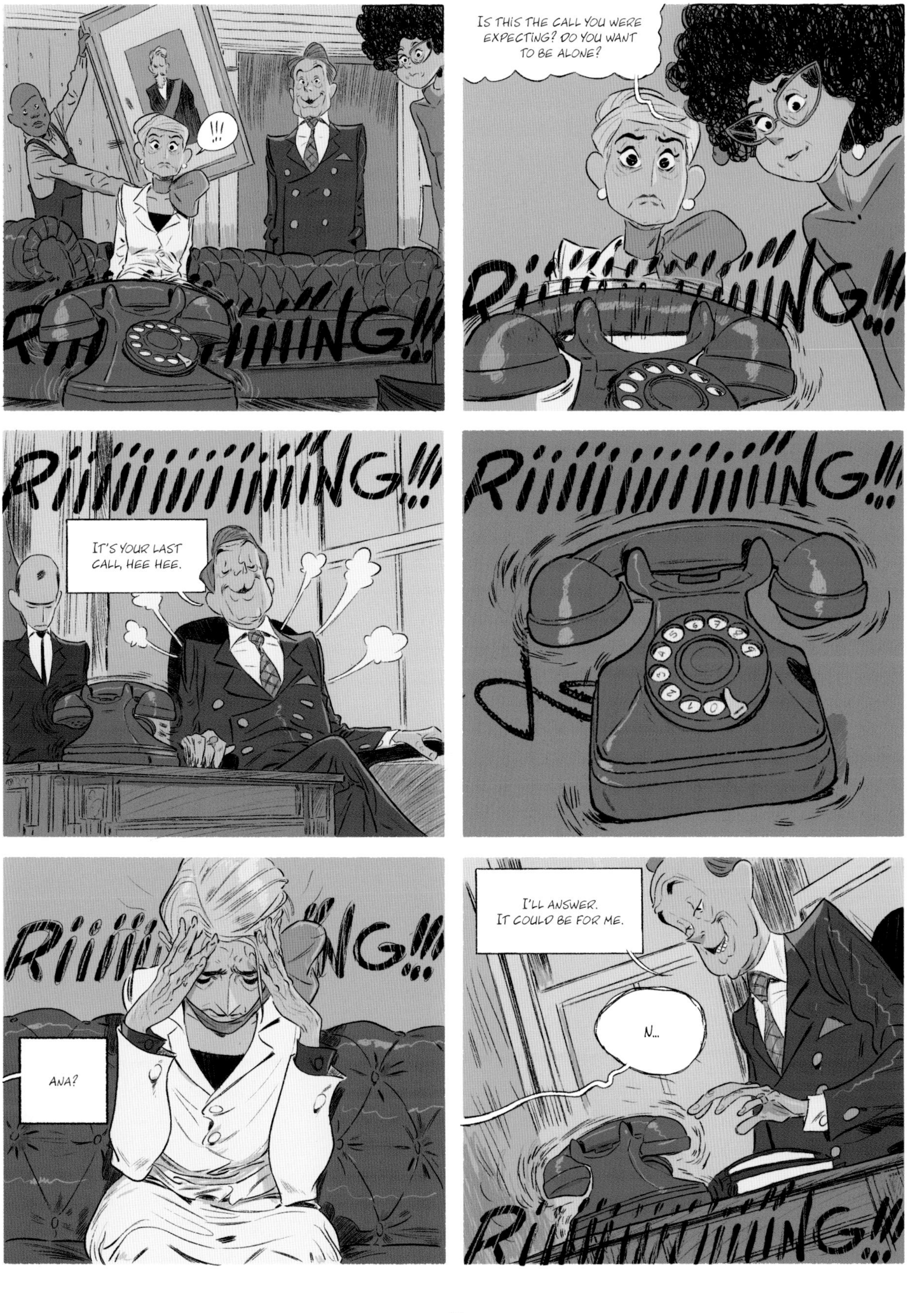
!!!
RIIIIIIIIIIING!!!
IS THIS THE CALL YOU WERE EXPECTING? DO YOU WANT TO BE ALONE?
RIIIIIIIIIIING!!!
RIIIIIIIIIIIIING!!!
IT'S YOUR LAST CALL, HEE HEE.
RIIIIIIIIIIIIING!!!
RIIIIING!!!
ANA?
I'LL ANSWER. IT COULD BE FOR ME.
N...
RIIIIIIIIIIING!!!

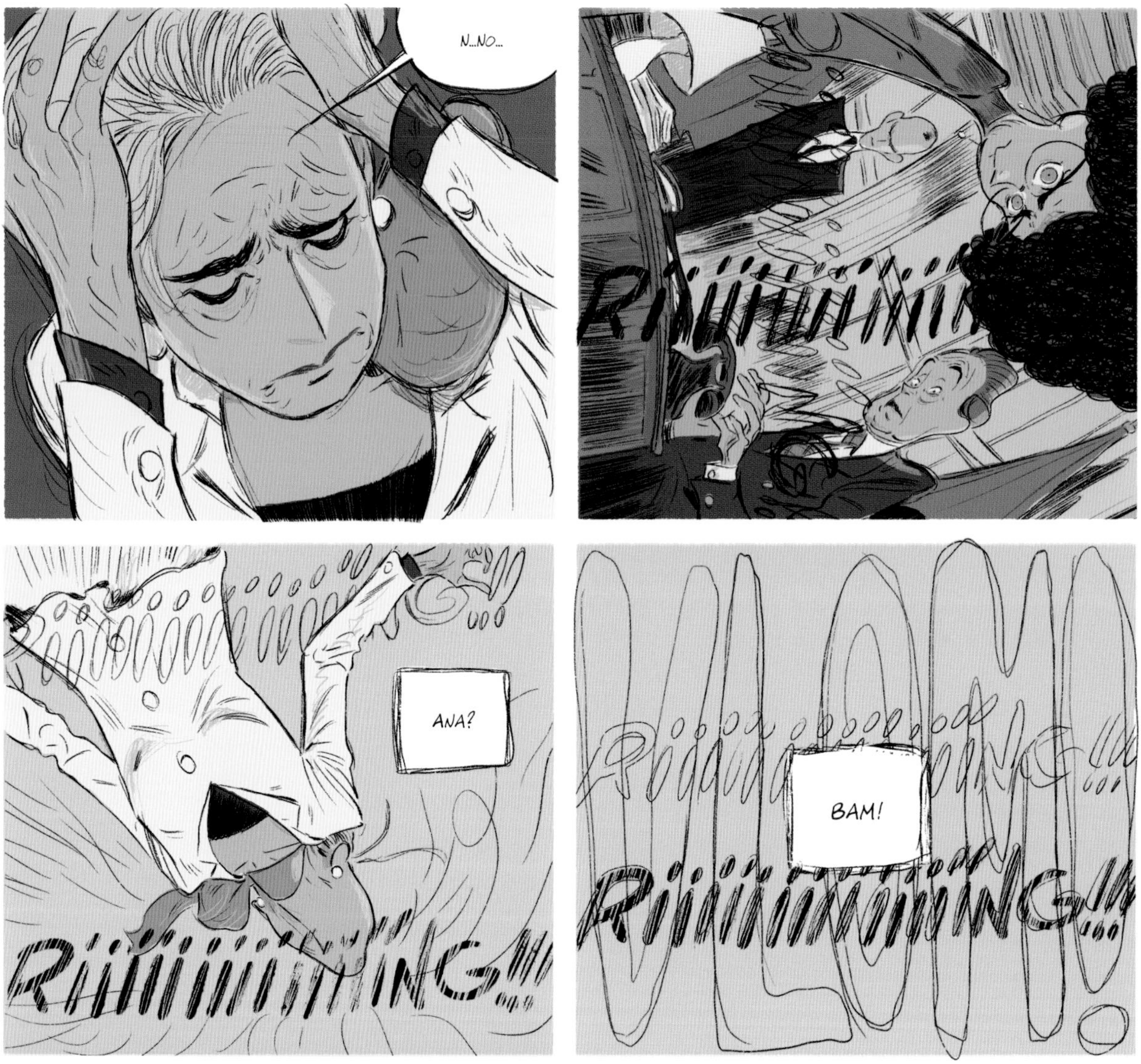
N...NO...
ANA?
BAM!

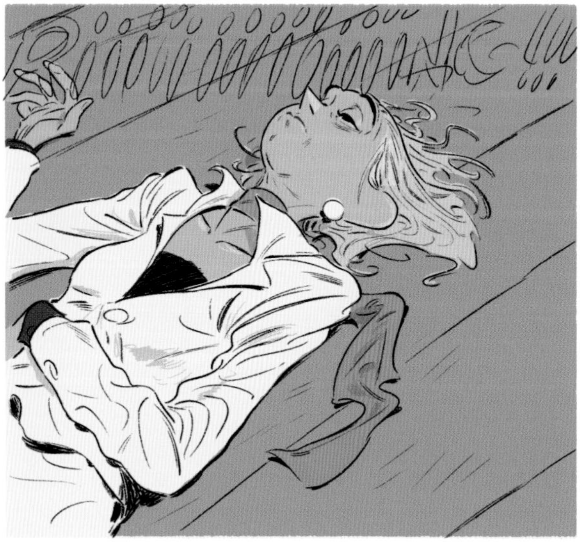

ANA?

CHAPTER
15

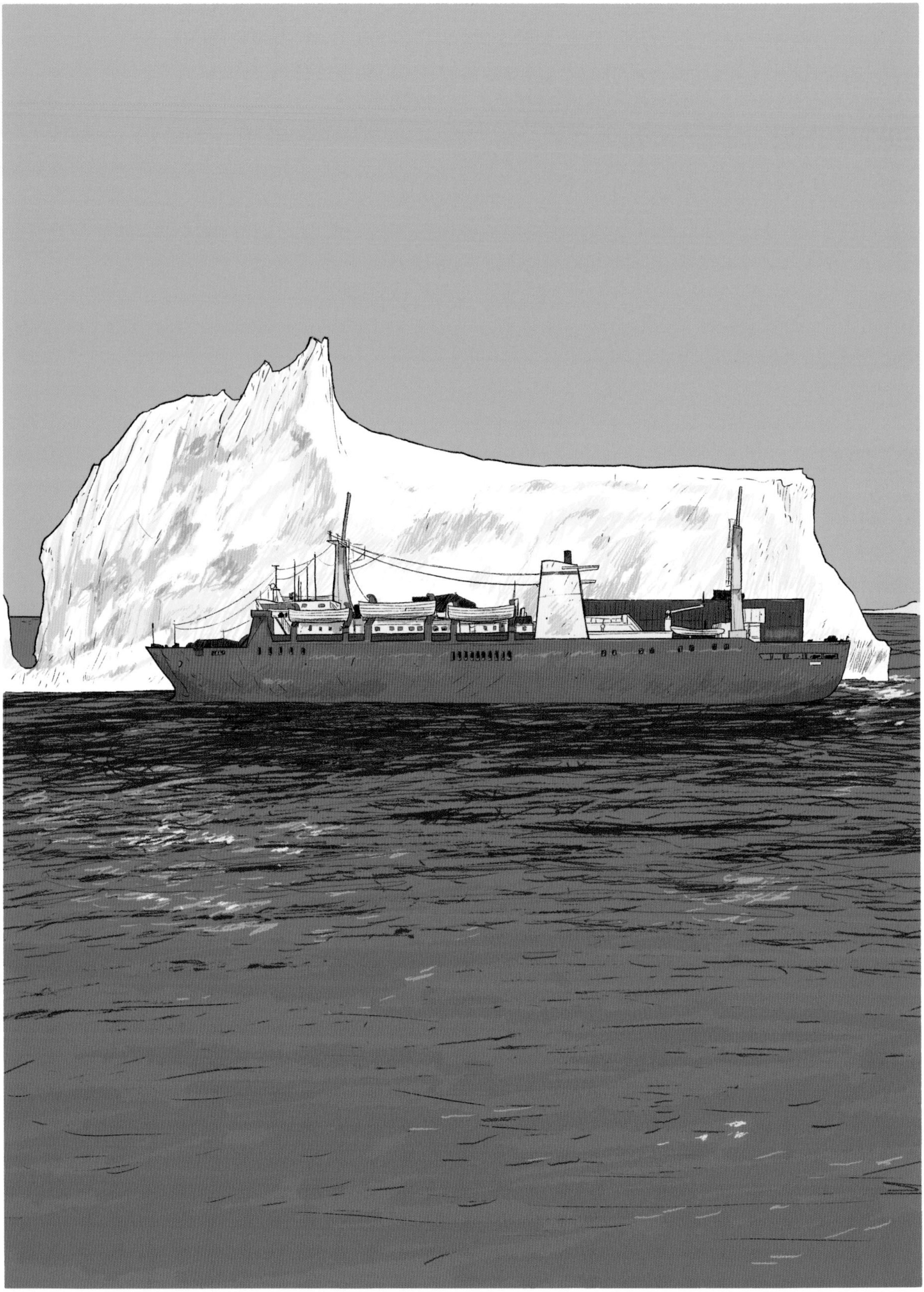

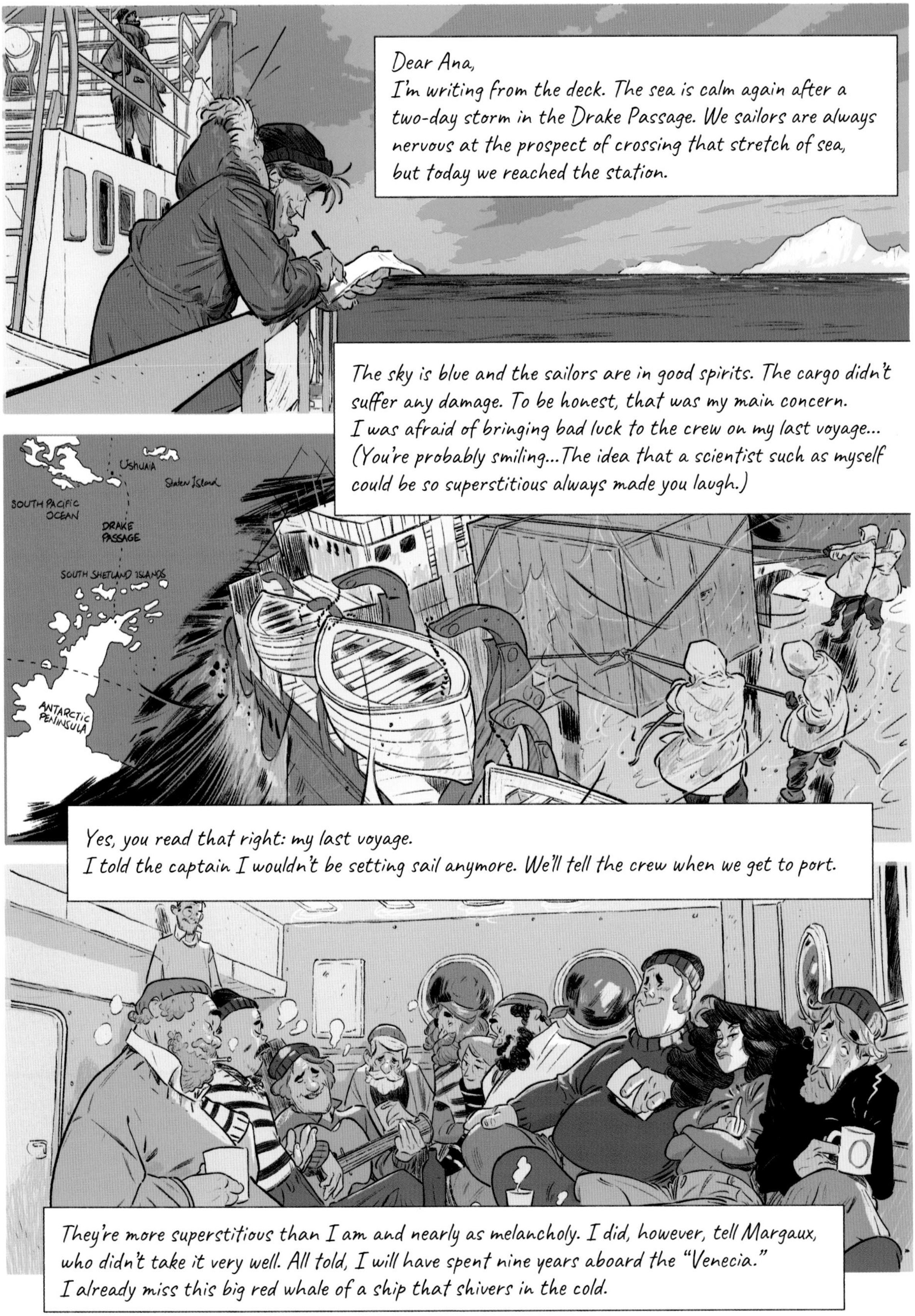
Dear Ana,
I'm writing from the deck. The sea is calm again after a two-day storm in the Drake Passage. We sailors are always nervous at the prospect of crossing that stretch of sea, but today we reached the station.
The sky is blue and the sailors are in good spirits. The cargo didn't suffer any damage. To be honest, that was my main concern. I was afraid of bringing bad luck to the crew on my last voyage... (You're probably smiling...The idea that a scientist such as myself could be so superstitious always made you laugh.)
Ushuaia
Staten Island
SOUTH PACIFIC OCEAN
DRAKE PASSAGE
SOUTH SHETLAND ISLANDS
ANTARCTIC PENINSULA
Yes, you read that right: my last voyage.
I told the captain I wouldn't be setting sail anymore. We'll tell the crew when we get to port.
They're more superstitious than I am and nearly as melancholy. I did, however, tell Margaux, who didn't take it very well. All told, I will have spent nine years aboard the "Venecia." I already miss this big red whale of a ship that shivers in the cold.

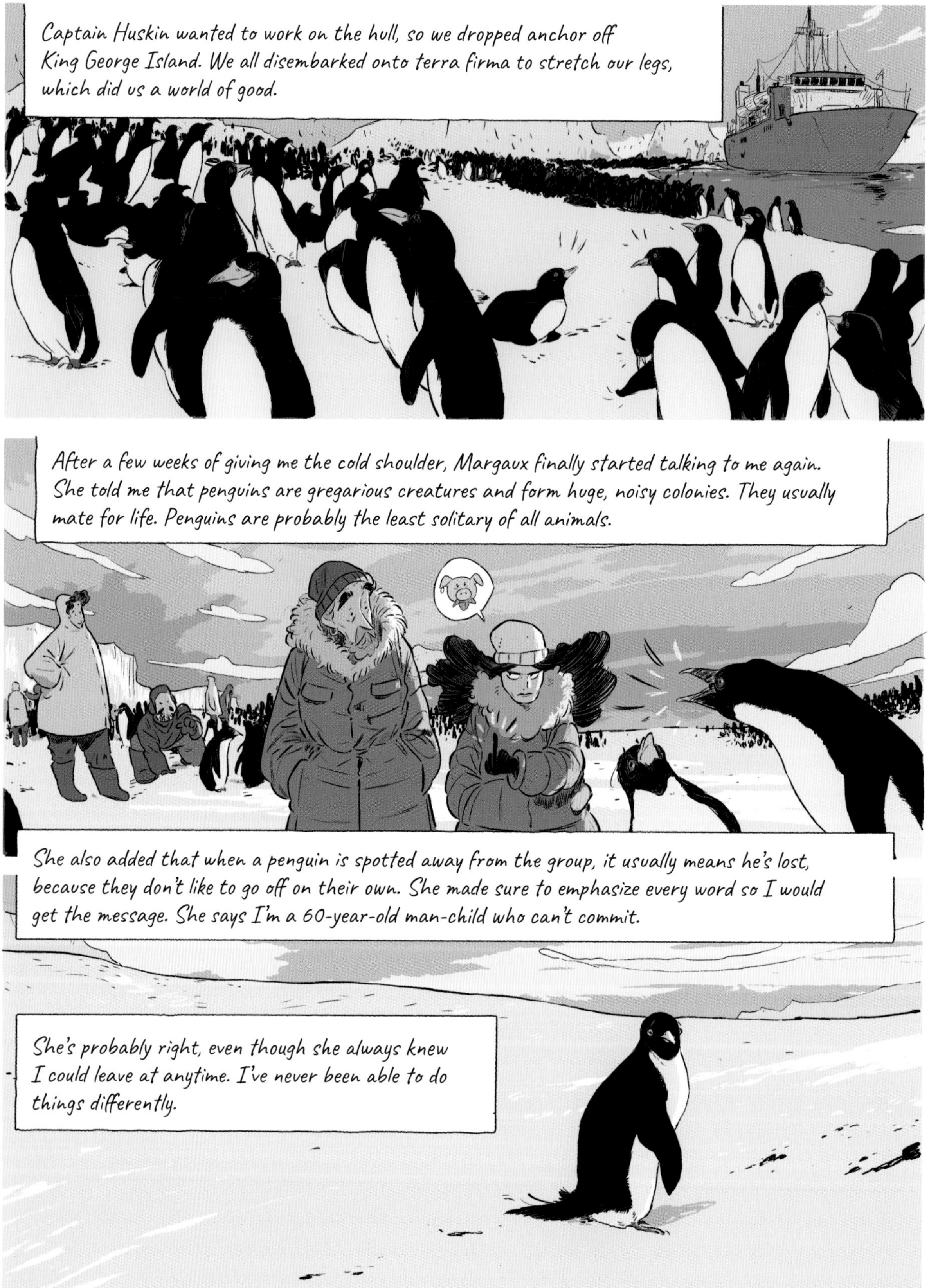
Captain Huskin wanted to work on the hull, so we dropped anchor off King George Island. We all disembarked onto terra firma to stretch our legs, which did us a world of good.
After a few weeks of giving me the cold shoulder, Margaux finally started talking to me again. She told me that penguins are gregarious creatures and form huge, noisy colonies. They usually mate for life. Penguins are probably the least solitary of all animals.
She also added that when a penguin is spotted away from the group, it usually means he's lost, because they don't like to go off on their own. She made sure to emphasize every word so I would get the message. She says I'm a 60-year-old man-child who can't commit.
She's probably right, even though she always knew I could leave at anytime. I've never been able to do things differently.

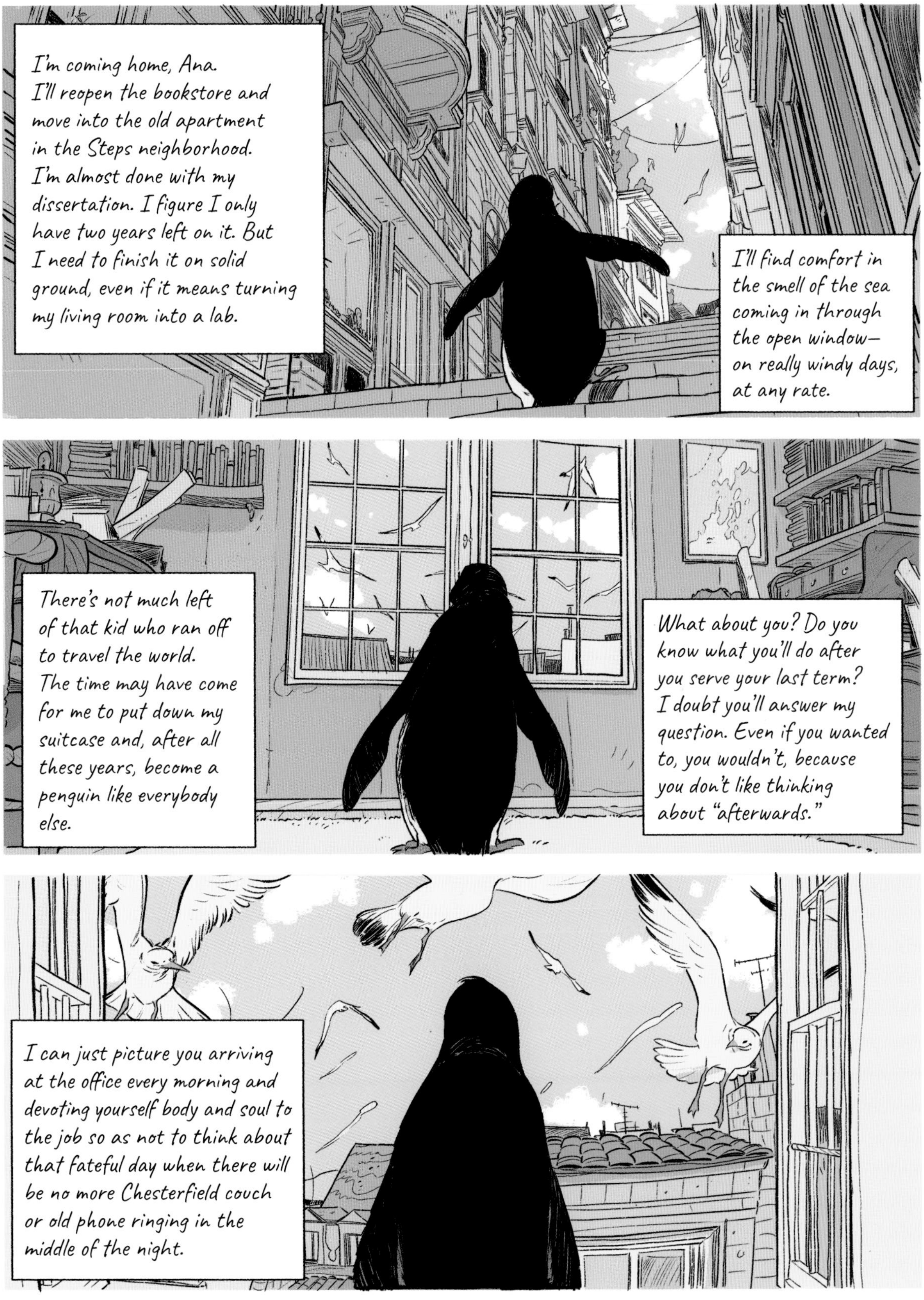
I'm coming home, Ana. I'll reopen the bookstore and move into the old apartment in the Steps neighborhood. I'm almost done with my dissertation. I figure I only have two years left on it. But I need to finish it on solid ground, even if it means turning my living room into a lab.
I'll find comfort in the smell of the sea coming in through the open window—on really windy days, at any rate.
There's not much left of that kid who ran off to travel the world. The time may have come for me to put down my suitcase and, after all these years, become a penguin like everybody else.
What about you? Do you know what you'll do after you serve your last term? I doubt you'll answer my question. Even if you wanted to, you wouldn't, because you don't like thinking about "afterwards."
I can just picture you arriving at the office every morning and devoting yourself body and soul to the job so as not to think about that fateful day when there will be no more Chesterfield couch or old phone ringing in the middle of the night.

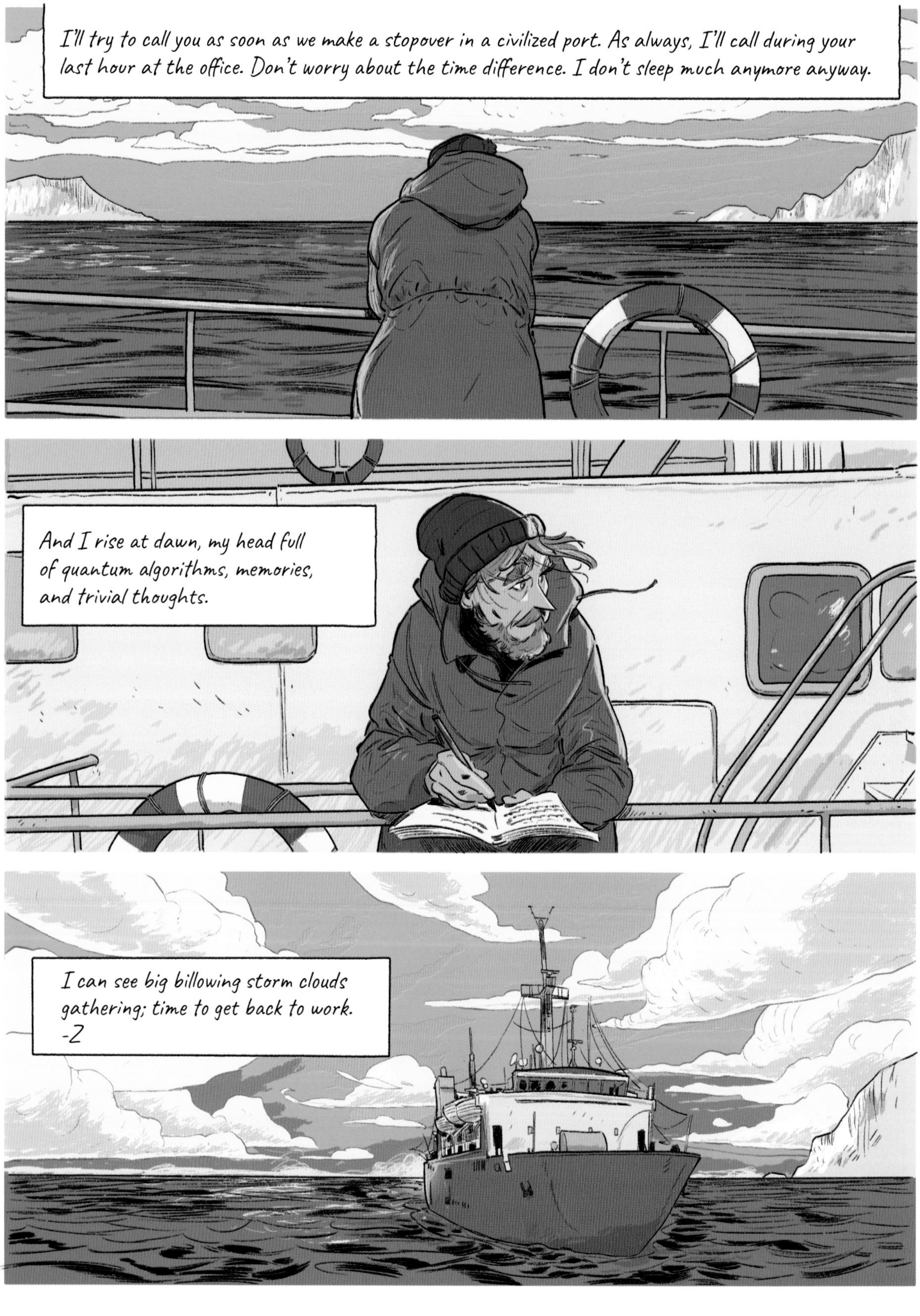
I'll try to call you as soon as we make a stopover in a civilized port. As always, I'll call during your last hour at the office. Don't worry about the time difference. I don't sleep much anymore anyway.
And I rise at dawn, my head full of quantum algorithms, memories, and trivial thoughts.
I can see big billowing storm clouds gathering; time to get back to work. -Z

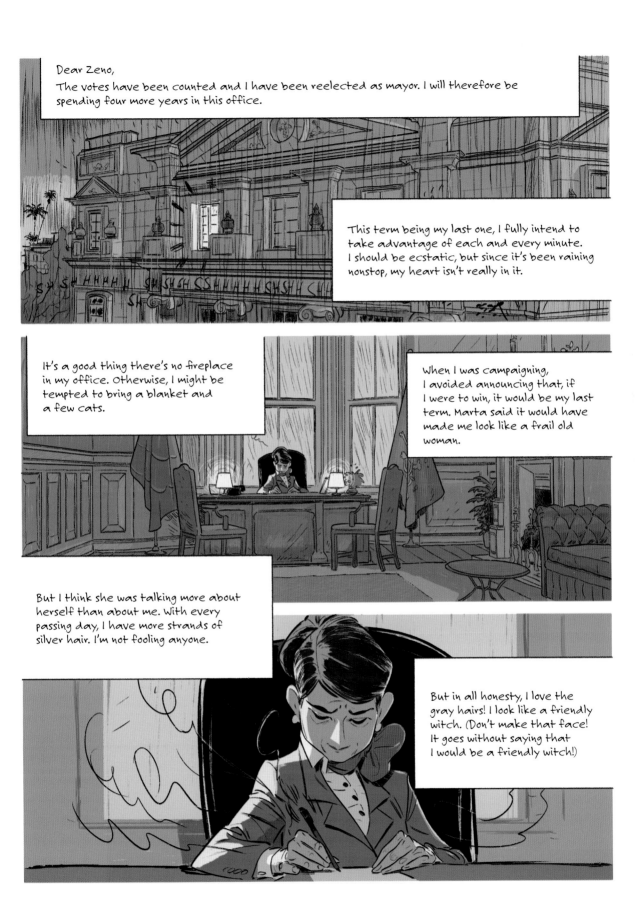

Dear Zeno,

The votes have been counted and I have been reelected as mayor. I will therefore be spending four more years in this office.

This term being my last one, I fully intend to take advantage of each and every minute. I should be ecstatic, but since it's been raining nonstop, my heart isn't really in it.

It's a good thing there's no fireplace in my office. Otherwise, I might be tempted to bring a blanket and a few cats.

When I was campaigning, I avoided announcing that, if I were to win, it would be my last term. Marta said it would have made me look like a frail old woman.

But I think she was talking more about herself than about me. With every passing day, I have more strands of silver hair. I'm not fooling anyone.

But in all honesty, I love the gray hairs! I look like a friendly witch. (Don't make that face! It goes without saying that I would be a friendly witch!)

53

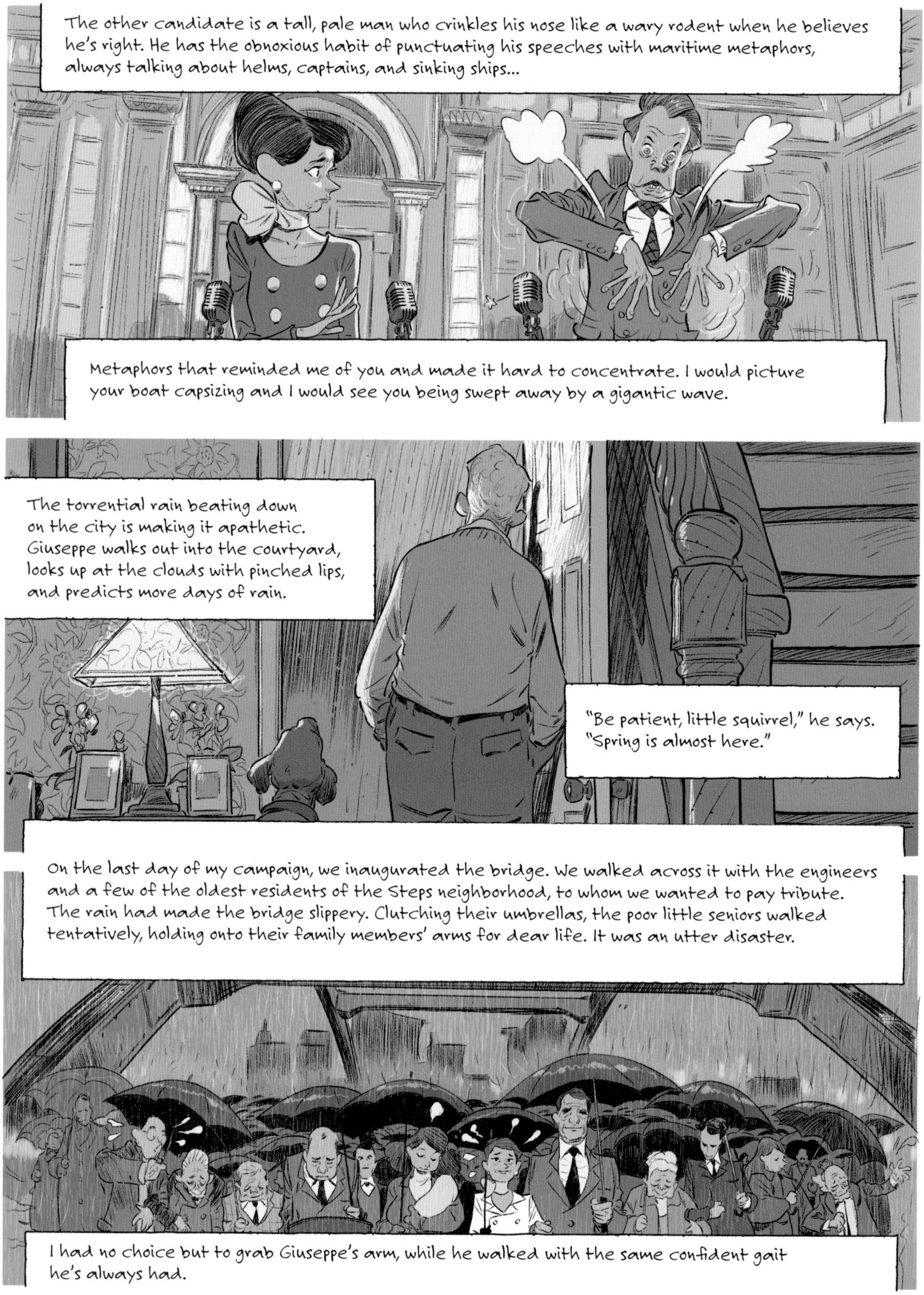
The other candidate is a tall, pale man who crinkles his nose like a wary rodent when he believes he's right. He has the obnoxious habit of punctuating his speeches with maritime metaphors, always talking about helms, captains, and sinking ships...
Metaphors that reminded me of you and made it hard to concentrate. I would picture your boat capsizing and I would see you being swept away by a gigantic wave.
The torrential rain beating down on the city is making it apathetic. Giuseppe walks out into the courtyard, looks up at the clouds with pinched lips, and predicts more days of rain.
"Be patient, little squirrel," he says. "Spring is almost here."
On the last day of my campaign, we inaugurated the bridge. We walked across it with the engineers and a few of the oldest residents of the Steps neighborhood, to whom we wanted to pay tribute. The rain had made the bridge slippery. Clutching their umbrellas, the poor little seniors walked tentatively, holding onto their family members' arms for dear life. It was an utter disaster.
I had no choice but to grab Giuseppe's arm, while he walked with the same confident gait he's always had.

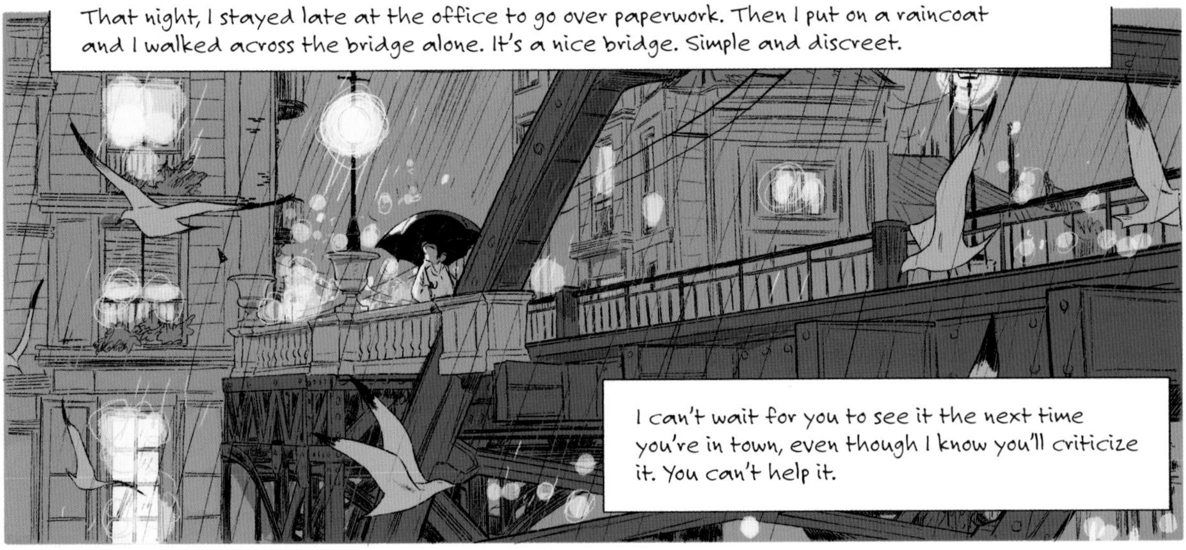
That night, I stayed late at the office to go over paperwork. Then I put on a raincoat and I walked across the bridge alone. It's a nice bridge. Simple and discreet.
I can't wait for you to see it the next time you're in town, even though I know you'll criticize it. You can't help it.

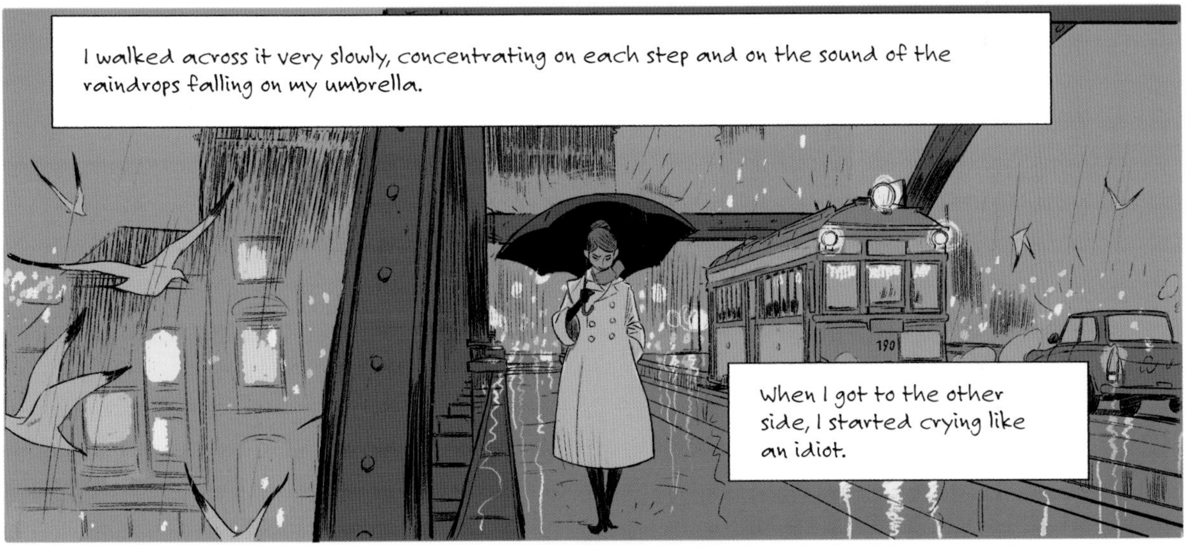
I walked across it very slowly, concentrating on each step and on the sound of the raindrops falling on my umbrella.
190
When I got to the other side, I started crying like an idiot.

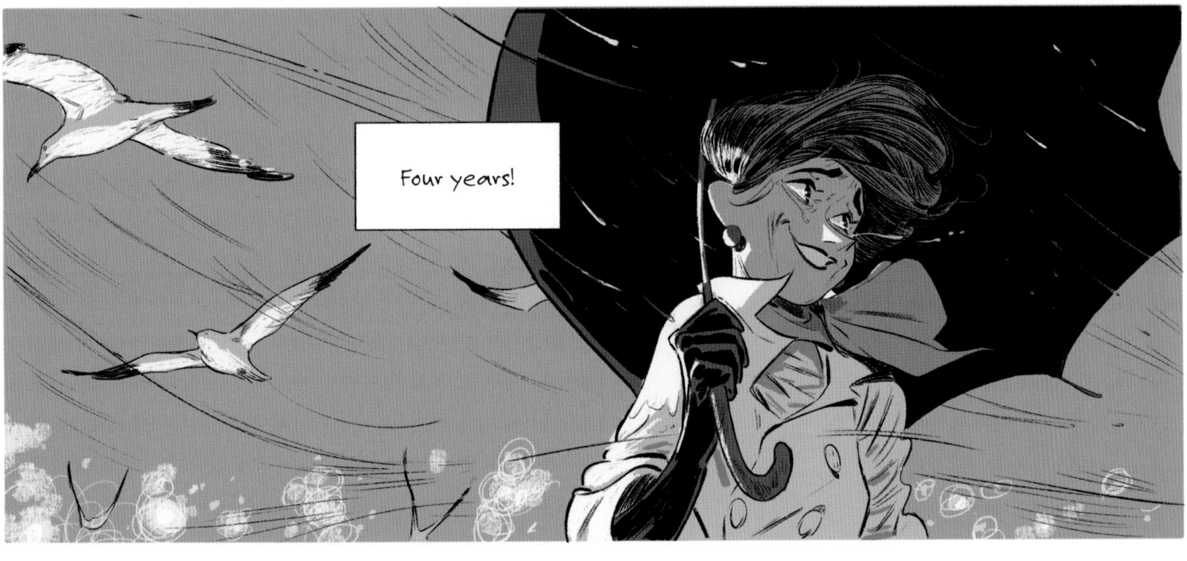
Four years!

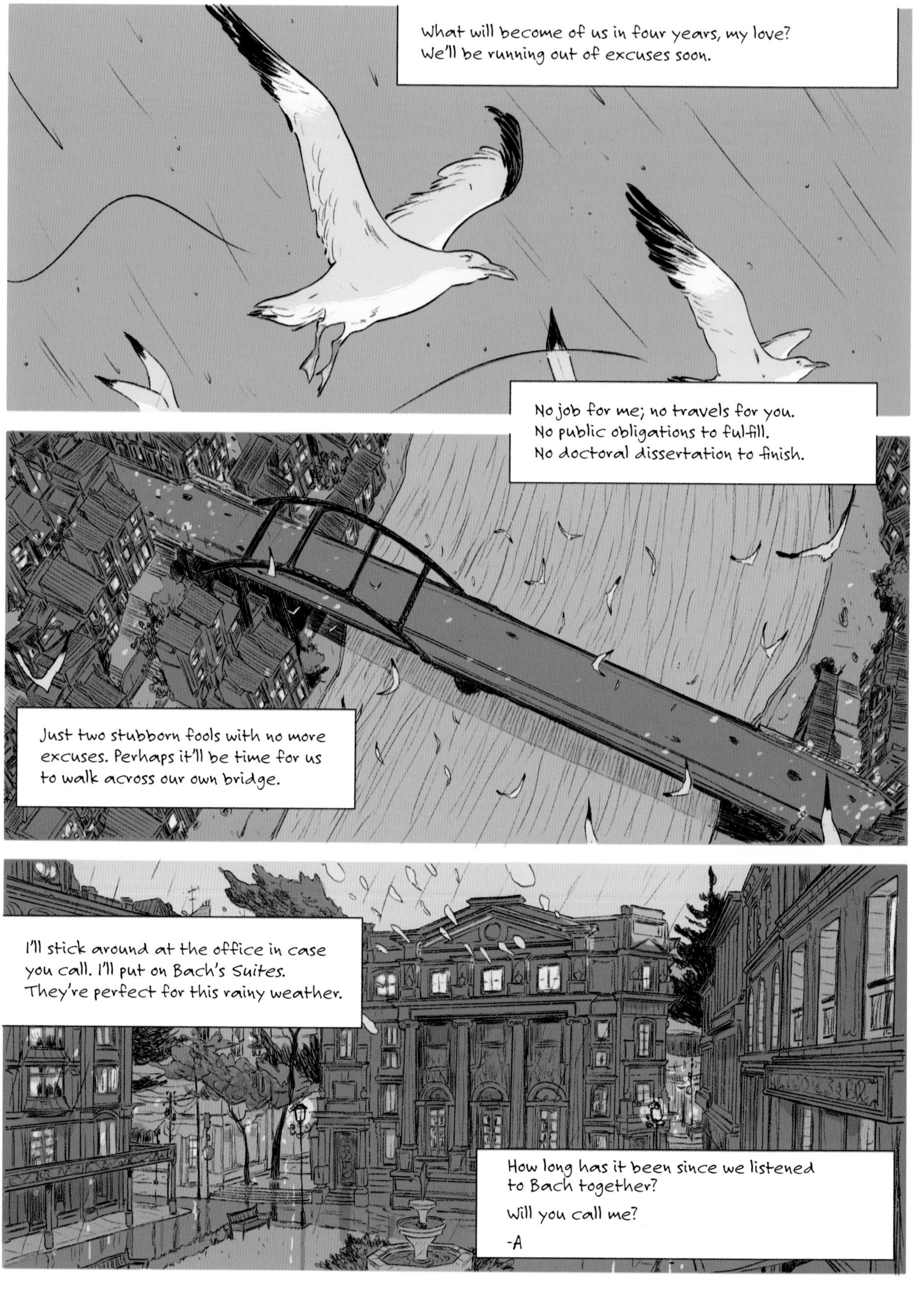
What will become of us in four years, my love? We'll be running out of excuses soon.
No job for me; no travels for you. No public obligations to ful-fill. No doctoral dissertation to finish.
Just two stubborn fools with no more excuses. Perhaps it'll be time for us to walk across our own bridge.
I'll stick around at the office in case you call. I'll put on Bach's Suites. They're perfect for this rainy weather.
How long has it been since we listened to Bach together?
Will you call me?
-A

CHAPTER
14

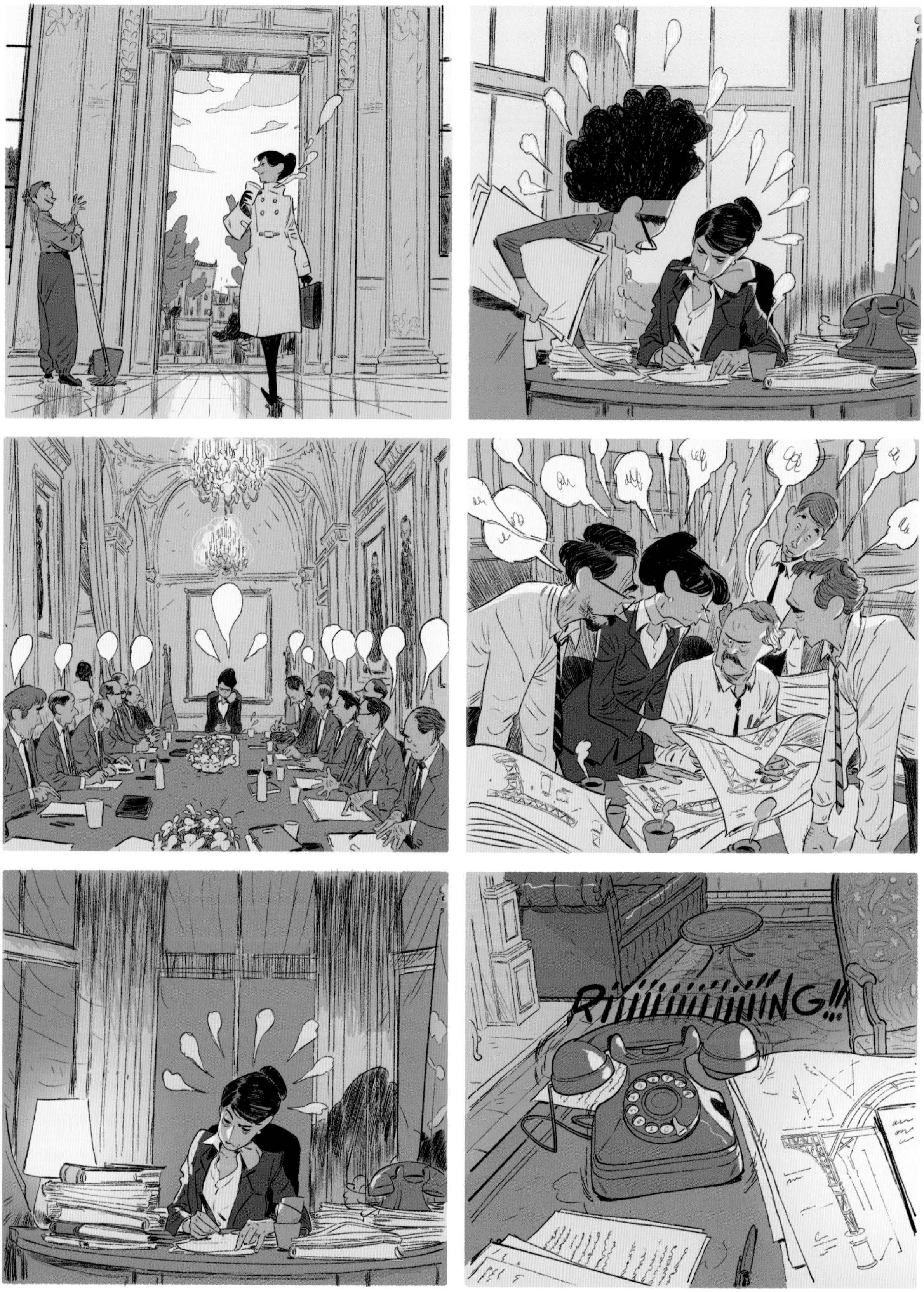
RIIIIIIIIIIIIIING!!!

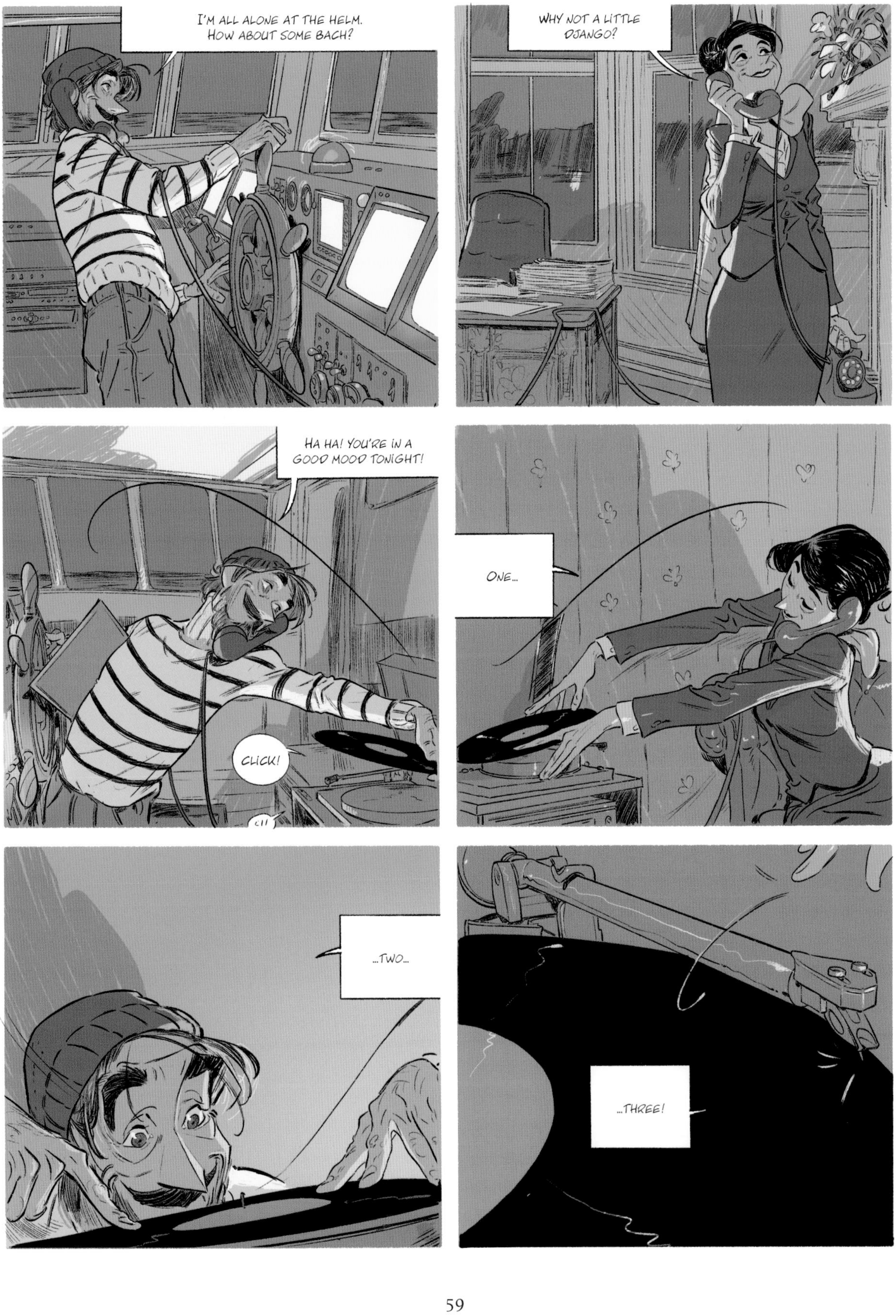
I'M ALL ALONE AT THE HELM. HOW ABOUT SOME BACH?
WHY NOT A LITTLE DJANGO?
HA HA! YOU'RE IN A GOOD MOOD TONIGHT!
CLICK!
ONE...
...TWO...
...THREE!

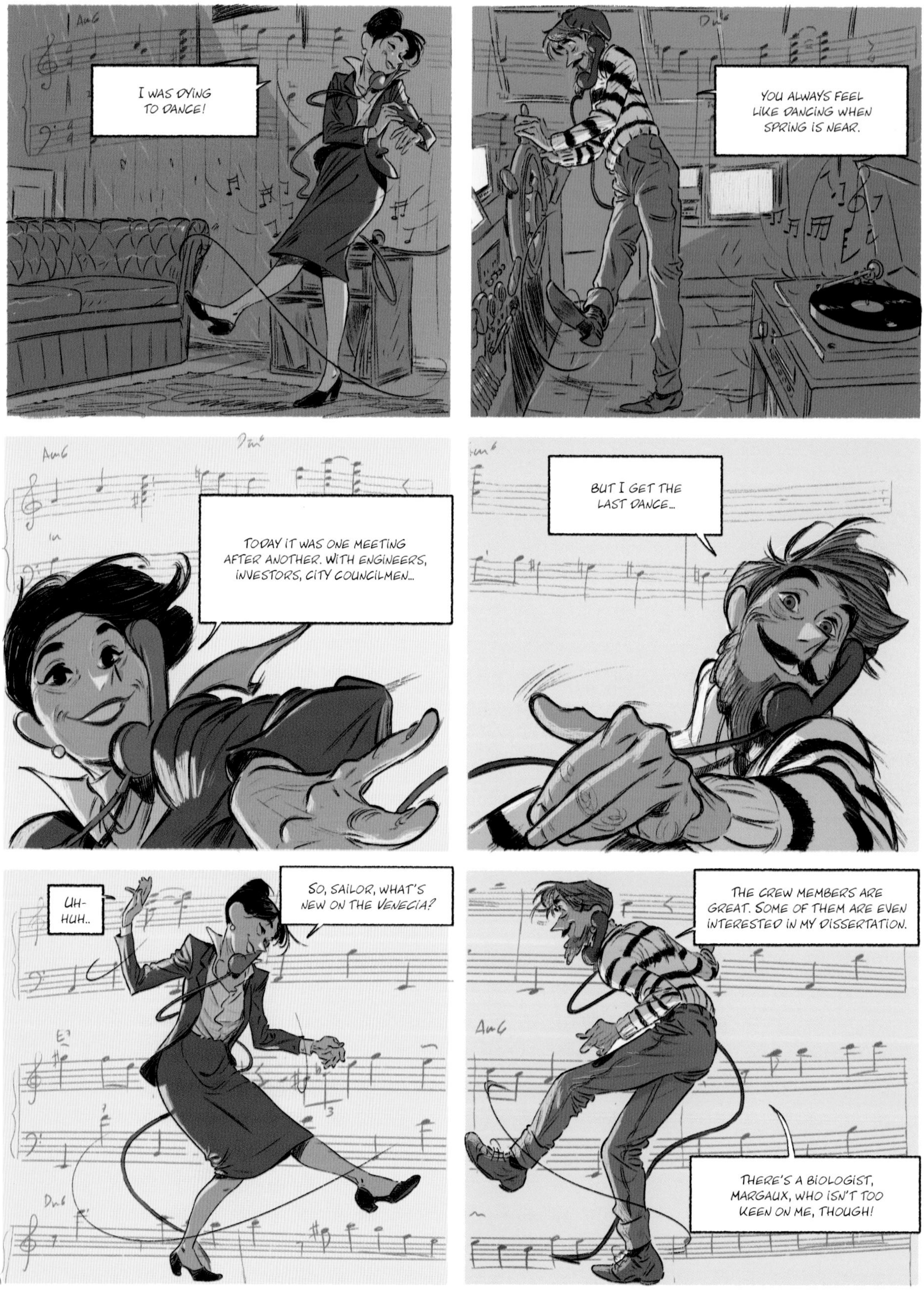
I WAS DYING TO DANCE!
YOU ALWAYS FEEL LIKE DANCING WHEN SPRING IS NEAR.
TODAY IT WAS ONE MEETING AFTER ANOTHER. WITH ENGINEERS, INVESTORS, CITY COUNCILMEN...
BUT I GET THE LAST DANCE...
UH-HUH..
SO, SAILOR, WHAT'S NEW ON THE VENECIA?
THE CREW MEMBERS ARE GREAT. SOME OF THEM ARE EVEN INTERESTED IN MY DISSERTATION.
THERE'S A BIOLOGIST, MARGAUX, WHO ISN'T TOO KEEN ON ME, THOUGH!

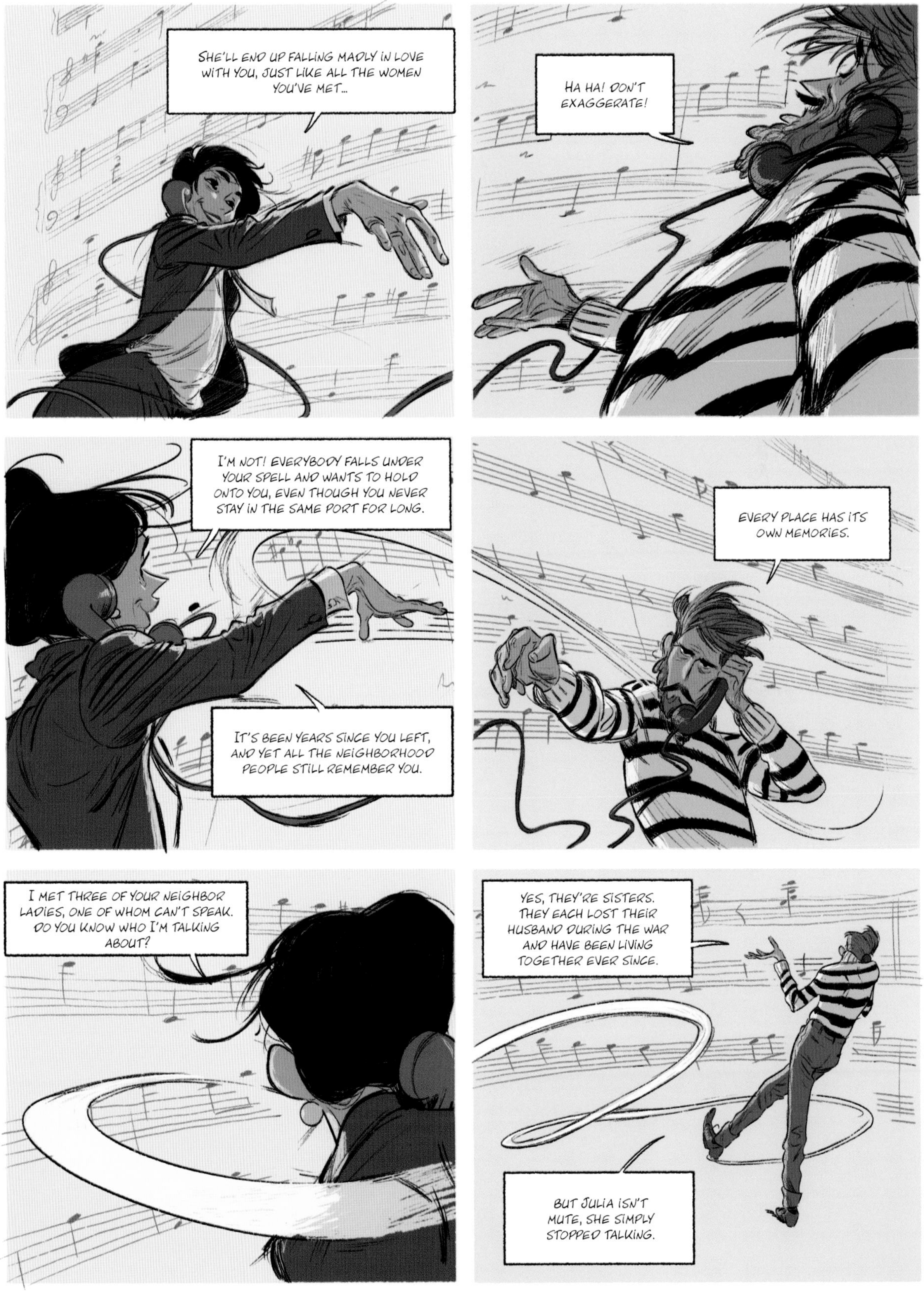
SHE'LL END UP FALLING MADLY IN LOVE WITH YOU, JUST LIKE ALL THE WOMEN YOU'VE MET...
HA HA! DON'T EXAGGERATE!
I'M NOT! EVERYBODY FALLS UNDER YOUR SPELL AND WANTS TO HOLD ONTO YOU, EVEN THOUGH YOU NEVER STAY IN THE SAME PORT FOR LONG.
IT'S BEEN YEARS SINCE YOU LEFT, AND YET ALL THE NEIGHBORHOOD PEOPLE STILL REMEMBER YOU.
EVERY PLACE HAS ITS OWN MEMORIES.
I MET THREE OF YOUR NEIGHBOR LADIES, ONE OF WHOM CAN'T SPEAK. DO YOU KNOW WHO I'M TALKING ABOUT?
YES, THEY'RE SISTERS. THEY EACH LOST THEIR HUSBAND DURING THE WAR AND HAVE BEEN LIVING TOGETHER EVER SINCE.
BUT JULIA ISN'T MUTE, SHE SIMPLY STOPPED TALKING.

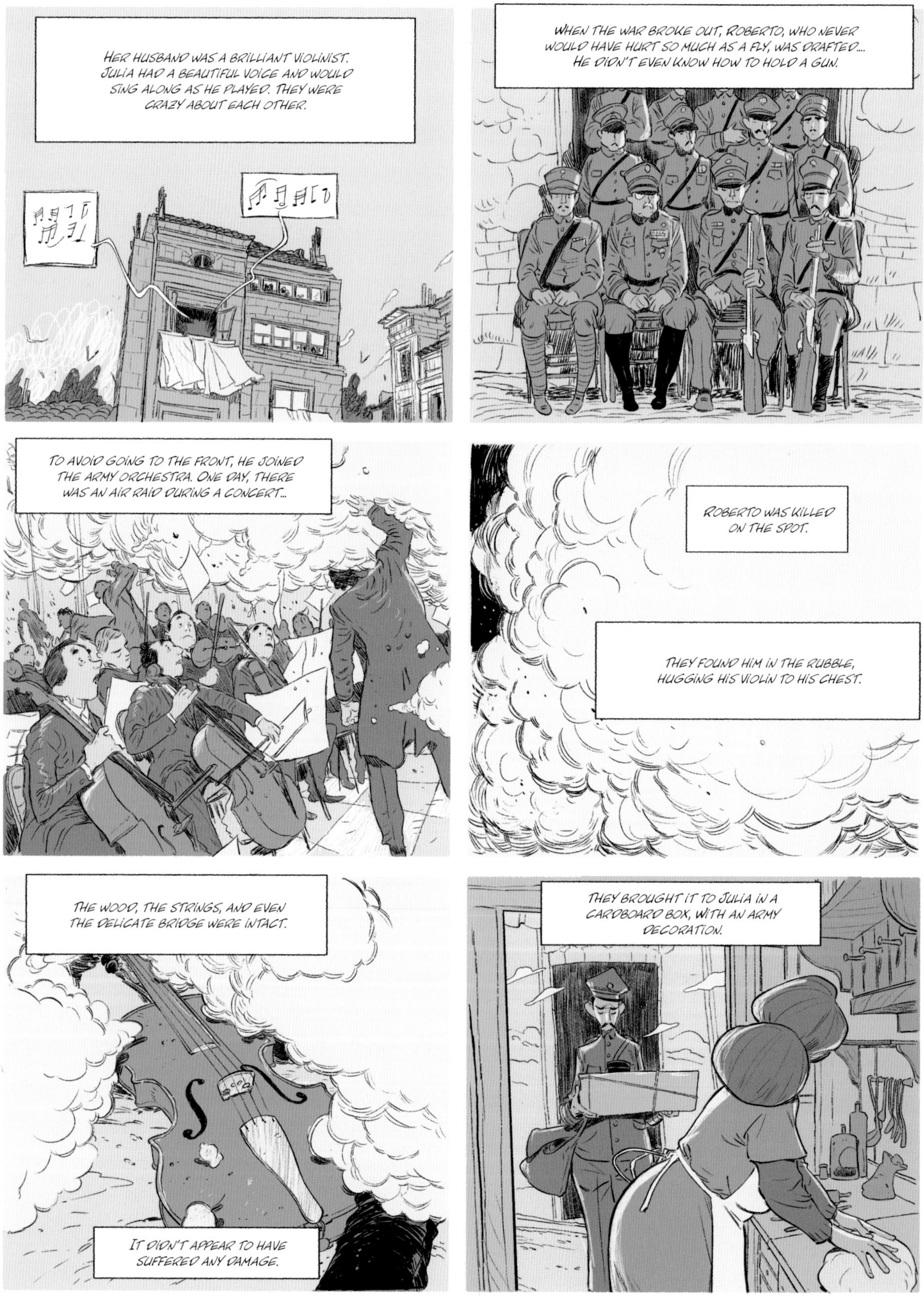
HER HUSBAND WAS A BRILLIANT VIOLINIST. JULIA HAD A BEAUTIFUL VOICE AND WOULD SING ALONG AS HE PLAYED. THEY WERE CRAZY ABOUT EACH OTHER.
WHEN THE WAR BROKE OUT, ROBERTO, WHO NEVER WOULD HAVE HURT SO MUCH AS A FLY, WAS DRAFTED.... HE DIDN'T EVEN KNOW HOW TO HOLD A GUN.
TO AVOID GOING TO THE FRONT, HE JOINED THE ARMY ORCHESTRA. ONE DAY, THERE WAS AN AIR RAID DURING A CONCERT...
ROBERTO WAS KILLED ON THE SPOT.
THEY FOUND HIM IN THE RUBBLE, HUGGING HIS VIOLIN TO HIS CHEST.
THE WOOD, THE STRINGS, AND EVEN THE DELICATE BRIDGE WERE INTACT.
IT DIDN'T APPEAR TO HAVE SUFFERED ANY DAMAGE.
THEY BROUGHT IT TO JULIA IN A CARDBOARD BOX, WITH AN ARMY DECORATION.

WHEN SHE TRIED TO PLAY IT IN MEMORY OF ROBERTO, THE VIOLIN HAD GONE MUTE. IT DIDN'T LET OUT A SOUND.

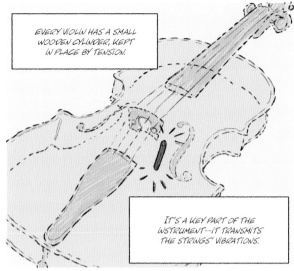

EVERY VIOLIN HAS A SMALL WOODEN CYLINDER, KEPT IN PLACE BY TENSION.

IT'S A KEY PART OF THE INSTRUMENT--IT TRANSMITS THE STRINGS' VIBRATIONS.

IT'S CALLED THE "SOUL OF THE VIOLIN." IT MUST'VE COME APART IN THE BLOW.

AFTER ROBERTO DIED, JULIA'S SOUL ALSO CAME APART.

SHE HASN'T SPOKEN A WORD SINCE THAT DAY...

A REAL TRAGEDY.

I'VE BROUGHT YOU DOWN, I'M SORRY.

NO, DON'T BE. THE STORY OF JULIA AND ROBERTO DESERVES TO BE TOLD. I'M GLAD YOU SHARED IT WITH ME.

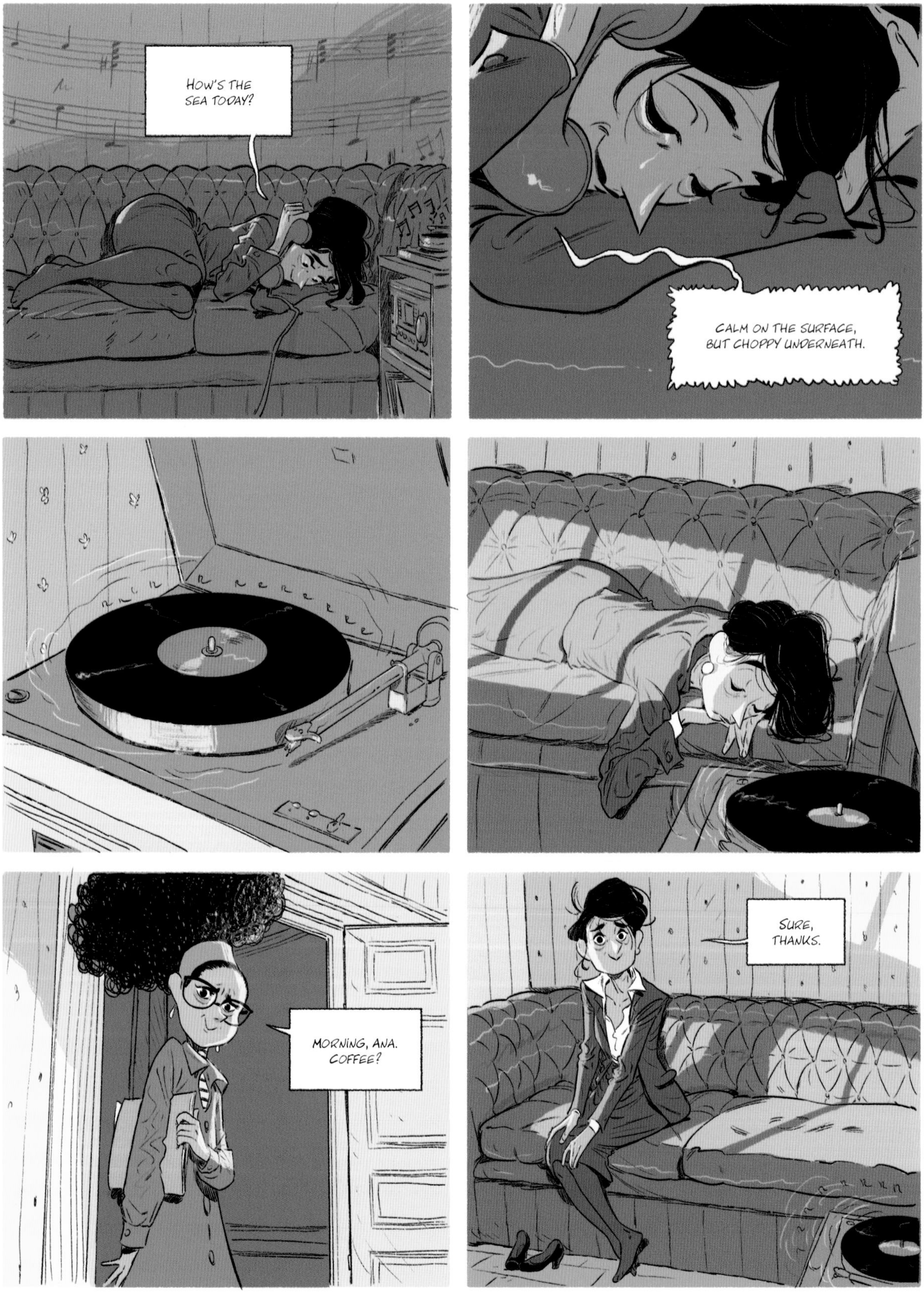
How's the sea today?
Calm on the surface, but choppy underneath.
Morning, Ana. Coffee?
Sure, thanks.

CHAPTER
13

FFLLLLSHHSHHHHHHH!!

YOU'VE BARELY BEEN ON BOARD TWO NIGHTS AND WE ALREADY HAVE ROUGH SEAS! I HOPE THIS ISN'T A BAD OMEN!

WHY WOULD IT BE A BAD OMEN?

WHAT KIND OF A QUESTION IS THAT? ARE YOU A SAILOR OR NOT?!

IT'S ONLY NATURAL FOR BOGDAN NOT TO KNOW ANYTHING ABOUT THE SEA, HE'S AN IDIOT. BUT YOU! I WAS EXPECTING MORE FROM OUR NEW BOATSWAIN!

THE NIGHT I MET OLENKA, THE MOON WAS JUST AS FULL, BUT THE WAVES WERE MUCH BIGGER!

IS OLENKA YOUR WIFE?

SHE'S BEEN MY WIFE THREE TIMES! WE GOT MARRIED THREE TIMES AND SHE KICKED ME OUT THREE TIMES!

ARE YOU MARRIED?

I'M NOT CUT OUT FOR MARRIAGE.

FFLLLLSHHSHHHHHHH

66

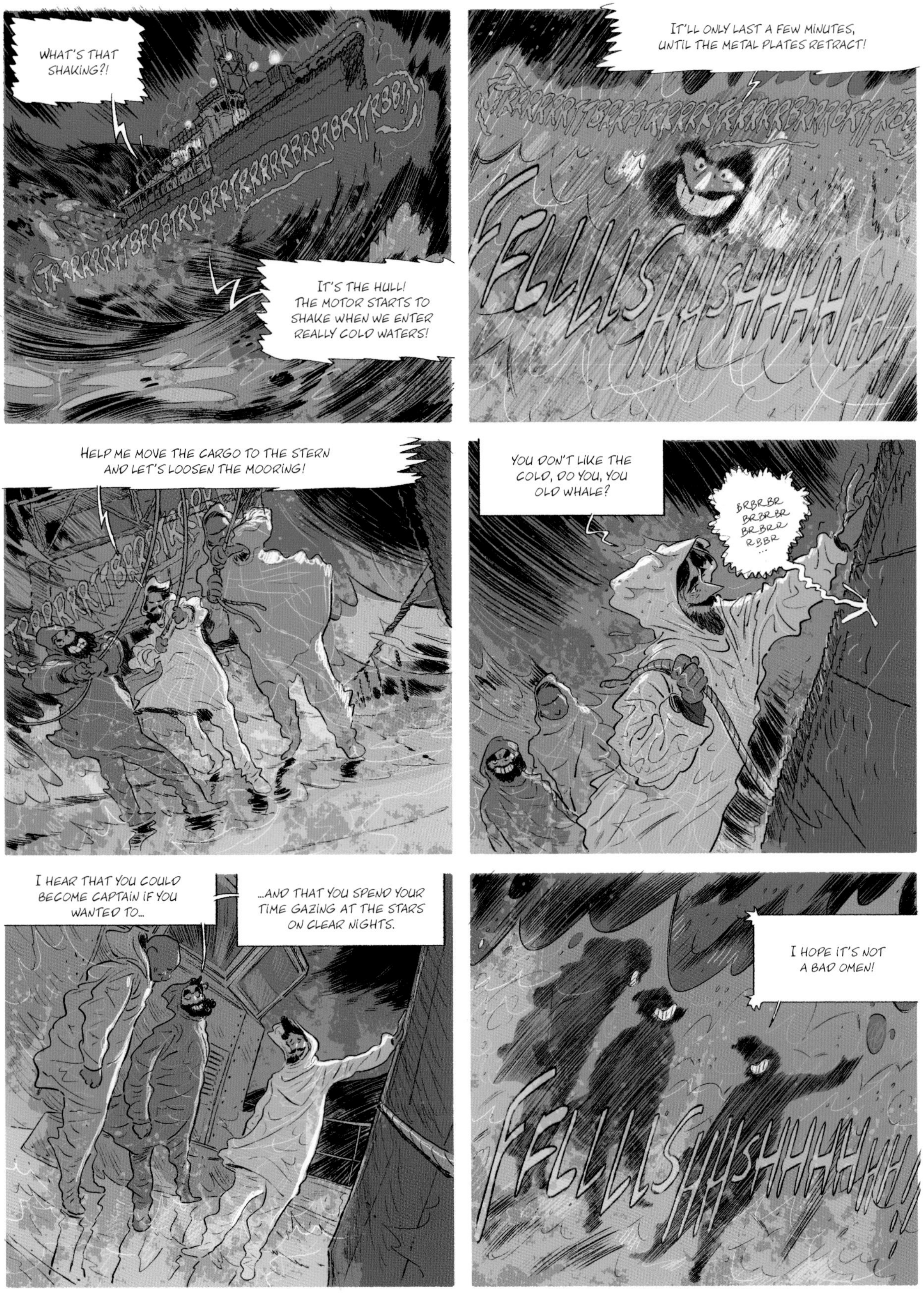

WHAT'S THAT SHAKING?!
IT'S THE HULL! THE MOTOR STARTS TO SHAKE WHEN WE ENTER REALLY COLD WATERS!
IT'LL ONLY LAST A FEW MINUTES, UNTIL THE METAL PLATES RETRACT!
HELP ME MOVE THE CARGO TO THE STERN AND LET'S LOOSEN THE MOORING!
YOU DON'T LIKE THE COLD, DO YOU, YOU OLD WHALE?
BRBRBR BRBRBR BRBRR RBBR ...
I HEAR THAT YOU COULD BECOME CAPTAIN IF YOU WANTED TO...
...AND THAT YOU SPEND YOUR TIME GAZING AT THE STARS ON CLEAR NIGHTS.
I HOPE IT'S NOT A BAD OMEN!

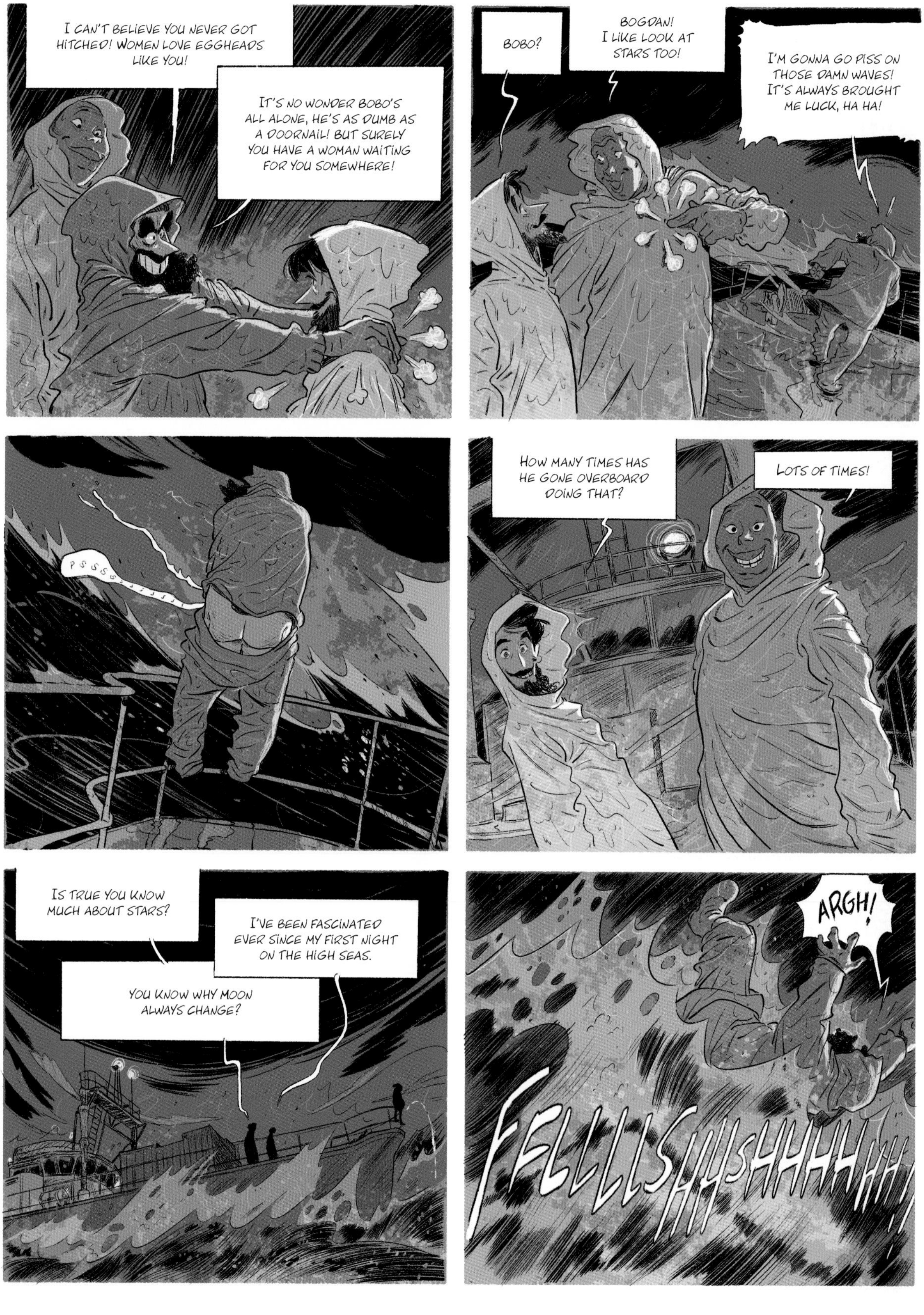
I CAN'T BELIEVE YOU NEVER GOT HITCHED! WOMEN LOVE EGGHEADS LIKE YOU!
IT'S NO WONDER BOBO'S ALL ALONE, HE'S AS DUMB AS A DOORNAIL! BUT SURELY YOU HAVE A WOMAN WAITING FOR YOU SOMEWHERE!
BOBO?
BOGDAN! I LIKE LOOK AT STARS TOO!
I'M GONNA GO PISS ON THOSE DAMN WAVES! IT'S ALWAYS BROUGHT ME LUCK, HA HA!
PSSSSSSSSS
HOW MANY TIMES HAS HE GONE OVERBOARD DOING THAT?
LOTS OF TIMES!
IS TRUE YOU KNOW MUCH ABOUT STARS?
I'VE BEEN FASCINATED EVER SINCE MY FIRST NIGHT ON THE HIGH SEAS.
YOU KNOW WHY MOON ALWAYS CHANGE?
ARGH!
FFLLLLSHHSHHHHHH!

PLEASE DON'T TELL THE CAPTAIN. HE FORBADE ME FROM PISSING IN THE WATER.

I NEVER GIVE AWAY A SECRET. IT'S BAD LUCK.

BOBO, THE MOON CHANGES BECAUSE IT'S ATTRACTED TO EARTH. IT'S CALLED ORBITING.

MOON AND EARTH WANT TO BE TOGETHER? SO WHY THEY NOT MEET?

A LONG TIME AGO, THE MOON AND EARTH EACH FOLLOWED THEIR OWN TRAJECTORIES.

ONE DAY THEY CROSSED PATHS AND WERE MUTUALLY ATTRACTED TO EACH OTHER, BUT NEITHER MANAGED TO STOP.

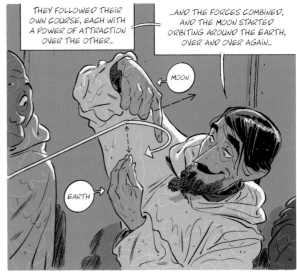

THEY FOLLOWED THEIR OWN COURSE, EACH WITH A POWER OF ATTRACTION OVER THE OTHER...

...AND THE FORCES COMBINED, AND THE MOON STARTED ORBITING AROUND THE EARTH, OVER AND OVER AGAIN...

MOON

EARTH

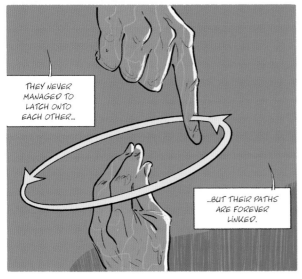

THEY NEVER MANAGED TO LATCH ONTO EACH OTHER...

...BUT THEIR PATHS ARE FOREVER LINKED.

SO MOON AND EARTH ALWAYS LIVE APART?

IT'S ACTUALLY THEIR WAY OF BEING TOGETHER. IF THEY EVER COLLIDED, THEY WOULD CAUSE A LOT OF DAMAGE.

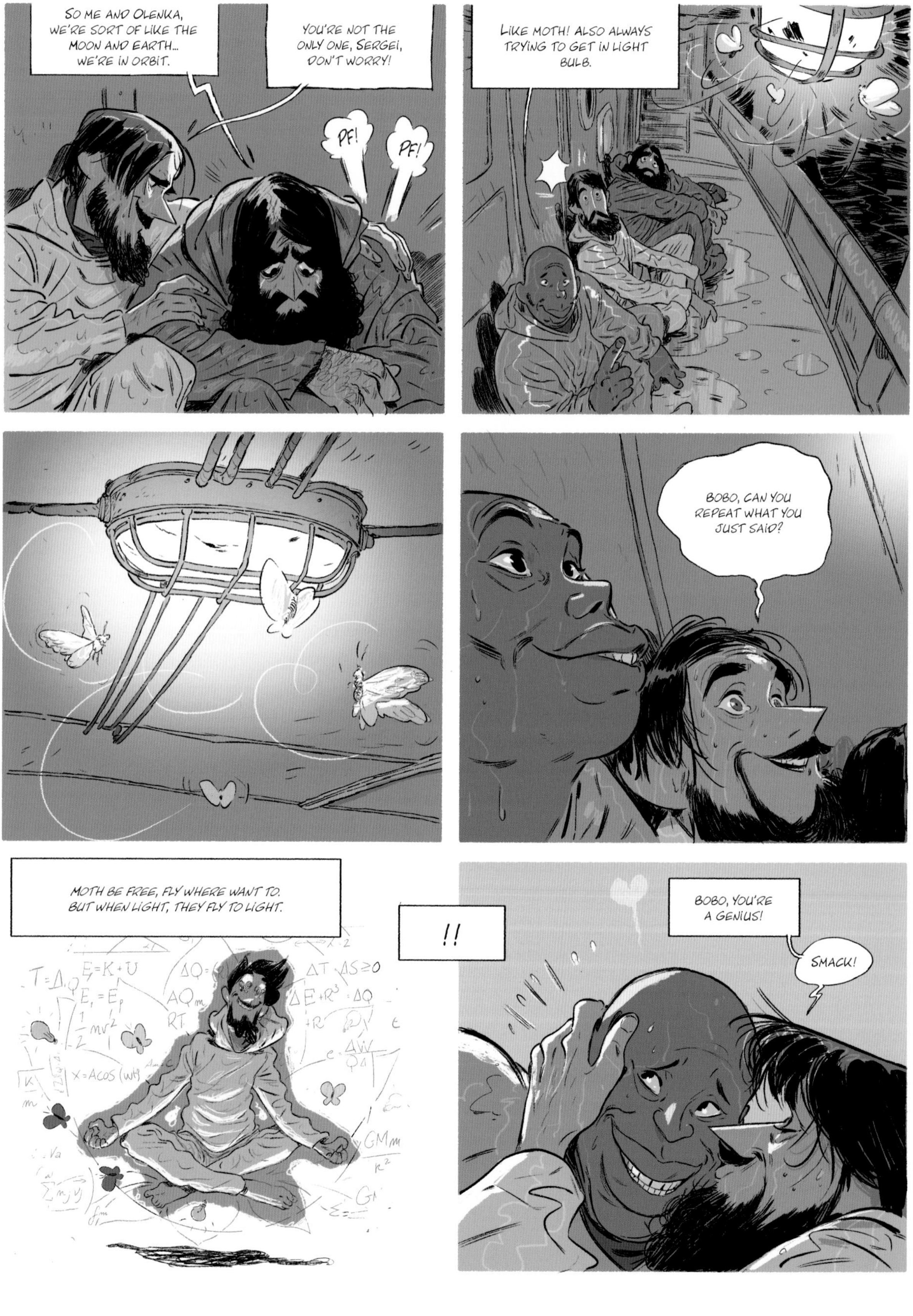
So me and Olenka, we're sort of like the moon and earth... we're in orbit.
You're not the only one, Sergei, don't worry!
PF!
PF!
Like moth! Also always trying to get in light bulb.
Bobo, can you repeat what you just said?
Moth be free, fly where want to. But when light, they fly to light.
!!
Bobo, you're a genius!
SMACK!

CHAPTER
12

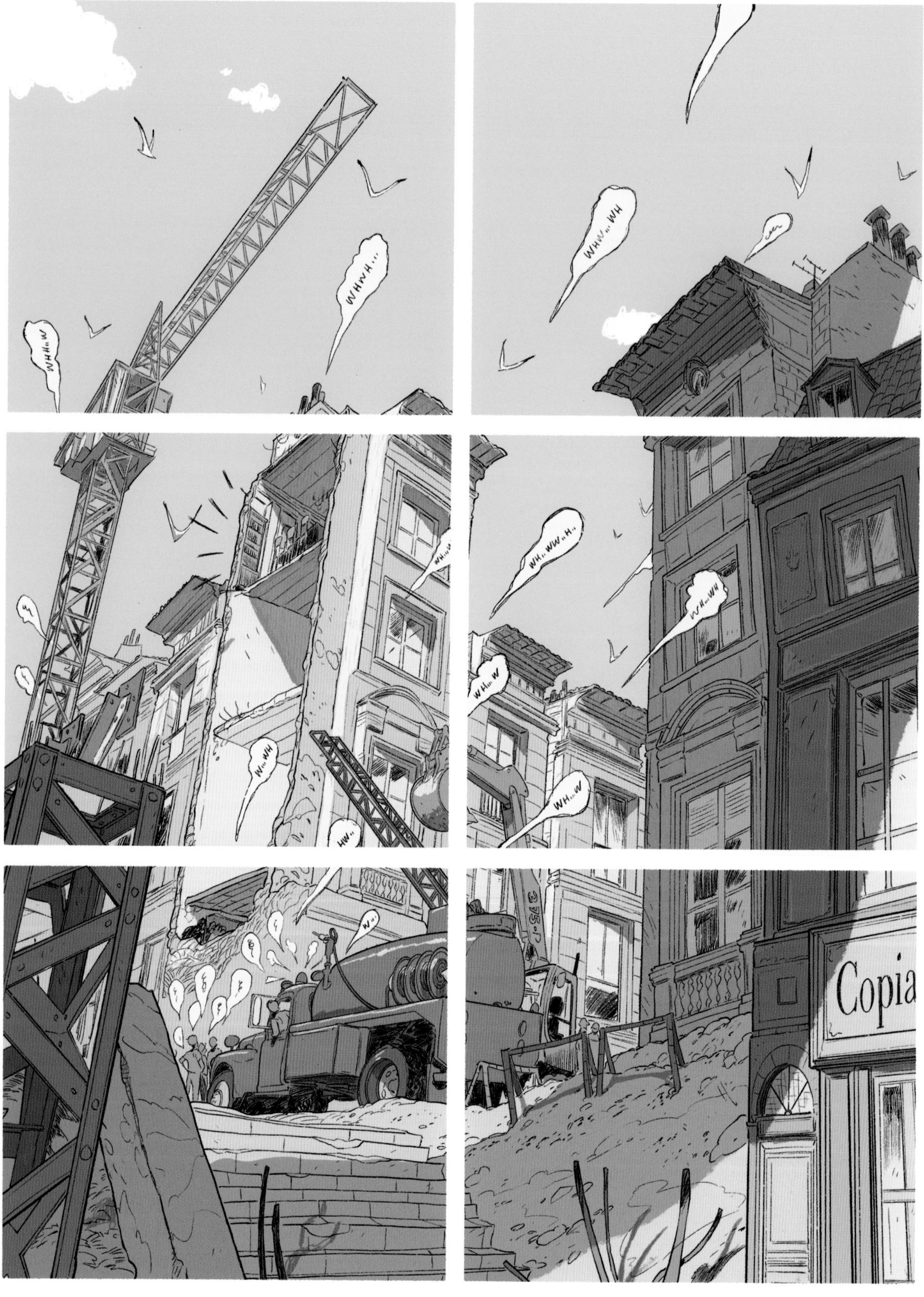
WHWH...
WHWW...WH
WH...WW...H...
WH...WH
WH...W
Copia

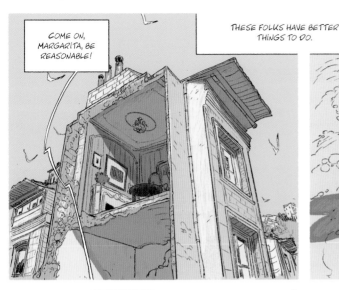

COME ON, MARGARITA, BE REASONABLE!

THESE FOLKS HAVE BETTER THINGS TO DO.

AND IT'S ALMOST LUNCHTIME! PLEASE...

WHAT'S GOING ON?

THE WOMAN ON THE FOURTH FLOOR WON'T COME DOWN. SHE'S BEEN UP THERE ALL MORNING AND WILL ONLY SPEAK TO THE MAYOR.

HAVE THEY BEEN COMPENSATED?

OF COURSE, AS HAVE ALL THE BUILDING'S OCCUPANTS. I WENT TO THE OFFICE TO GET THE FILE WE HAVE ON IT. OH, AND YOU GOT ANOTHER ONE OF THOSE LETTERS WITHOUT A RETURN ADDRESS...

THANKS MARTA, YOU CAN GO HOME. IT'S SATURDAY, AND BESIDES, IT'S YOUR ANNIVERSARY.

ARE YOU SURE YOU DON'T NEED ME ANYMORE?

YES, I'M FINE, DON'T WORRY. HAVE A GREAT WEEKEND!

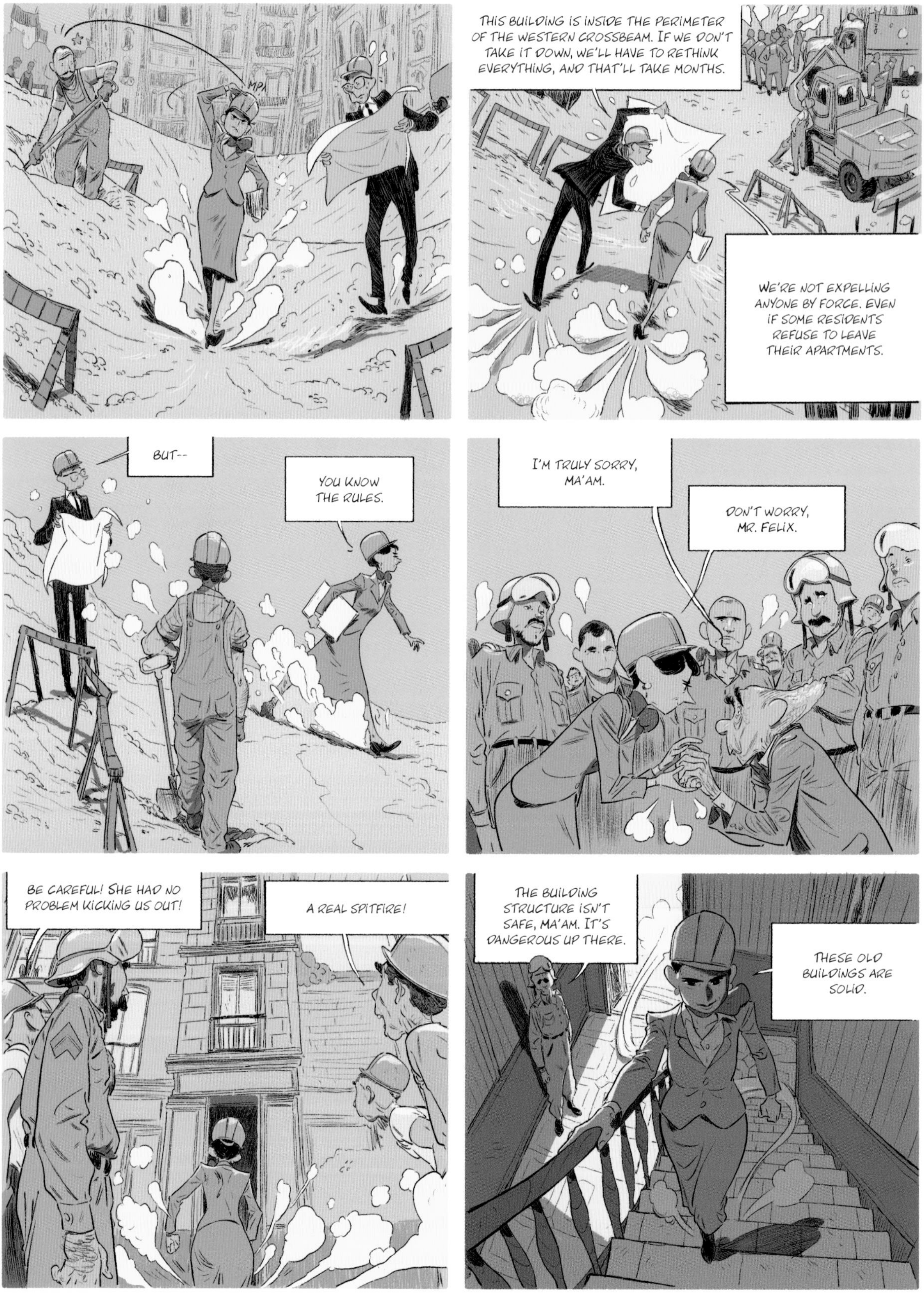
MPA
THIS BUILDING IS INSIDE THE PERIMETER OF THE WESTERN CROSSBEAM. IF WE DON'T TAKE IT DOWN, WE'LL HAVE TO RETHINK EVERYTHING, AND THAT'LL TAKE MONTHS.
WE'RE NOT EXPELLING ANYONE BY FORCE. EVEN IF SOME RESIDENTS REFUSE TO LEAVE THEIR APARTMENTS.
BUT--
YOU KNOW THE RULES.
I'M TRULY SORRY, MA'AM.
DON'T WORRY, MR. FELIX.
BE CAREFUL! SHE HAD NO PROBLEM KICKING US OUT!
A REAL SPITFIRE!
THE BUILDING STRUCTURE ISN'T SAFE, MA'AM. IT'S DANGEROUS UP THERE.
THESE OLD BUILDINGS ARE SOLID.

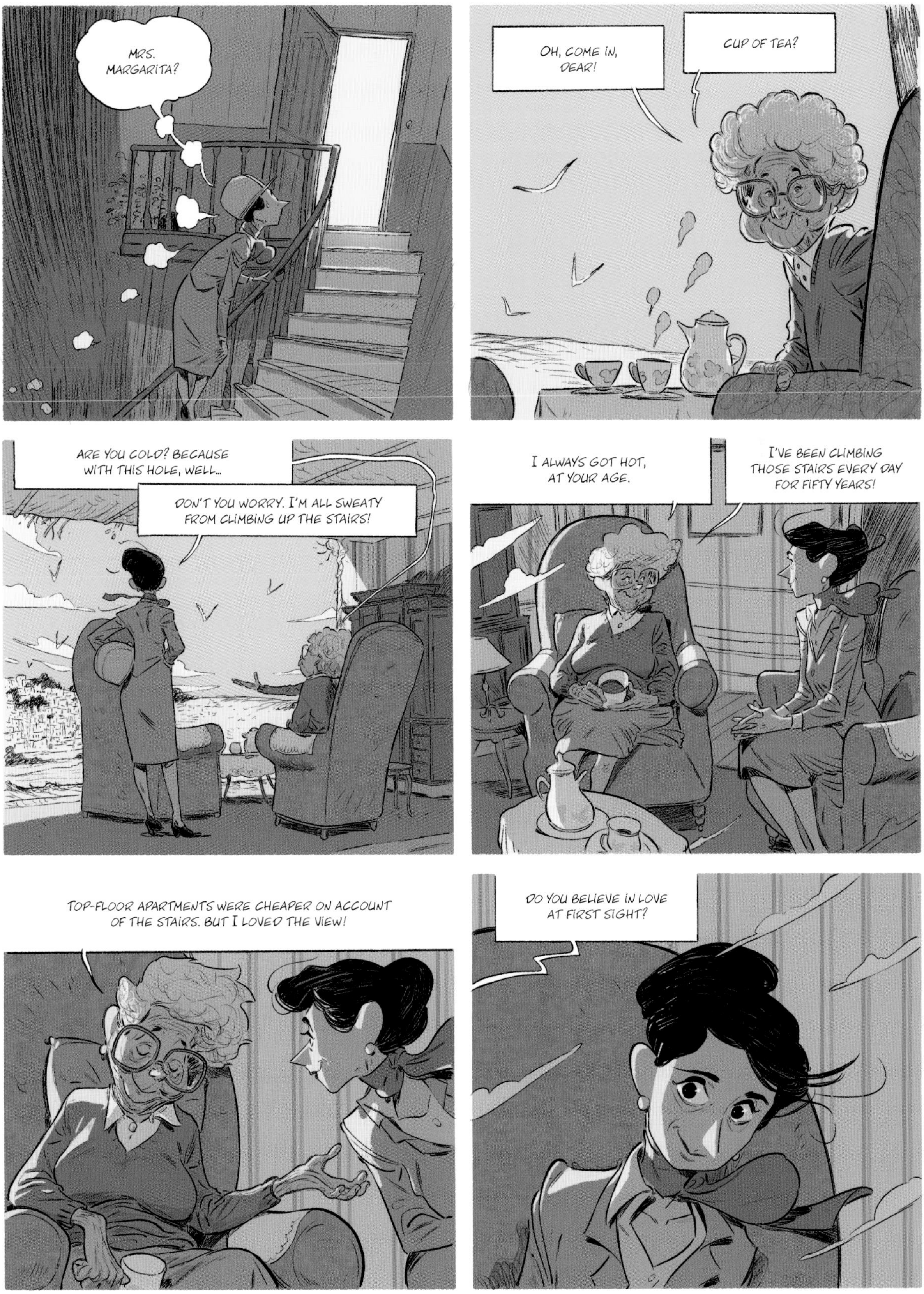
MRS. MARGARITA?
OH, COME IN, DEAR!
CUP OF TEA?
ARE YOU COLD? BECAUSE WITH THIS HOLE, WELL...
DON'T YOU WORRY. I'M ALL SWEATY FROM CLIMBING UP THE STAIRS!
I ALWAYS GOT HOT, AT YOUR AGE.
I'VE BEEN CLIMBING THOSE STAIRS EVERY DAY FOR FIFTY YEARS!
TOP-FLOOR APARTMENTS WERE CHEAPER ON ACCOUNT OF THE STAIRS. BUT I LOVED THE VIEW!
DO YOU BELIEVE IN LOVE AT FIRST SIGHT?

MRS. MARGARITA, WHEN CONSTRUCTION IS FINISHED, THE NEIGHBORHOOD WON'T BE THE SAME ANYMORE. MOST OF YOUR NEIGHBORS TOOK THE MONEY AND LEFT.

FELIX'S CHILDREN SAY WE SHOULD MOVE TO A GROUND-LEVEL HOME IN THE SUBURBS, BUT I'VE ALWAYS LIVED IN THIS NEIGHBORHOOD.

THEY'RE NOT MY KIDS, SEE. I WAS FELIX'S SECOND'S WIFE. I NEVER HAD CHILDREN MYSELF. WHAT ABOUT YOU?

YES, A TEENAGER. BUT SHE'S NOT ALWAYS MY BIGGEST FAN.

COME NOW, I BET SHE ADMIRES YOU VERY MUCH!

MRS. MARGARITA, I'M AFRAID YOU DON'T UNDERSTAND THE SITUATION. THE BRIDGE WILL PASS RIGHT UNDER YOUR HOUSE. IT WILL BE HIDEOUS.

AT MY AGE, LOOKS DON'T MATTER.

BUT YOU ACCEPTED OUR OFFER.

BECAUSE FELIX INSISTED. BUT THEN I REMEMBERED THE BOTANICAL GARDEN THAT WAS DEMOLISHED LAST YEAR, AND IT MADE ME SAD. I DON'T WANT MY APARTMENT TO SUFFER THE SAME FATE.

IT MADE ME SAD AS WELL. BUT THE GREENHOUSE WAS IN SUCH A TERRIBLE STATE THAT IT HAD TO BE DESTROYED EITHER WAY.

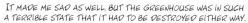

I SUPPOSE WE ALL GET OLD EVENTUALLY.

THIS IS THE MONEY YOU GAVE US TO LEAVE OUR APARTMENT.

FELIX TOOK A BIT TO GO BUY HIMSELF SOME SHOES, BUT I PUT IT BACK IN THE ENVELOPE ON TUESDAY.

POOR FELIX, HE'S VERY WORRIED ABOUT MY HEALTH.

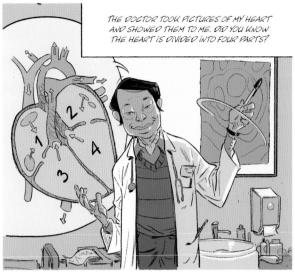

THE DOCTOR TOOK PICTURES OF MY HEART AND SHOWED THEM TO ME. DID YOU KNOW THE HEART IS DIVIDED INTO FOUR PARTS?

IT'S STRANGE...I ALWAYS THOUGHT OF THE HEART AS A LITTLE BOX IN WHICH WE PUT EVERYTHING WE LOVE...

...BUT IT'S REALLY FOUR SEPARATE DRAWERS.

WHAT DO YOU THINK?

I THINK THAT NOT ALL HEARTS WORK THE SAME WAY.

YOU'RE PROBABLY RIGHT, BUT I WAS TALKING ABOUT THE APARTMENT. NOW THAT YOU KNOW ME A BIT BETTER, I WOULD LIKE TO HEAR YOUR OPINION.

ANOTHER CUP OF TEA?

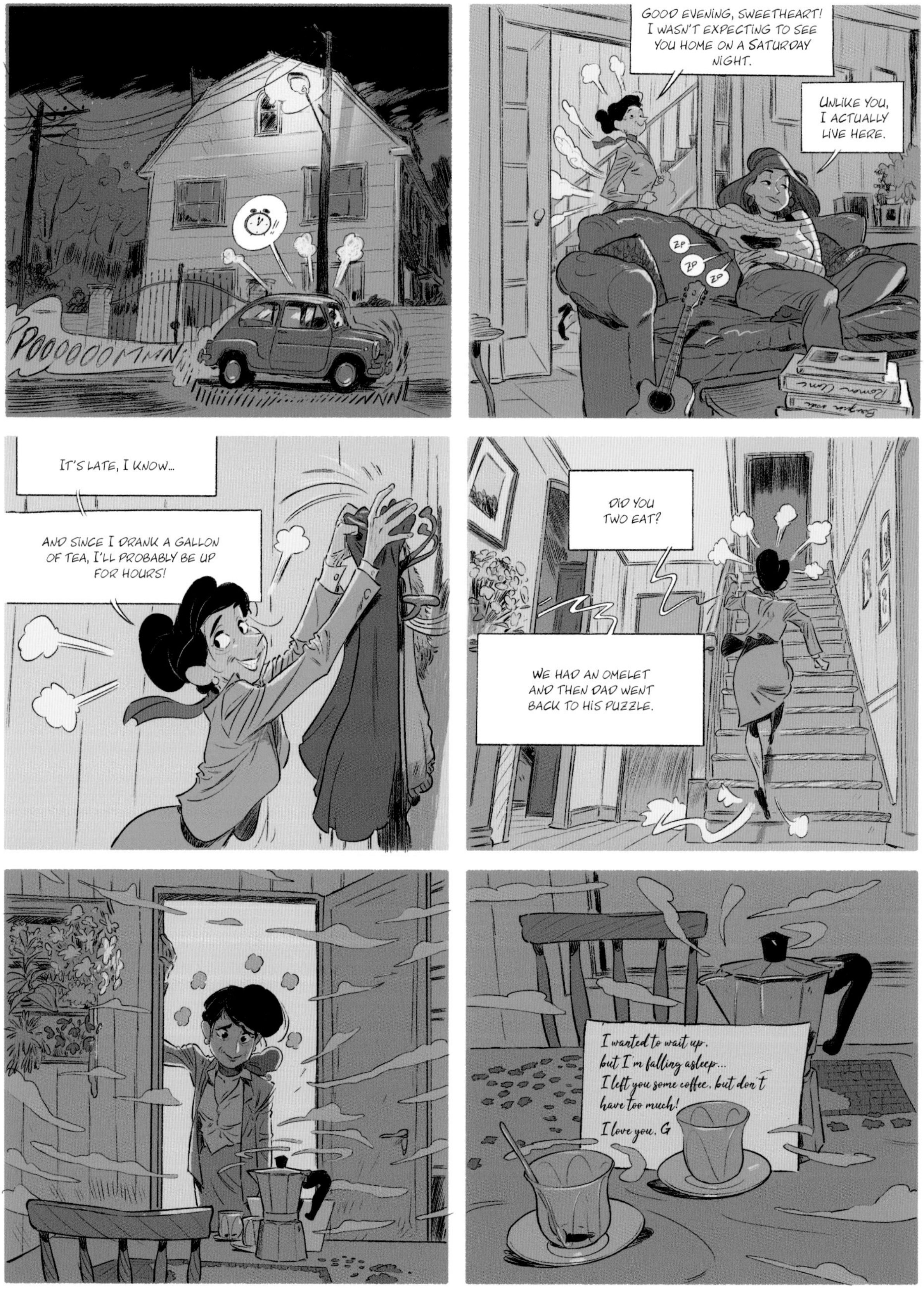
POOOOOOMMN
GOOD EVENING, SWEETHEART! I WASN'T EXPECTING TO SEE YOU HOME ON A SATURDAY NIGHT.
UNLIKE YOU, I ACTUALLY LIVE HERE.
ZP
ZP
ZP
IT'S LATE, I KNOW...
AND SINCE I DRANK A GALLON OF TEA, I'LL PROBABLY BE UP FOR HOURS!
DID YOU TWO EAT?
WE HAD AN OMELET AND THEN DAD WENT BACK TO HIS PUZZLE.
I wanted to wait up,
but I'm falling asleep...
I left you some coffee, but don't
have too much!
I love you. G

CHAPTER
11

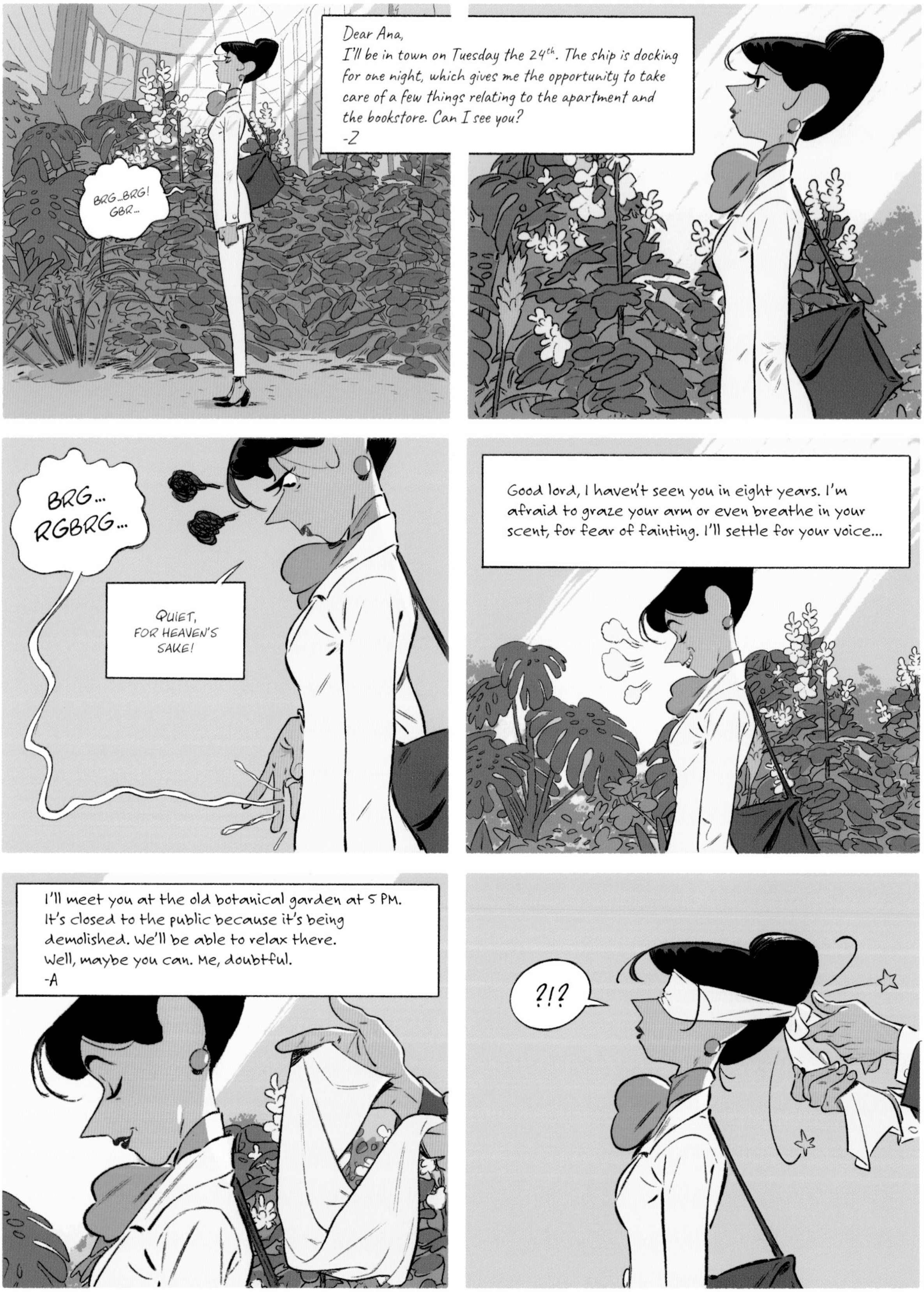

Dear Ana,
I'll be in town on Tuesday the 24th. The ship is docking for one night, which gives me the opportunity to take care of a few things relating to the apartment and the bookstore. Can I see you?
-Z
BRG...BRG! GBR...
BRG... RGBRG...
QUIET, FOR HEAVEN'S SAKE!
Good lord, I haven't seen you in eight years. I'm afraid to graze your arm or even breathe in your scent, for fear of fainting. I'll settle for your voice...
I'll meet you at the old botanical garden at 5 PM. It's closed to the public because it's being demolished. We'll be able to relax there. Well, maybe you can. Me, doubtful.
-A
?!?

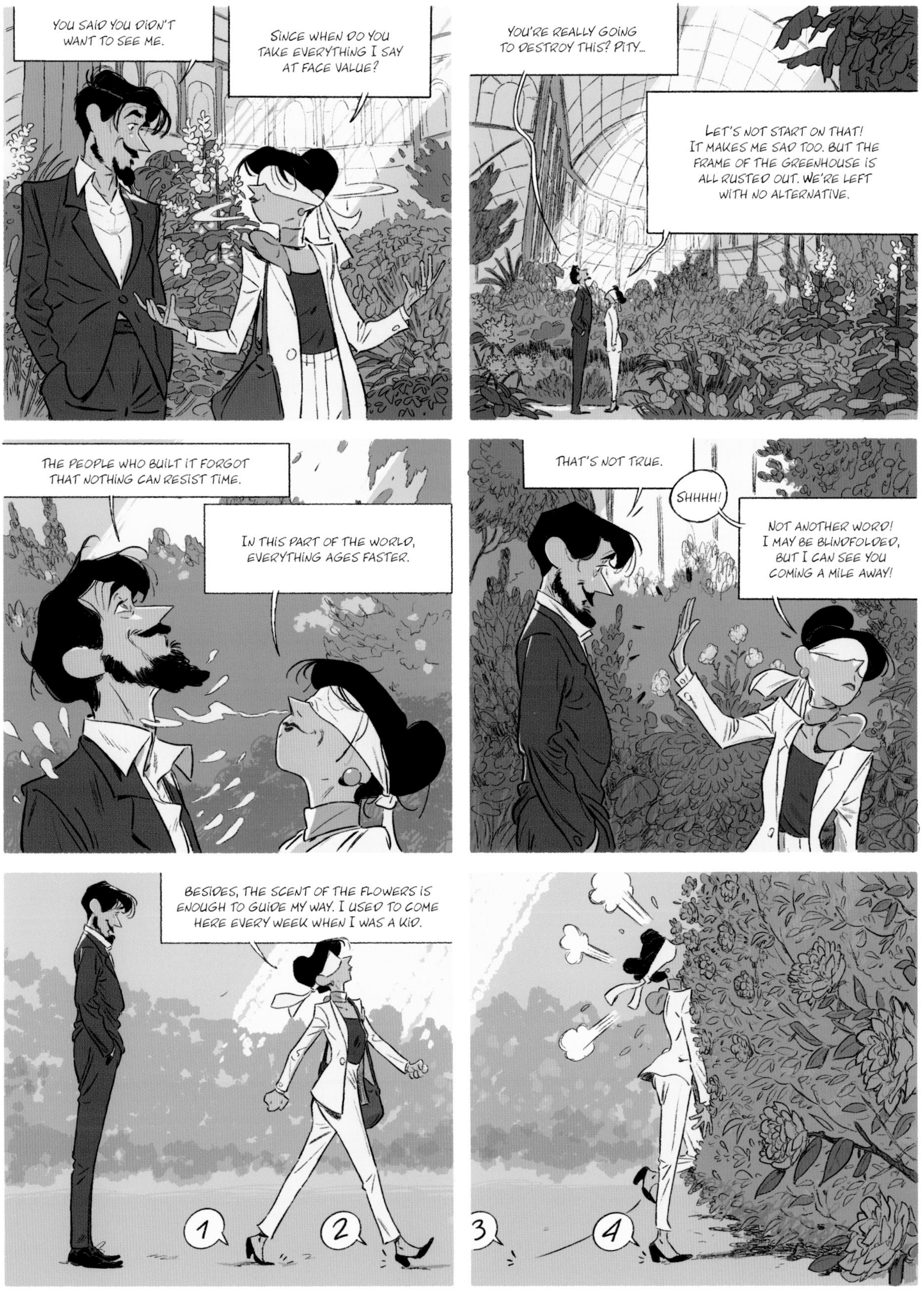

YOU SAID YOU DIDN'T WANT TO SEE ME.
SINCE WHEN DO YOU TAKE EVERYTHING I SAY AT FACE VALUE?
YOU'RE REALLY GOING TO DESTROY THIS? PITY...
LET'S NOT START ON THAT! IT MAKES ME SAD TOO. BUT THE FRAME OF THE GREENHOUSE IS ALL RUSTED OUT. WE'RE LEFT WITH NO ALTERNATIVE.
THE PEOPLE WHO BUILT IT FORGOT THAT NOTHING CAN RESIST TIME.
IN THIS PART OF THE WORLD, EVERYTHING AGES FASTER.
THAT'S NOT TRUE.
SHHHH!
NOT ANOTHER WORD! I MAY BE BLINDFOLDED, BUT I CAN SEE YOU COMING A MILE AWAY!
BESIDES, THE SCENT OF THE FLOWERS IS ENOUGH TO GUIDE MY WAY. I USED TO COME HERE EVERY WEEK WHEN I WAS A KID.
1
2
3
4

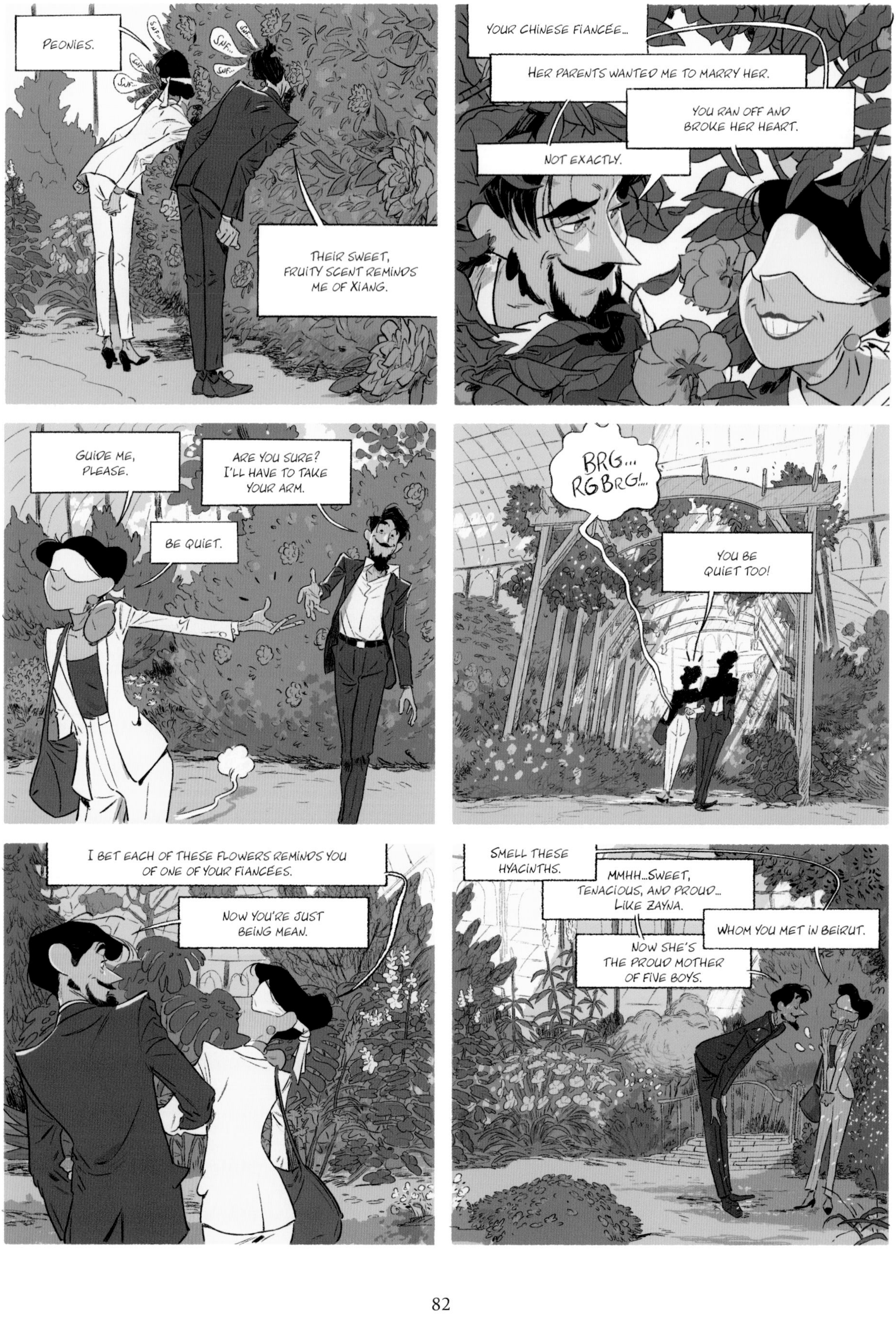
PEONIES.
SNF...
SNF...
SNF...
SNF...
SNF...
SNF...
THEIR SWEET, FRUITY SCENT REMINDS ME OF XIANG.
YOUR CHINESE FIANCÉE...
HER PARENTS WANTED ME TO MARRY HER.
YOU RAN OFF AND BROKE HER HEART.
NOT EXACTLY.
GUIDE ME, PLEASE.
ARE YOU SURE? I'LL HAVE TO TAKE YOUR ARM.
BE QUIET.
BRG... RGBRG!...
YOU BE QUIET TOO!
I BET EACH OF THESE FLOWERS REMINDS YOU OF ONE OF YOUR FIANCÉES.
NOW YOU'RE JUST BEING MEAN.
SMELL THESE HYACINTHS.
MMHH...SWEET, TENACIOUS, AND PROUD... LIKE ZAYNA.
WHOM YOU MET IN BEIRUT.
NOW SHE'S THE PROUD MOTHER OF FIVE BOYS.

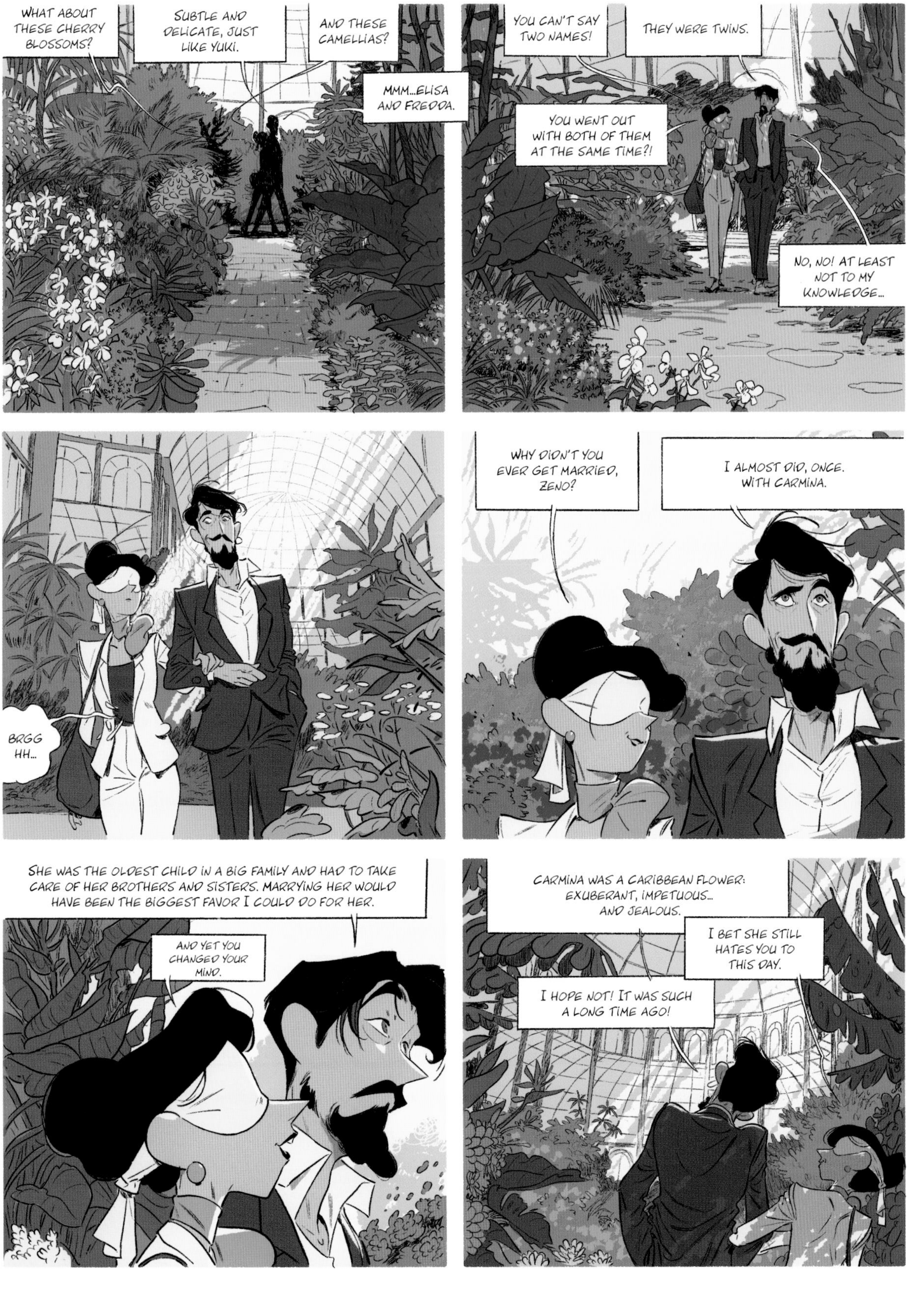
WHAT ABOUT THESE CHERRY BLOSSOMS?
SUBTLE AND DELICATE, JUST LIKE YUKI.
AND THESE CAMELLIAS?
MMM...ELISA AND FREDDA.
YOU CAN'T SAY TWO NAMES!
THEY WERE TWINS.
YOU WENT OUT WITH BOTH OF THEM AT THE SAME TIME?!
NO, NO! AT LEAST NOT TO MY KNOWLEDGE...
BRGG HH...
WHY DIDN'T YOU EVER GET MARRIED, ZENO?
I ALMOST DID, ONCE. WITH CARMINA.
SHE WAS THE OLDEST CHILD IN A BIG FAMILY AND HAD TO TAKE CARE OF HER BROTHERS AND SISTERS. MARRYING HER WOULD HAVE BEEN THE BIGGEST FAVOR I COULD DO FOR HER.
AND YET YOU CHANGED YOUR MIND.
CARMINA WAS A CARIBBEAN FLOWER: EXUBERANT, IMPETUOUS... AND JEALOUS.
I BET SHE STILL HATES YOU TO THIS DAY.
I HOPE NOT! IT WAS SUCH A LONG TIME AGO!

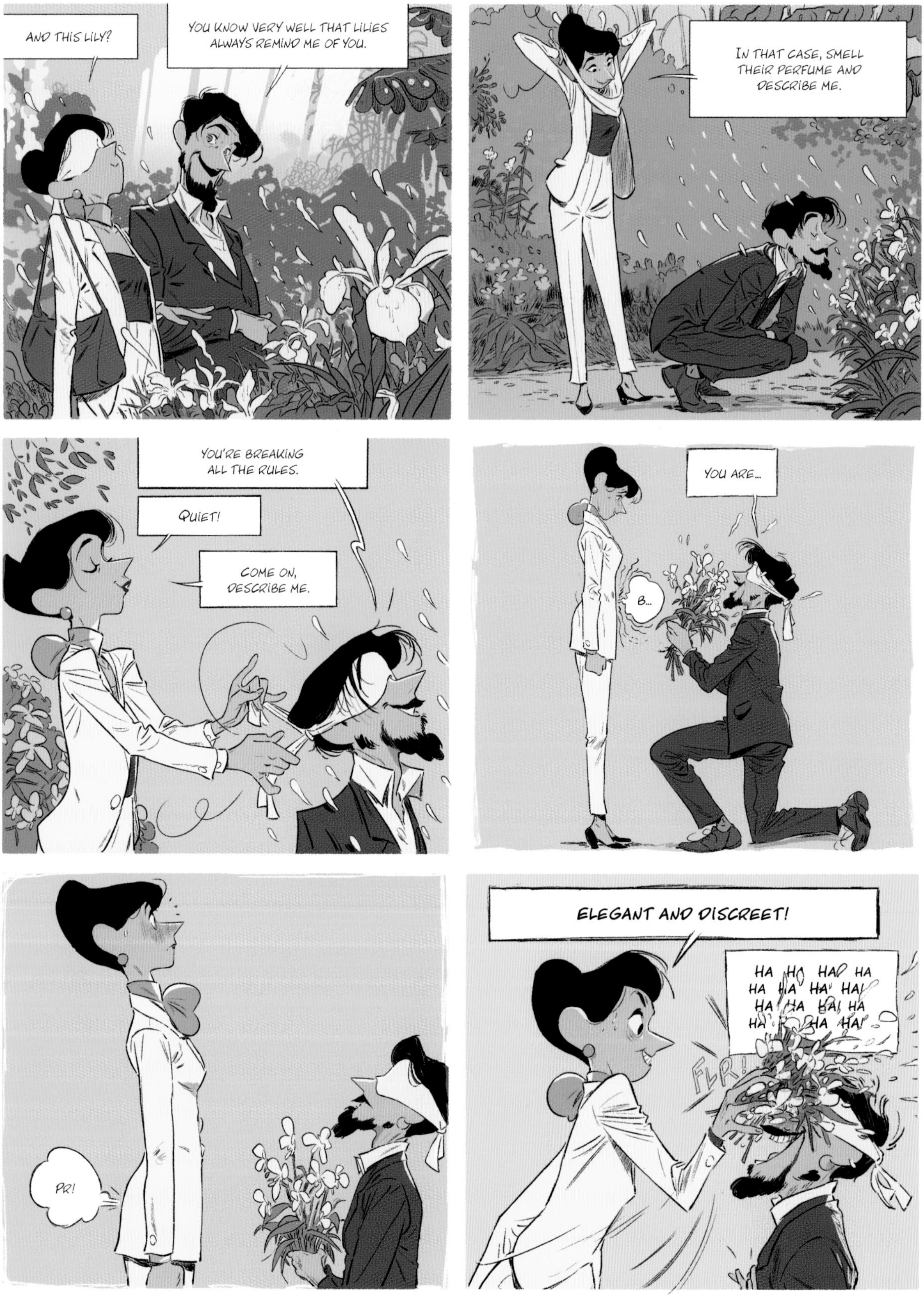
AND THIS LILY?
YOU KNOW VERY WELL THAT LILIES ALWAYS REMIND ME OF YOU.
IN THAT CASE, SMELL THEIR PERFUME AND DESCRIBE ME.
YOU'RE BREAKING ALL THE RULES.
QUIET!
COME ON, DESCRIBE ME.
YOU ARE...
B...
PR!
ELEGANT AND DISCREET!
HA HA HA HA HA HA HA HA HA HA HA HA HA HA HA HA
FLR!

CHAPTER
10

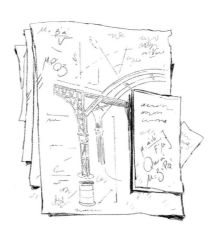

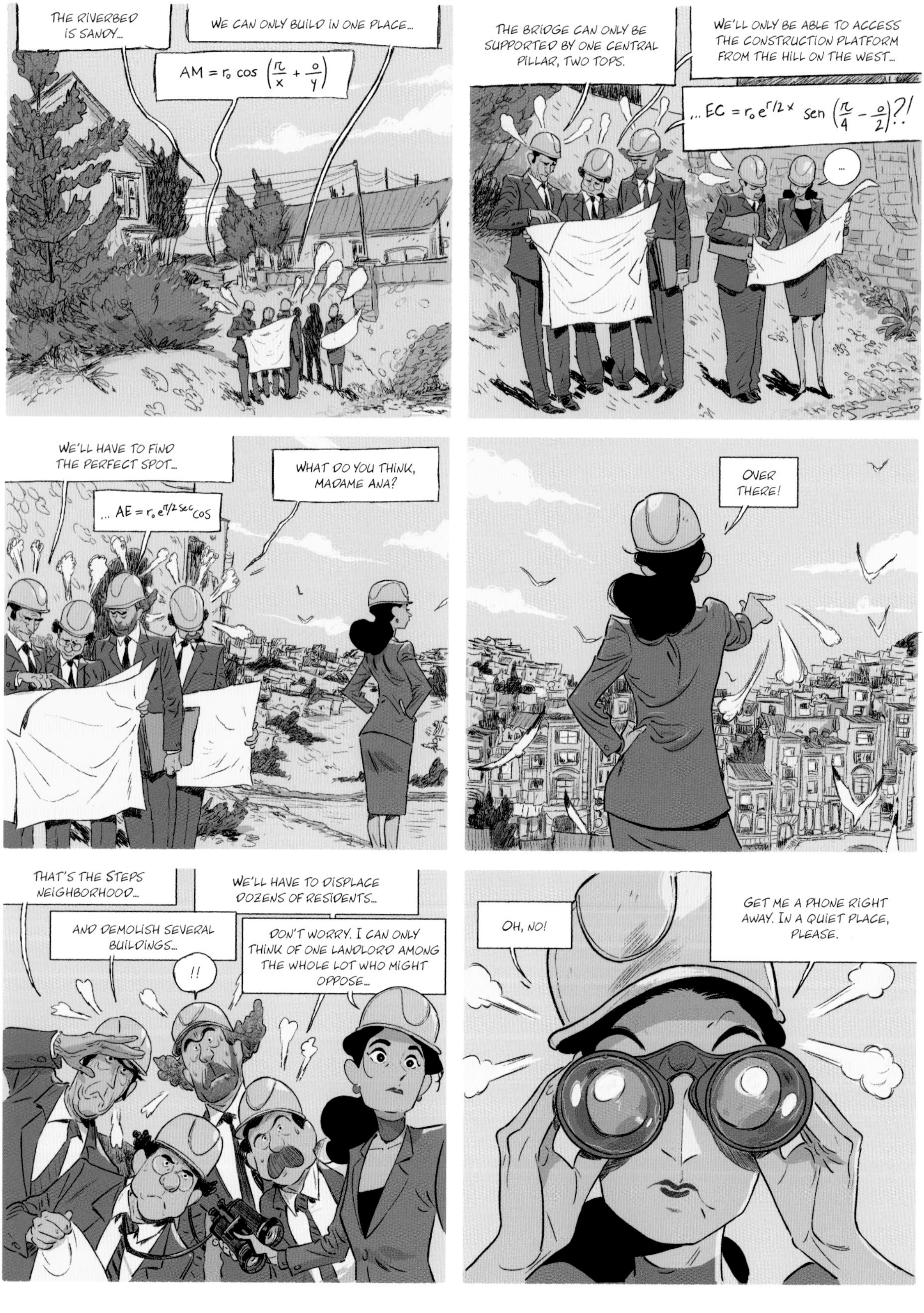
THE RIVERBED IS SANDY...
WE CAN ONLY BUILD IN ONE PLACE...
$AM = r_0 \cos\left(\frac{\pi}{x} + \frac{o}{y}\right)$
THE BRIDGE CAN ONLY BE SUPPORTED BY ONE CENTRAL PILLAR, TWO TOPS.
WE'LL ONLY BE ABLE TO ACCESS THE CONSTRUCTION PLATFORM FROM THE HILL ON THE WEST...
... $EC = r_0 e^{r/2x}$ sen $\left(\frac{\pi}{4} - \frac{o}{2}\right)$?!
...
WE'LL HAVE TO FIND THE PERFECT SPOT...
... $AE = r_0 e^{\pi/2 \sec} \cos$
WHAT DO YOU THINK, MADAME ANA?
OVER THERE!
THAT'S THE STEPS NEIGHBORHOOD...
WE'LL HAVE TO DISPLACE DOZENS OF RESIDENTS...
AND DEMOLISH SEVERAL BUILDINGS...
!!
DON'T WORRY. I CAN ONLY THINK OF ONE LANDLORD AMONG THE WHOLE LOT WHO MIGHT OPPOSE...
OH, NO!
GET ME A PHONE RIGHT AWAY. IN A QUIET PLACE, PLEASE.

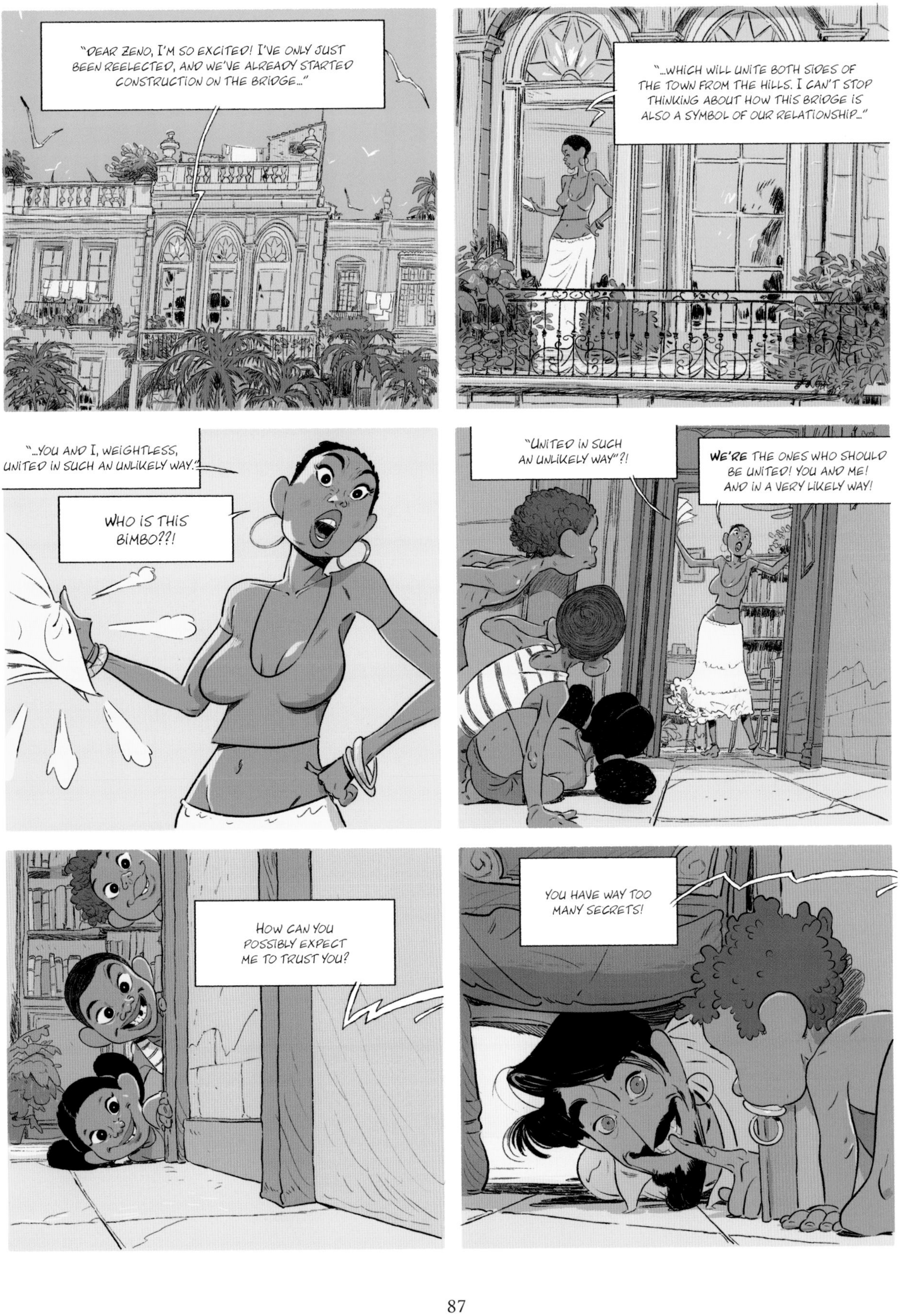
"DEAR ZENO, I'M SO EXCITED! I'VE ONLY JUST BEEN REELECTED, AND WE'VE ALREADY STARTED CONSTRUCTION ON THE BRIDGE..."
"...WHICH WILL UNITE BOTH SIDES OF THE TOWN FROM THE HILLS. I CAN'T STOP THINKING ABOUT HOW THIS BRIDGE IS ALSO A SYMBOL OF OUR RELATIONSHIP..."
"...YOU AND I, WEIGHTLESS, UNITED IN SUCH AN UNLIKELY WAY."
WHO IS THIS BIMBO??!
"UNITED IN SUCH AN UNLIKELY WAY"?!
WE'RE THE ONES WHO SHOULD BE UNITED! YOU AND ME! AND IN A VERY LIKELY WAY!
HOW CAN YOU POSSIBLY EXPECT ME TO TRUST YOU?
YOU HAVE WAY TOO MANY SECRETS!

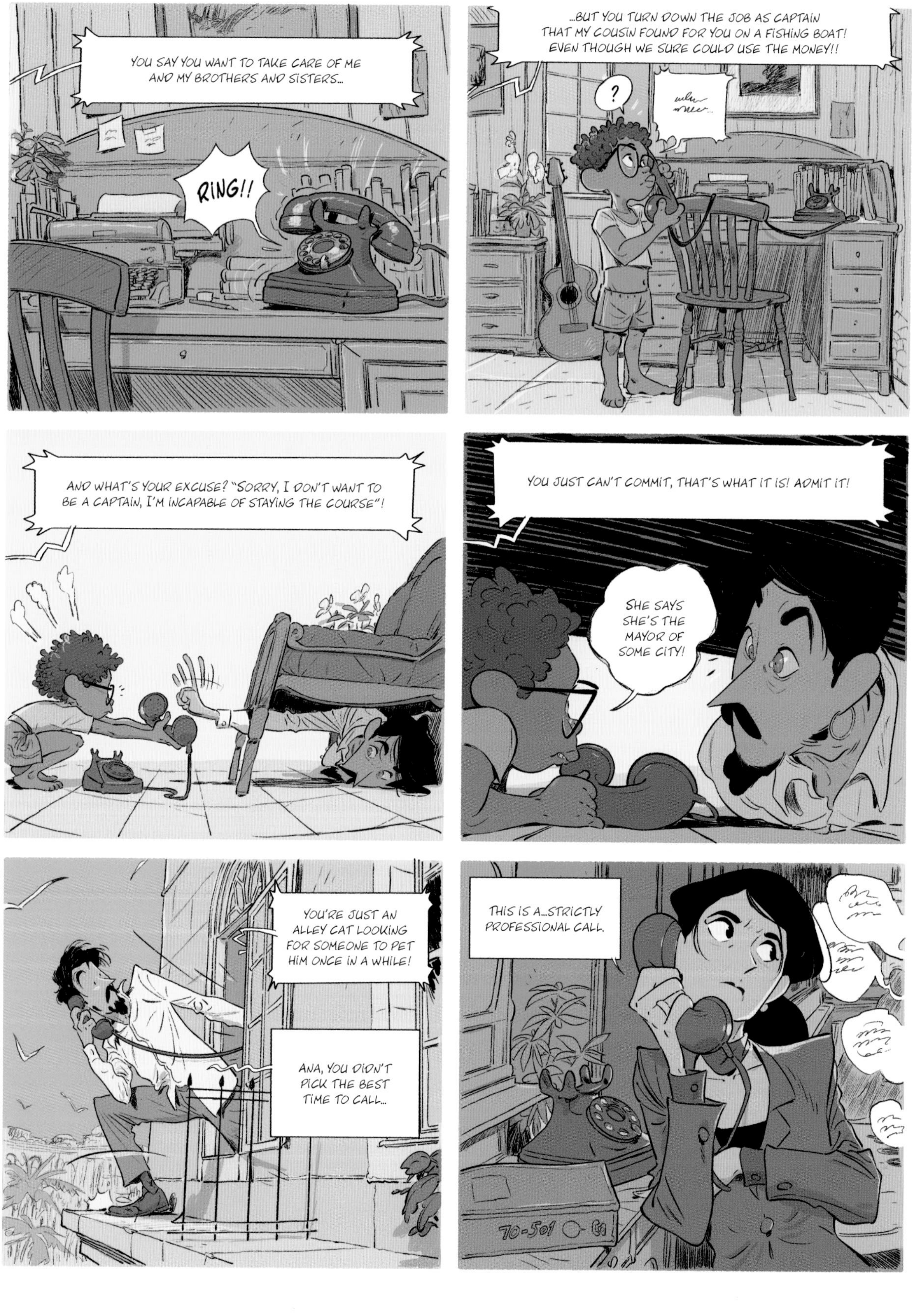

YOU SAY YOU WANT TO TAKE CARE OF ME AND MY BROTHERS AND SISTERS...
RING!!
...BUT YOU TURN DOWN THE JOB AS CAPTAIN THAT MY COUSIN FOUND FOR YOU ON A FISHING BOAT! EVEN THOUGH WE SURE COULD USE THE MONEY!!
?
AND WHAT'S YOUR EXCUSE? "SORRY, I DON'T WANT TO BE A CAPTAIN, I'M INCAPABLE OF STAYING THE COURSE"!
YOU JUST CAN'T COMMIT, THAT'S WHAT IT IS! ADMIT IT!
SHE SAYS SHE'S THE MAYOR OF SOME CITY!
YOU'RE JUST AN ALLEY CAT LOOKING FOR SOMEONE TO PET HIM ONCE IN A WHILE!
ANA, YOU DIDN'T PICK THE BEST TIME TO CALL...
THIS IS A...STRICTLY PROFESSIONAL CALL.
70-501

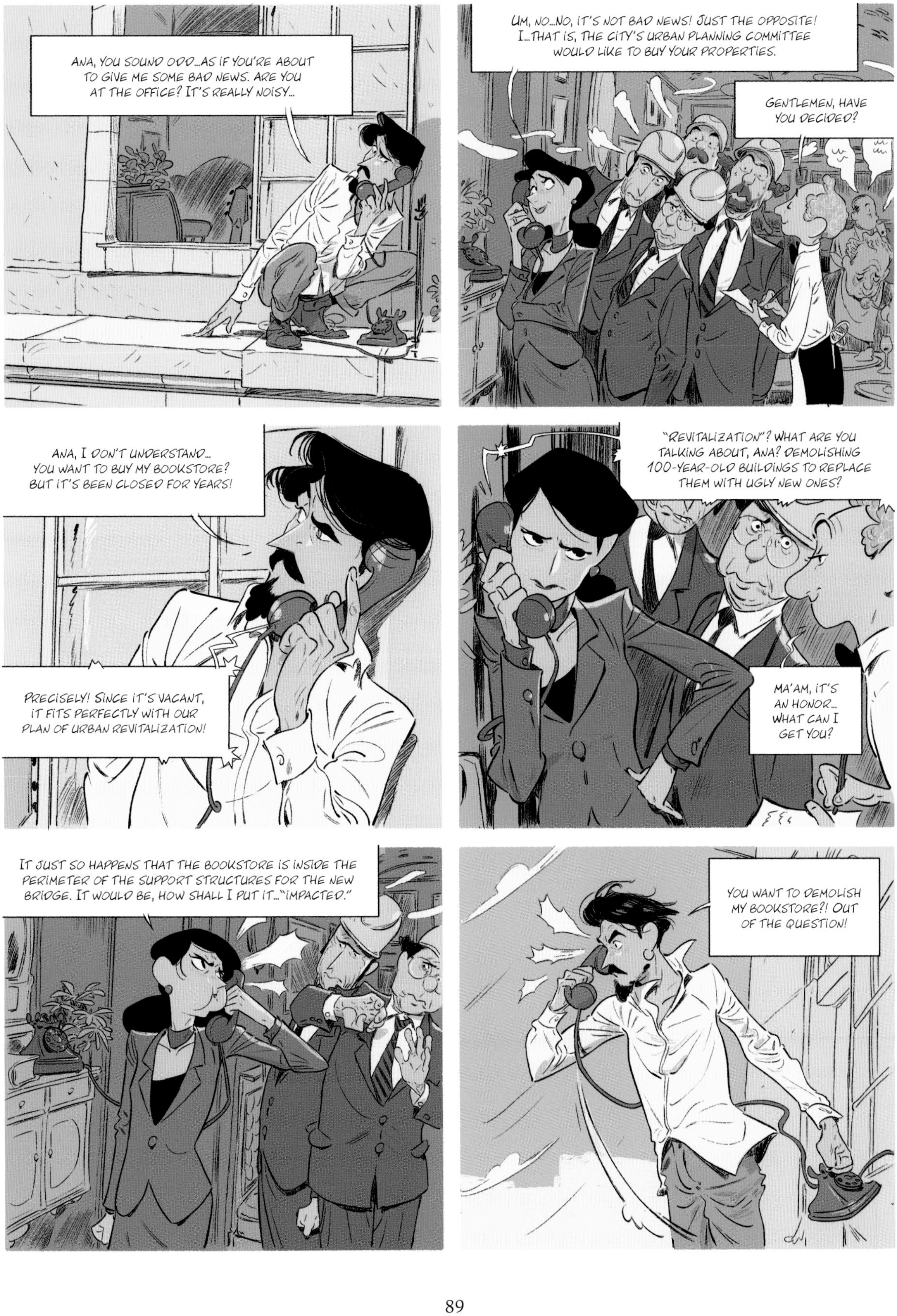

ANA, YOU SOUND ODD...AS IF YOU'RE ABOUT TO GIVE ME SOME BAD NEWS. ARE YOU AT THE OFFICE? IT'S REALLY NOISY...
UM, NO...NO, IT'S NOT BAD NEWS! JUST THE OPPOSITE! I...THAT IS, THE CITY'S URBAN PLANNING COMMITTEE WOULD LIKE TO BUY YOUR PROPERTIES.
GENTLEMEN, HAVE YOU DECIDED?
ANA, I DON'T UNDERSTAND... YOU WANT TO BUY MY BOOKSTORE? BUT IT'S BEEN CLOSED FOR YEARS!
PRECISELY! SINCE IT'S VACANT, IT FITS PERFECTLY WITH OUR PLAN OF URBAN REVITALIZATION!
"REVITALIZATION"? WHAT ARE YOU TALKING ABOUT, ANA? DEMOLISHING 100-YEAR-OLD BUILDINGS TO REPLACE THEM WITH UGLY NEW ONES?
MA'AM, IT'S AN HONOR... WHAT CAN I GET YOU?
IT JUST SO HAPPENS THAT THE BOOKSTORE IS INSIDE THE PERIMETER OF THE SUPPORT STRUCTURES FOR THE NEW BRIDGE. IT WOULD BE, HOW SHALL I PUT IT..."IMPACTED."
YOU WANT TO DEMOLISH MY BOOKSTORE?! OUT OF THE QUESTION!

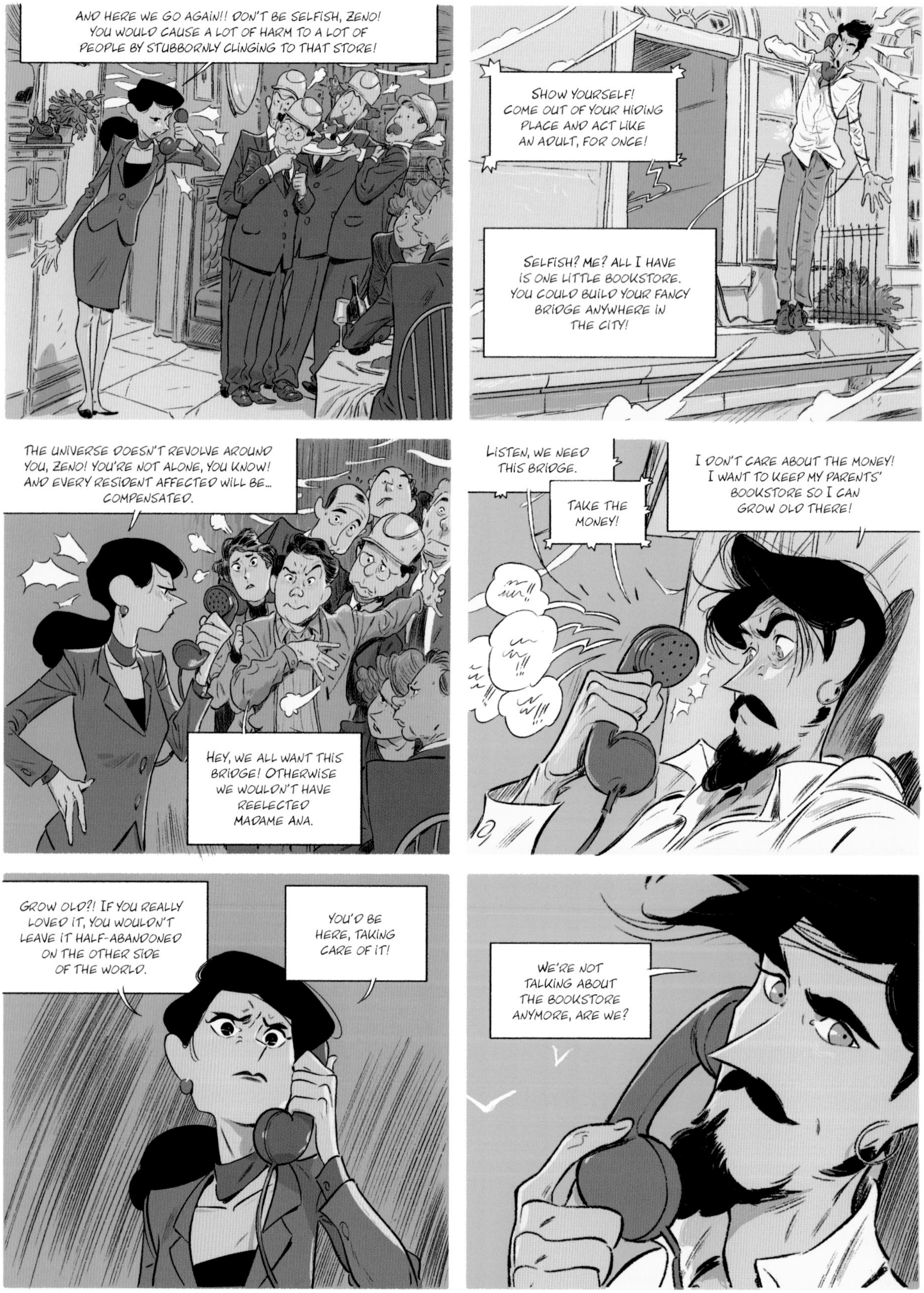
AND HERE WE GO AGAIN!! DON'T BE SELFISH, ZENO! YOU WOULD CAUSE A LOT OF HARM TO A LOT OF PEOPLE BY STUBBORNLY CLINGING TO THAT STORE!
SHOW YOURSELF! COME OUT OF YOUR HIDING PLACE AND ACT LIKE AN ADULT, FOR ONCE!
SELFISH? ME? ALL I HAVE IS ONE LITTLE BOOKSTORE. YOU COULD BUILD YOUR FANCY BRIDGE ANYWHERE IN THE CITY!
THE UNIVERSE DOESN'T REVOLVE AROUND YOU, ZENO! YOU'RE NOT ALONE, YOU KNOW! AND EVERY RESIDENT AFFECTED WILL BE... COMPENSATED.
HEY, WE ALL WANT THIS BRIDGE! OTHERWISE WE WOULDN'T HAVE REELECTED MADAME ANA.
LISTEN, WE NEED THIS BRIDGE.
TAKE THE MONEY!
I DON'T CARE ABOUT THE MONEY! I WANT TO KEEP MY PARENTS' BOOKSTORE SO I CAN GROW OLD THERE!
GROW OLD?! IF YOU REALLY LOVED IT, YOU WOULDN'T LEAVE IT HALF-ABANDONED ON THE OTHER SIDE OF THE WORLD.
YOU'D BE HERE, TAKING CARE OF IT!
WE'RE NOT TALKING ABOUT THE BOOKSTORE ANYMORE, ARE WE?

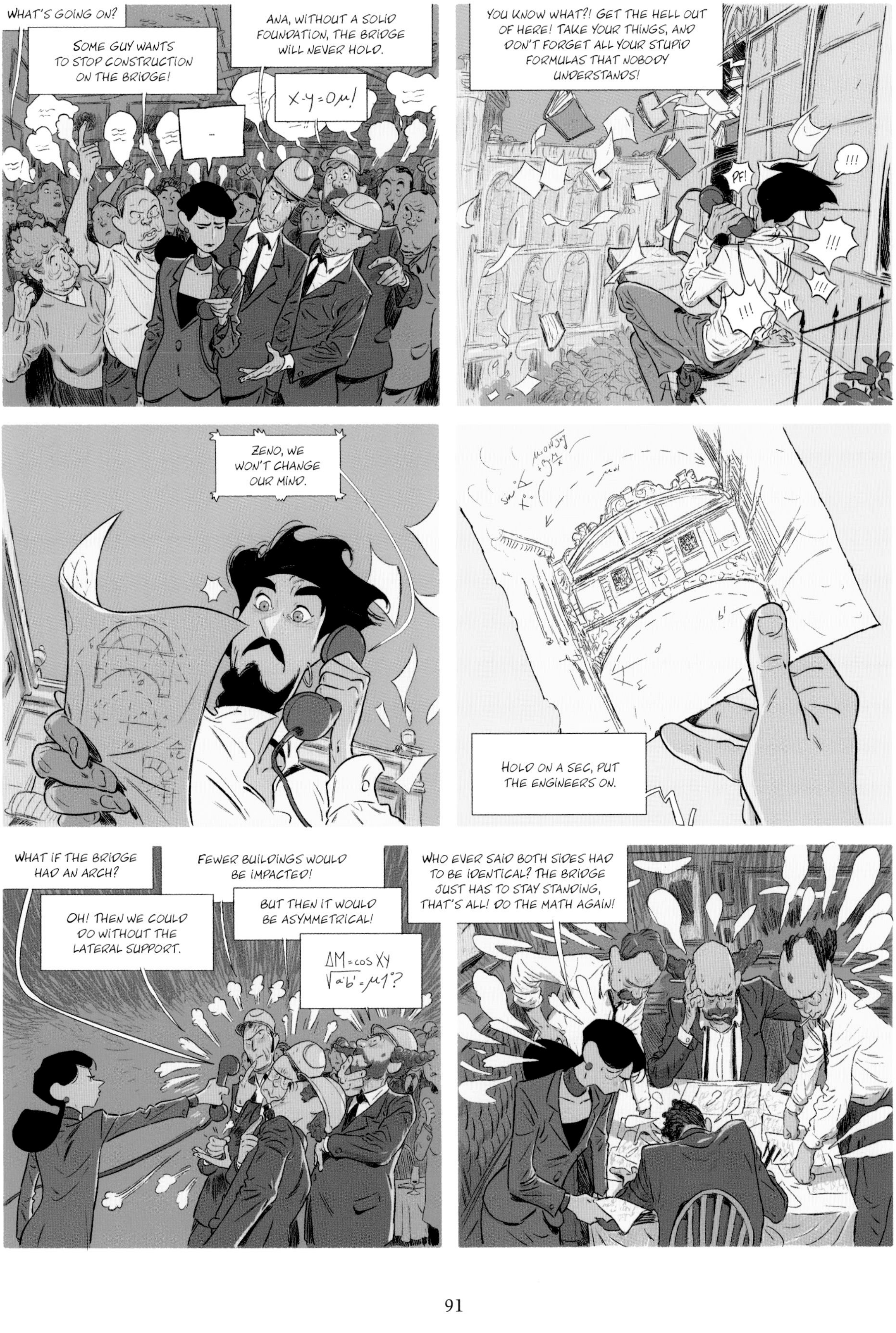

WHAT'S GOING ON?
SOME GUY WANTS TO STOP CONSTRUCTION ON THE BRIDGE!
ANA, WITHOUT A SOLID FOUNDATION, THE BRIDGE WILL NEVER HOLD.
X-Y=0μ!
...
YOU KNOW WHAT?! GET THE HELL OUT OF HERE! TAKE YOUR THINGS, AND DON'T FORGET ALL YOUR STUPID FORMULAS THAT NOBODY UNDERSTANDS!
PF!
!!!
!!!
!!!
!!!
ZENO, WE WON'T CHANGE OUR MIND.
HOLD ON A SEC, PUT THE ENGINEERS ON.
WHAT IF THE BRIDGE HAD AN ARCH?
OH! THEN WE COULD DO WITHOUT THE LATERAL SUPPORT.
FEWER BUILDINGS WOULD BE IMPACTED!
BUT THEN IT WOULD BE ASYMMETRICAL!
ΔM=cos XY √a·b'=μ1°?
WHO EVER SAID BOTH SIDES HAD TO BE IDENTICAL? THE BRIDGE JUST HAS TO STAY STANDING, THAT'S ALL! DO THE MATH AGAIN!

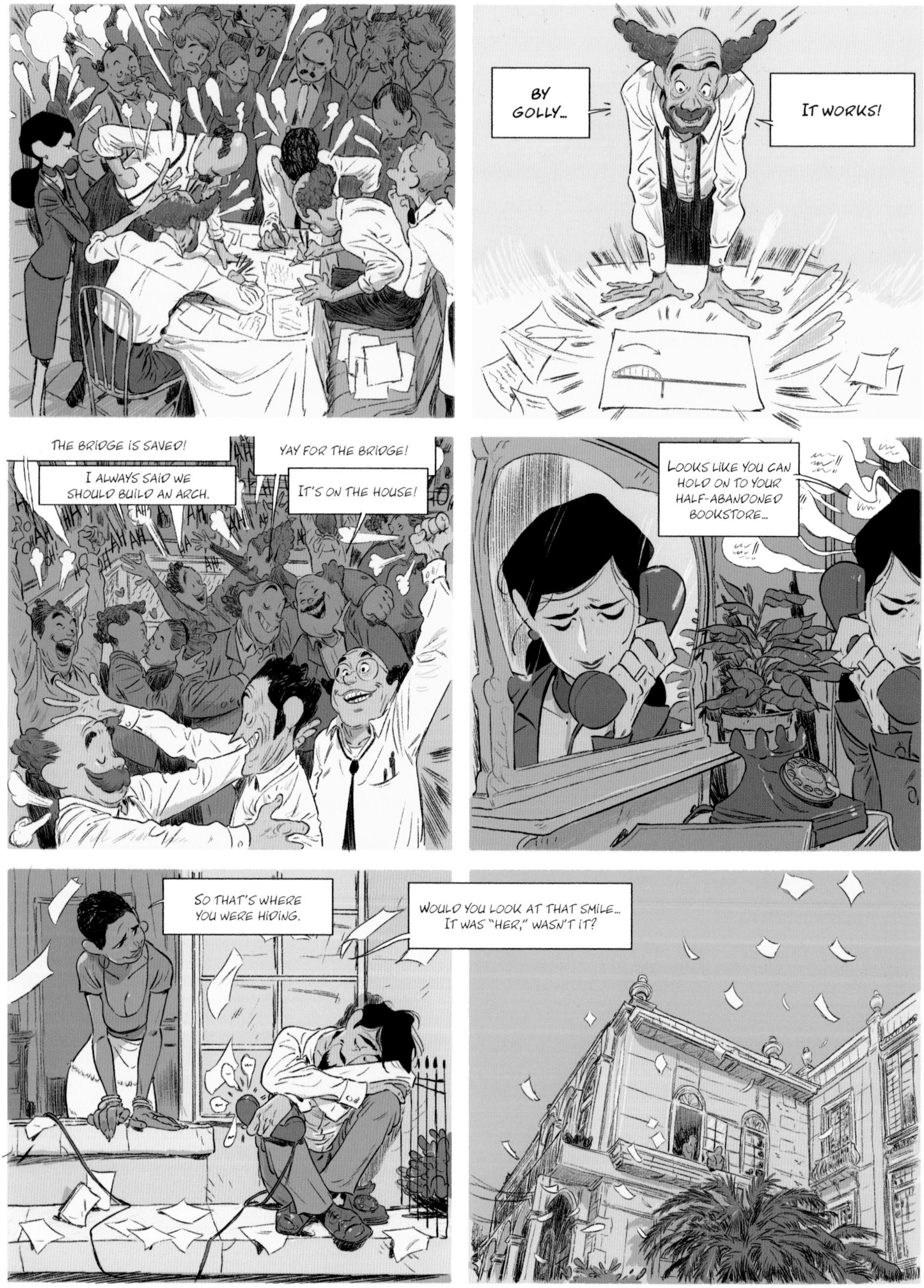
BY GOLLY...
IT WORKS!
THE BRIDGE IS SAVED!
I ALWAYS SAID WE SHOULD BUILD AN ARCH.
YAY FOR THE BRIDGE!
IT'S ON THE HOUSE!
LOOKS LIKE YOU CAN HOLD ON TO YOUR HALF-ABANDONED BOOKSTORE...
SO THAT'S WHERE YOU WERE HIDING.
WOULD YOU LOOK AT THAT SMILE... IT WAS "HER," WASN'T IT?

CHAPTER
9

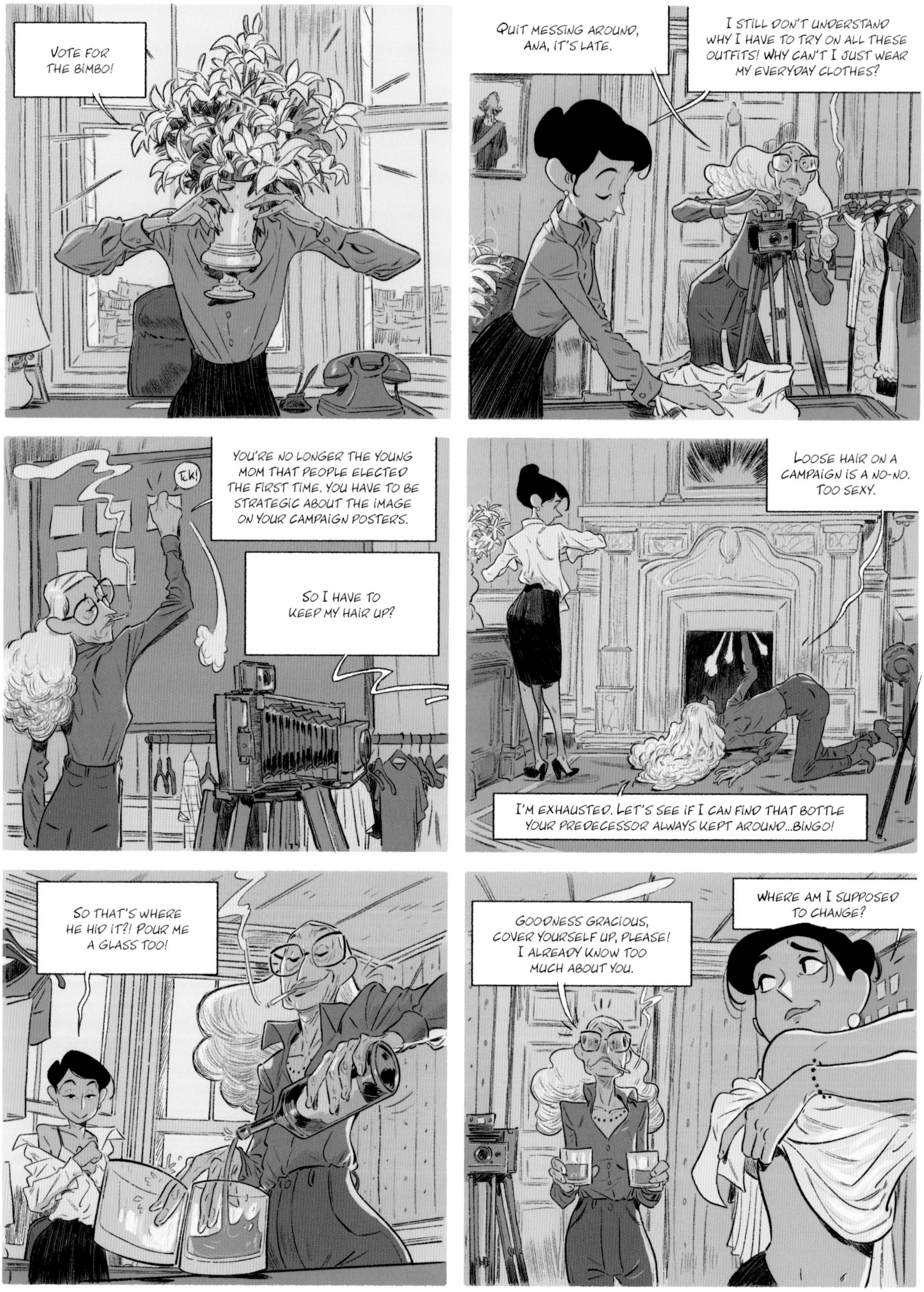
VOTE FOR THE BIMBO!
QUIT MESSING AROUND, ANA, IT'S LATE.
I STILL DON'T UNDERSTAND WHY I HAVE TO TRY ON ALL THESE OUTFITS! WHY CAN'T I JUST WEAR MY EVERYDAY CLOTHES?
YOU'RE NO LONGER THE YOUNG MOM THAT PEOPLE ELECTED THE FIRST TIME. YOU HAVE TO BE STRATEGIC ABOUT THE IMAGE ON YOUR CAMPAIGN POSTERS.
TCK!
SO I HAVE TO KEEP MY HAIR UP?
LOOSE HAIR ON A CAMPAIGN IS A NO-NO. TOO SEXY.
I'M EXHAUSTED. LET'S SEE IF I CAN FIND THAT BOTTLE YOUR PREDECESSOR ALWAYS KEPT AROUND...BINGO!
SO THAT'S WHERE HE HID IT?! POUR ME A GLASS TOO!
GOODNESS GRACIOUS, COVER YOURSELF UP, PLEASE! I ALREADY KNOW TOO MUCH ABOUT YOU.
WHERE AM I SUPPOSED TO CHANGE?

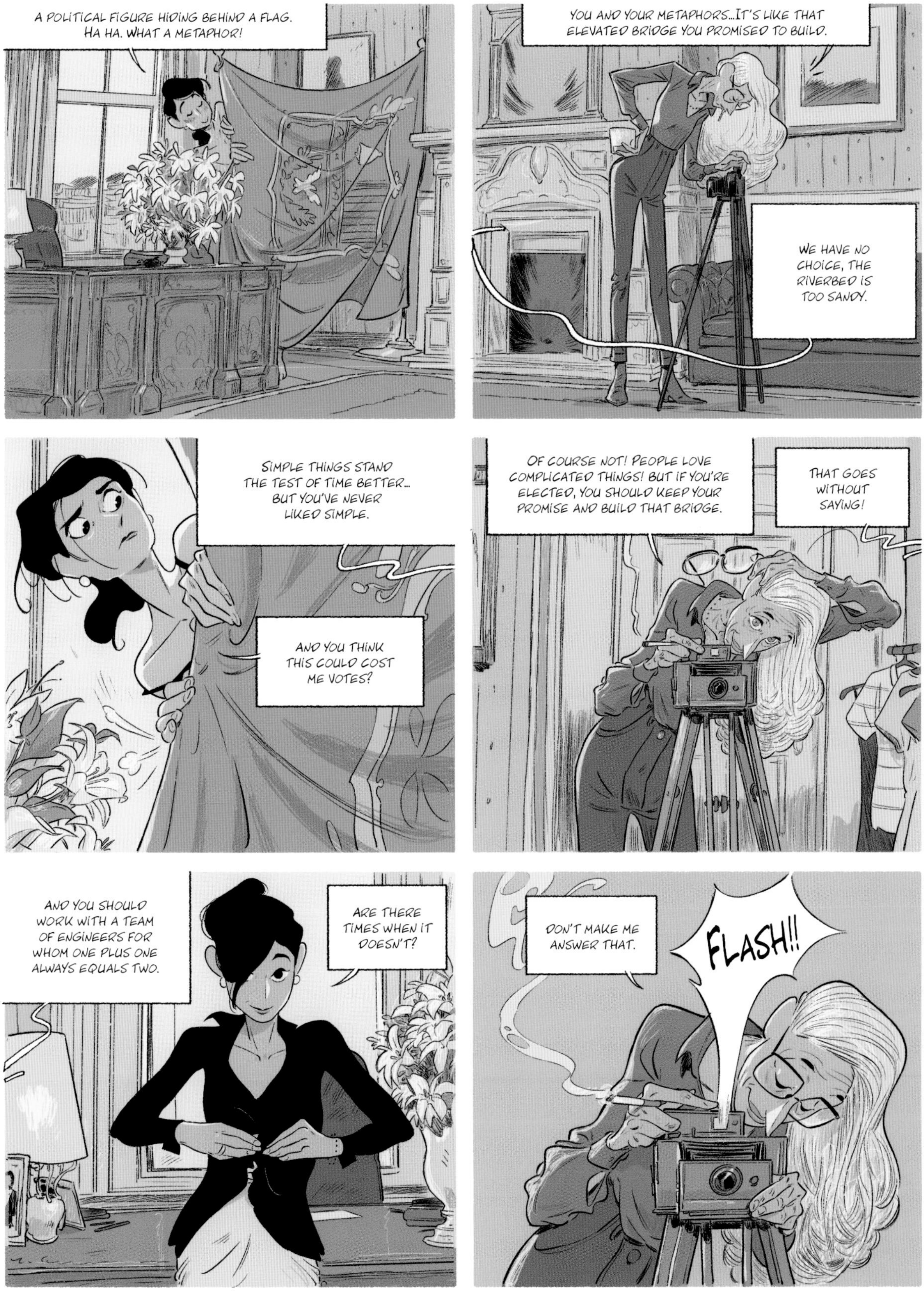
A POLITICAL FIGURE HIDING BEHIND A FLAG. HA HA. WHAT A METAPHOR!
YOU AND YOUR METAPHORS...IT'S LIKE THAT ELEVATED BRIDGE YOU PROMISED TO BUILD.
WE HAVE NO CHOICE, THE RIVERBED IS TOO SANDY.
SIMPLE THINGS STAND THE TEST OF TIME BETTER... BUT YOU'VE NEVER LIKED SIMPLE.
AND YOU THINK THIS COULD COST ME VOTES?
OF COURSE NOT! PEOPLE LOVE COMPLICATED THINGS! BUT IF YOU'RE ELECTED, YOU SHOULD KEEP YOUR PROMISE AND BUILD THAT BRIDGE.
THAT GOES WITHOUT SAYING!
AND YOU SHOULD WORK WITH A TEAM OF ENGINEERS FOR WHOM ONE PLUS ONE ALWAYS EQUALS TWO.
ARE THERE TIMES WHEN IT DOESN'T?
DON'T MAKE ME ANSWER THAT.
FLASH!!

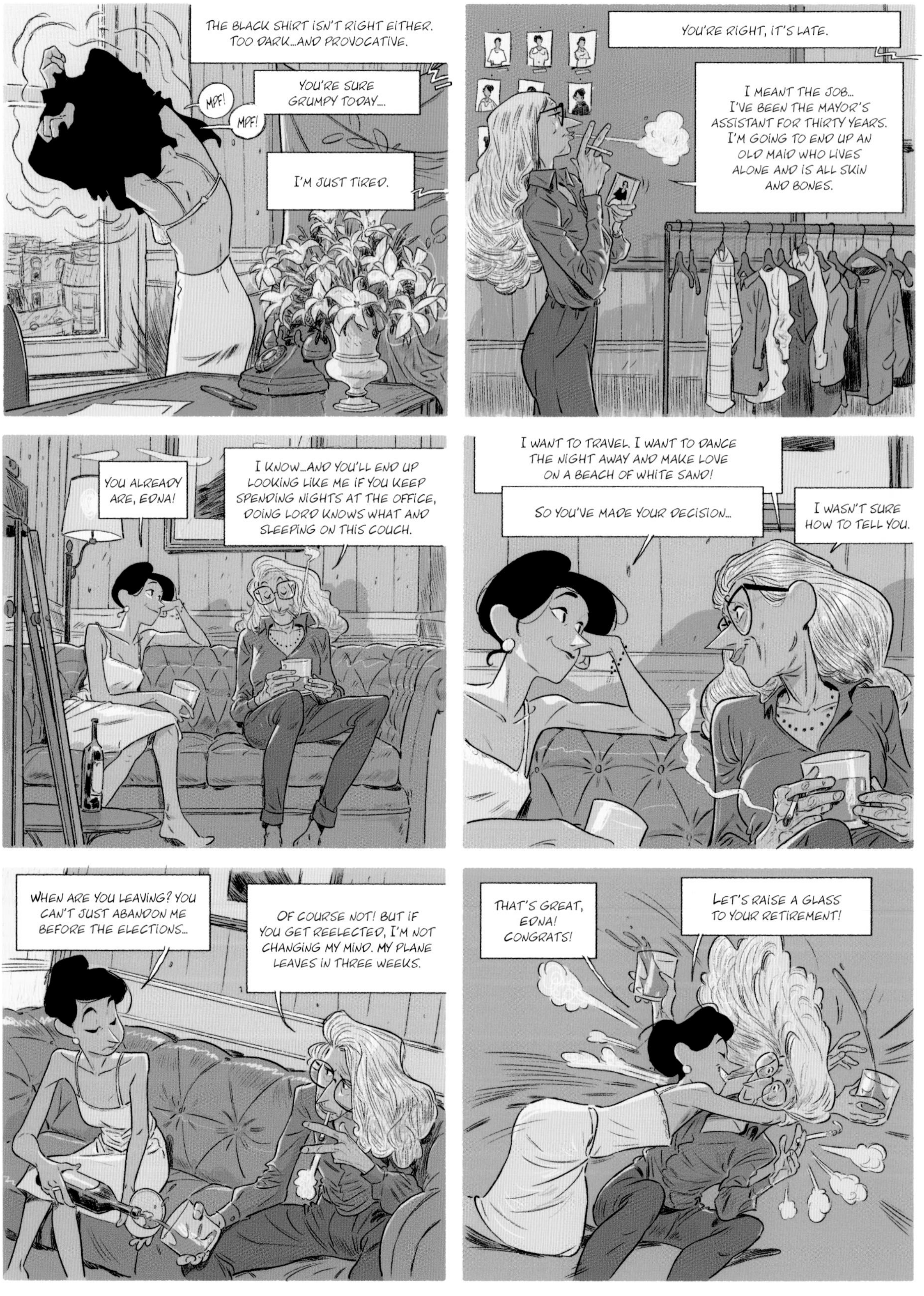
THE BLACK SHIRT ISN'T RIGHT EITHER. TOO DARK...AND PROVOCATIVE.
YOU'RE SURE GRUMPY TODAY....
MPF!
MPF!
I'M JUST TIRED.
YOU'RE RIGHT, IT'S LATE.
I MEANT THE JOB... I'VE BEEN THE MAYOR'S ASSISTANT FOR THIRTY YEARS. I'M GOING TO END UP AN OLD MAID WHO LIVES ALONE AND IS ALL SKIN AND BONES.
YOU ALREADY ARE, EDNA!
I KNOW...AND YOU'LL END UP LOOKING LIKE ME IF YOU KEEP SPENDING NIGHTS AT THE OFFICE, DOING LORD KNOWS WHAT AND SLEEPING ON THIS COUCH.
I WANT TO TRAVEL. I WANT TO DANCE THE NIGHT AWAY AND MAKE LOVE ON A BEACH OF WHITE SAND!
SO YOU'VE MADE YOUR DECISION...
I WASN'T SURE HOW TO TELL YOU.
WHEN ARE YOU LEAVING? YOU CAN'T JUST ABANDON ME BEFORE THE ELECTIONS...
OF COURSE NOT! BUT IF YOU GET REELECTED, I'M NOT CHANGING MY MIND. MY PLANE LEAVES IN THREE WEEKS.
THAT'S GREAT, EDNA! CONGRATS!
LET'S RAISE A GLASS TO YOUR RETIREMENT!

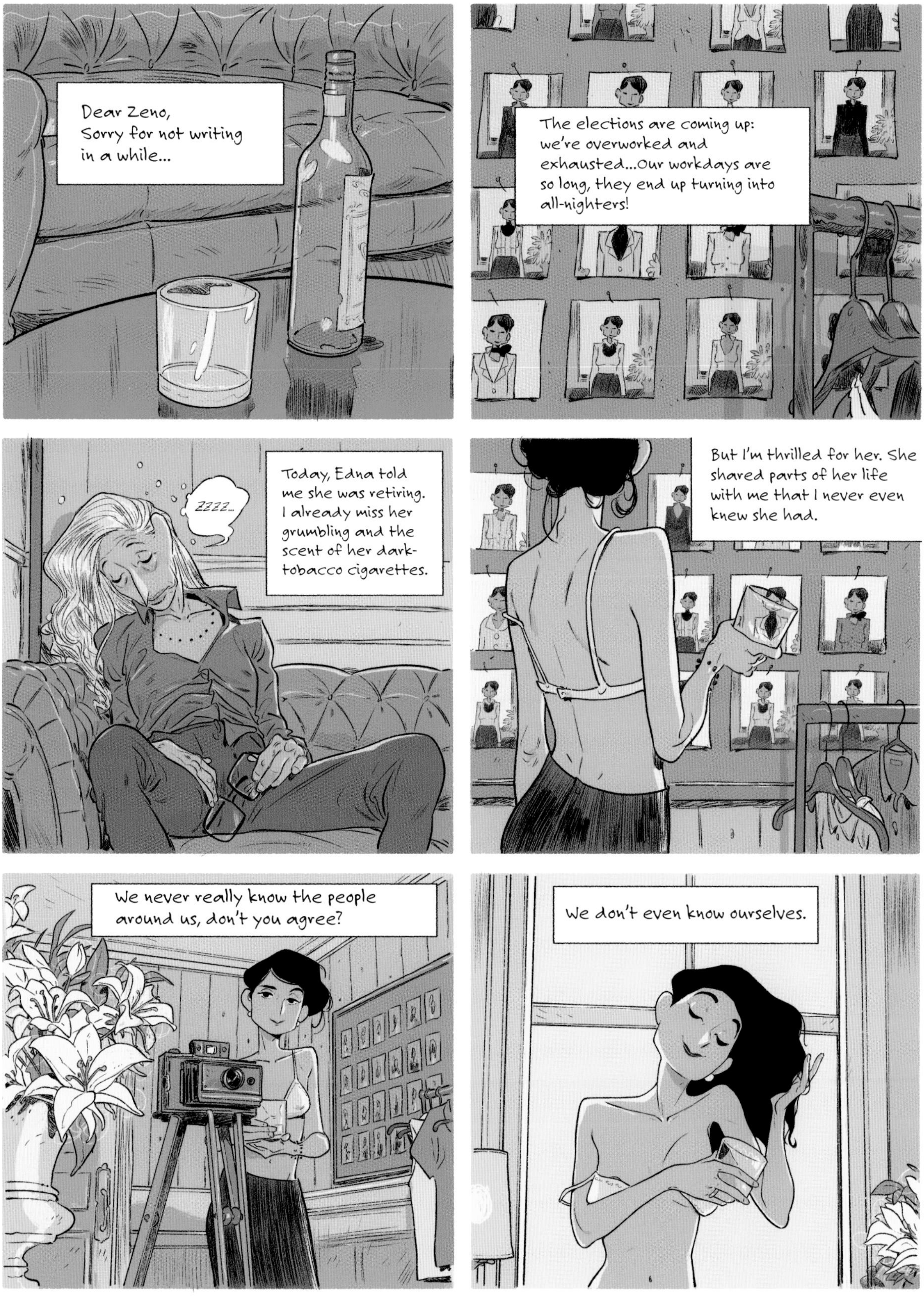
Dear Zeno,
Sorry for not writing in a while...
The elections are coming up: we're overworked and exhausted...Our workdays are so long, they end up turning into all-nighters!
Today, Edna told me she was retiring. I already miss her grumbling and the scent of her dark-tobacco cigarettes.
ZZZZ...
But I'm thrilled for her. She shared parts of her life with me that I never even knew she had.
We never really know the people around us, don't you agree?
We don't even know ourselves.

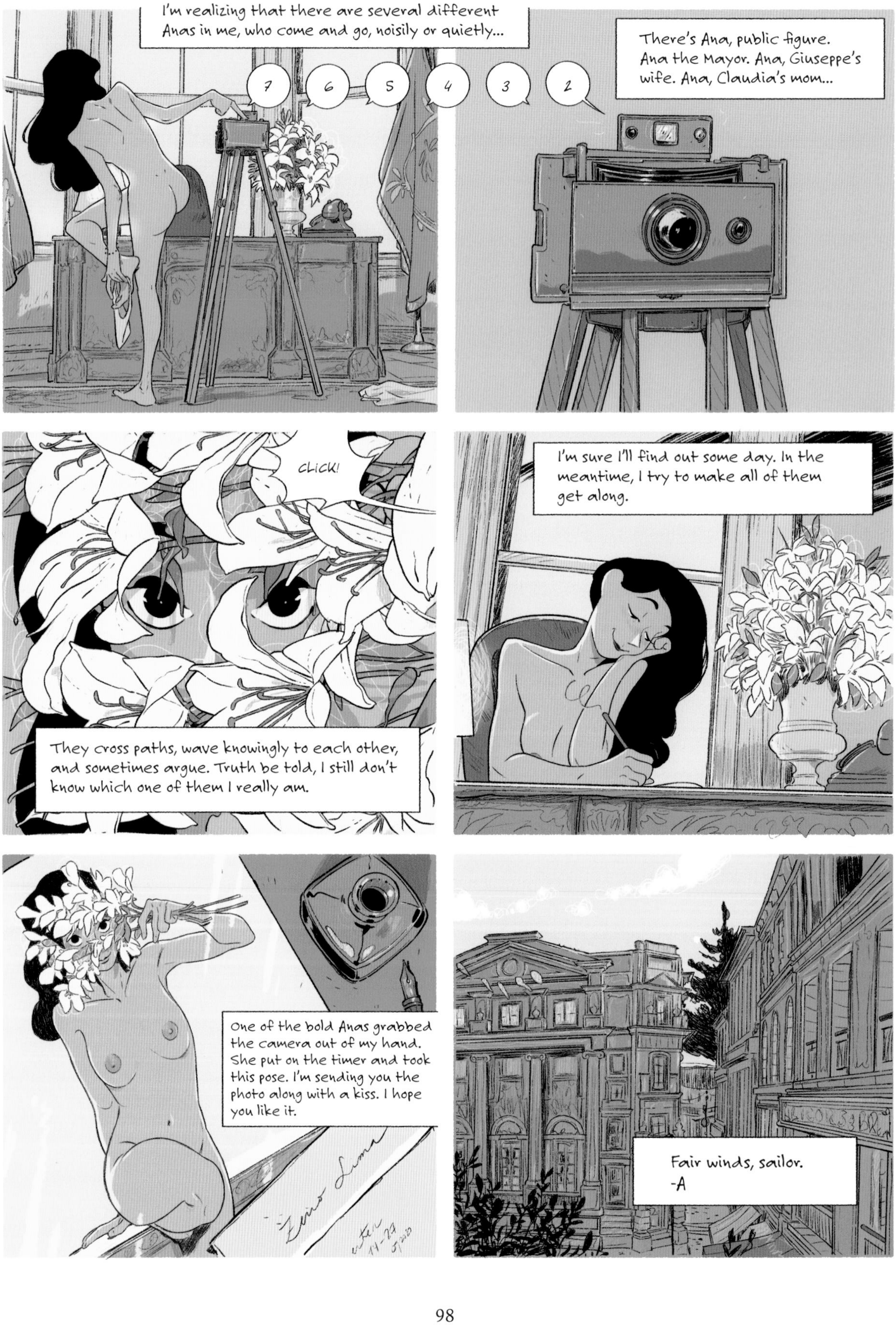

I'm realizing that there are several different Anas in me, who come and go, noisily or quietly...
7
6
5
4
3
2
There's Ana, public figure. Ana the Mayor. Ana, Giuseppe's wife. Ana, Claudia's mom...
CLICK!
They cross paths, wave knowingly to each other, and sometimes argue. Truth be told, I still don't know which one of them I really am.
I'm sure I'll find out some day. In the meantime, I try to make all of them get along.
One of the bold Anas grabbed the camera out of my hand. She put on the timer and took this pose. I'm sending you the photo along with a kiss. I hope you like it.
Fair winds, sailor.
-A

CHAPTER
8

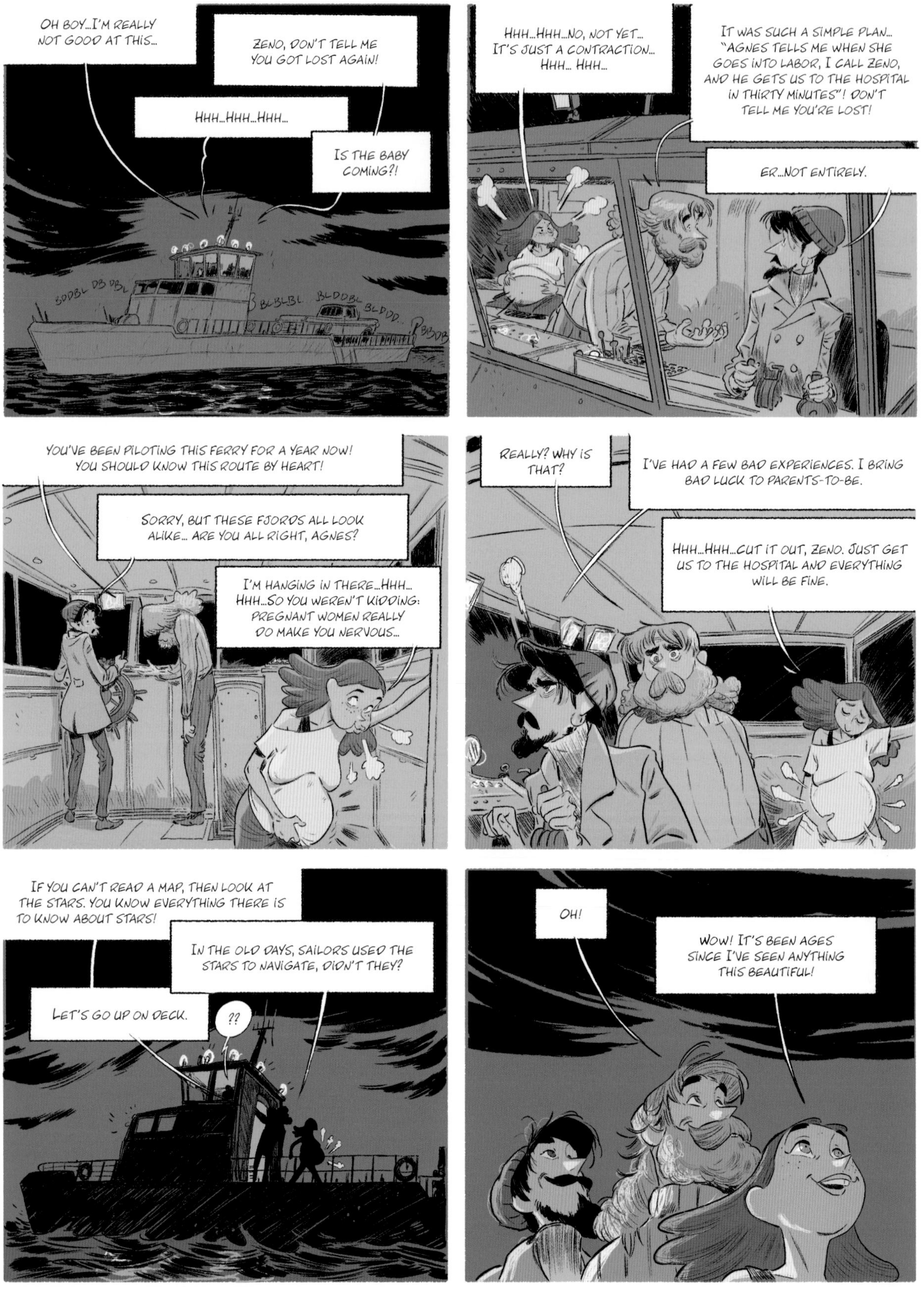

OH BOY...I'M REALLY NOT GOOD AT THIS...
ZENO, DON'T TELL ME YOU GOT LOST AGAIN!
HHH...HHH...HHH...
IS THE BABY COMING?!
HHH...HHH...NO, NOT YET... IT'S JUST A CONTRACTION... HHH... HHH...
IT WAS SUCH A SIMPLE PLAN... "AGNES TELLS ME WHEN SHE GOES INTO LABOR, I CALL ZENO, AND HE GETS US TO THE HOSPITAL IN THIRTY MINUTES"! DON'T TELL ME YOU'RE LOST!
ER...NOT ENTIRELY.
YOU'VE BEEN PILOTING THIS FERRY FOR A YEAR NOW! YOU SHOULD KNOW THIS ROUTE BY HEART!
SORRY, BUT THESE FJORDS ALL LOOK ALIKE... ARE YOU ALL RIGHT, AGNES?
I'M HANGING IN THERE...HHH... HHH...SO YOU WEREN'T KIDDING: PREGNANT WOMEN REALLY DO MAKE YOU NERVOUS...
REALLY? WHY IS THAT?
I'VE HAD A FEW BAD EXPERIENCES. I BRING BAD LUCK TO PARENTS-TO-BE.
HHH...HHH...CUT IT OUT, ZENO. JUST GET US TO THE HOSPITAL AND EVERYTHING WILL BE FINE.
IF YOU CAN'T READ A MAP, THEN LOOK AT THE STARS. YOU KNOW EVERYTHING THERE IS TO KNOW ABOUT STARS!
IN THE OLD DAYS, SAILORS USED THE STARS TO NAVIGATE, DIDN'T THEY?
LET'S GO UP ON DECK.
??
OH!
WOW! IT'S BEEN AGES SINCE I'VE SEEN ANYTHING THIS BEAUTIFUL!

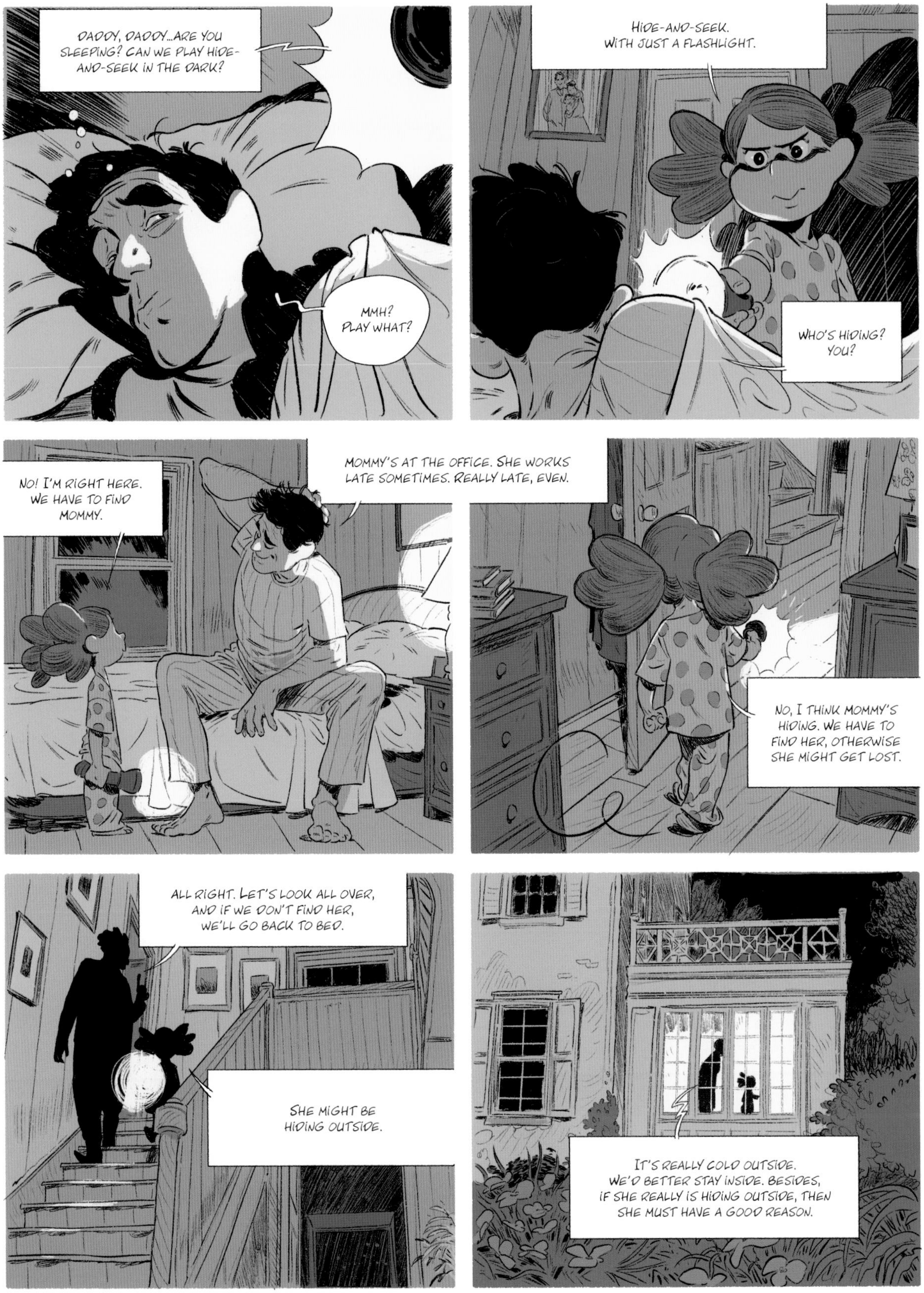
DADDY, DADDY...ARE YOU SLEEPING? CAN WE PLAY HIDE-AND-SEEK IN THE DARK?
MMH? PLAY WHAT?
HIDE-AND-SEEK. WITH JUST A FLASHLIGHT.
WHO'S HIDING? YOU?
NO! I'M RIGHT HERE. WE HAVE TO FIND MOMMY.
MOMMY'S AT THE OFFICE. SHE WORKS LATE SOMETIMES. REALLY LATE, EVEN.
NO, I THINK MOMMY'S HIDING. WE HAVE TO FIND HER, OTHERWISE SHE MIGHT GET LOST.
ALL RIGHT. LET'S LOOK ALL OVER, AND IF WE DON'T FIND HER, WE'LL GO BACK TO BED.
SHE MIGHT BE HIDING OUTSIDE.
IT'S REALLY COLD OUTSIDE. WE'D BETTER STAY INSIDE. BESIDES, IF SHE REALLY IS HIDING OUTSIDE, THEN SHE MUST HAVE A GOOD REASON.

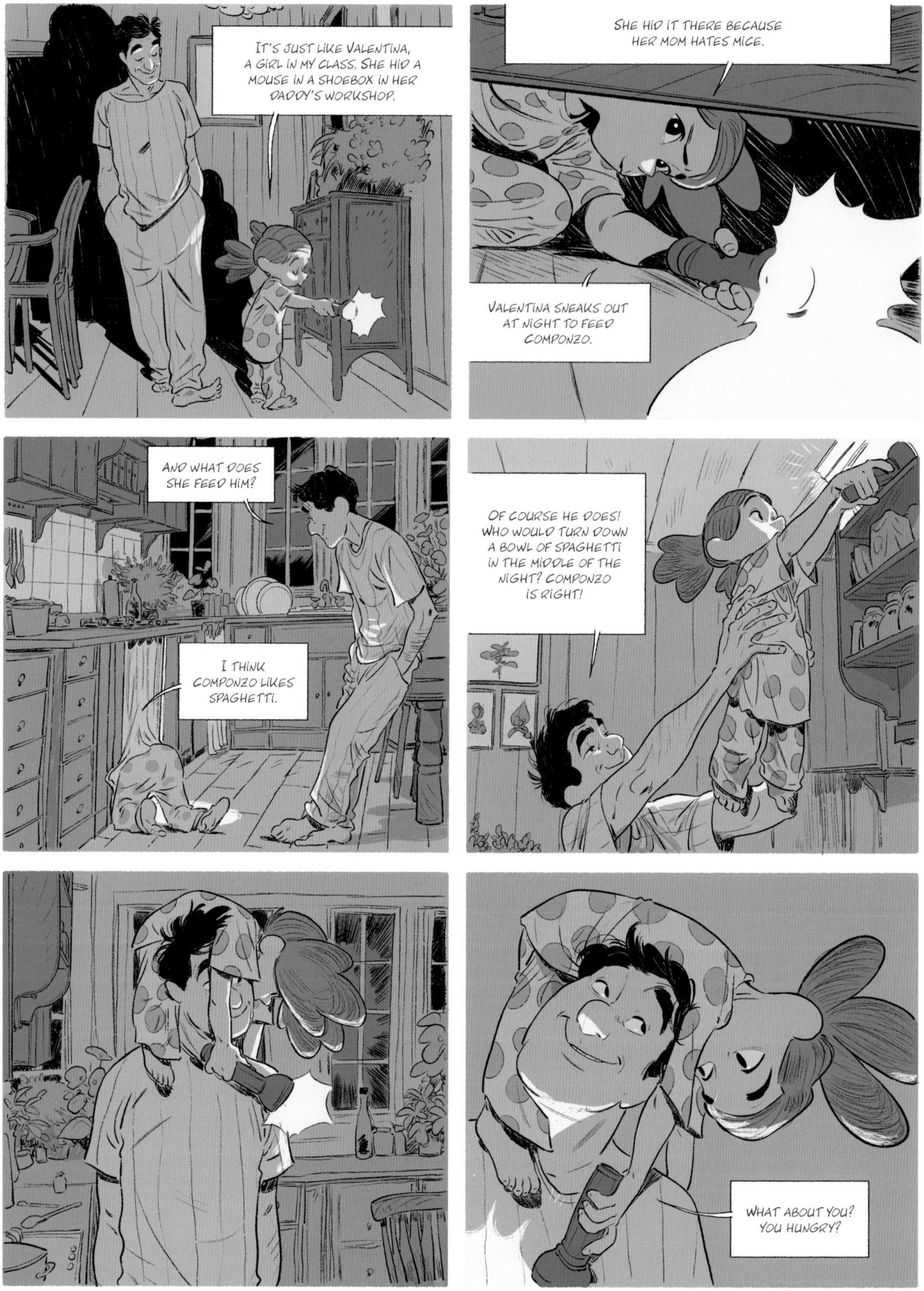
IT'S JUST LIKE VALENTINA, A GIRL IN MY CLASS. SHE HID A MOUSE IN A SHOEBOX IN HER DADDY'S WORKSHOP.
SHE HID IT THERE BECAUSE HER MOM HATES MICE.
VALENTINA SNEAKS OUT AT NIGHT TO FEED COMPONZO.
AND WHAT DOES SHE FEED HIM?
I THINK COMPONZO LIKES SPAGHETTI.
OF COURSE HE DOES! WHO WOULD TURN DOWN A BOWL OF SPAGHETTI IN THE MIDDLE OF THE NIGHT? COMPONZO IS RIGHT!
WHAT ABOUT YOU? YOU HUNGRY?

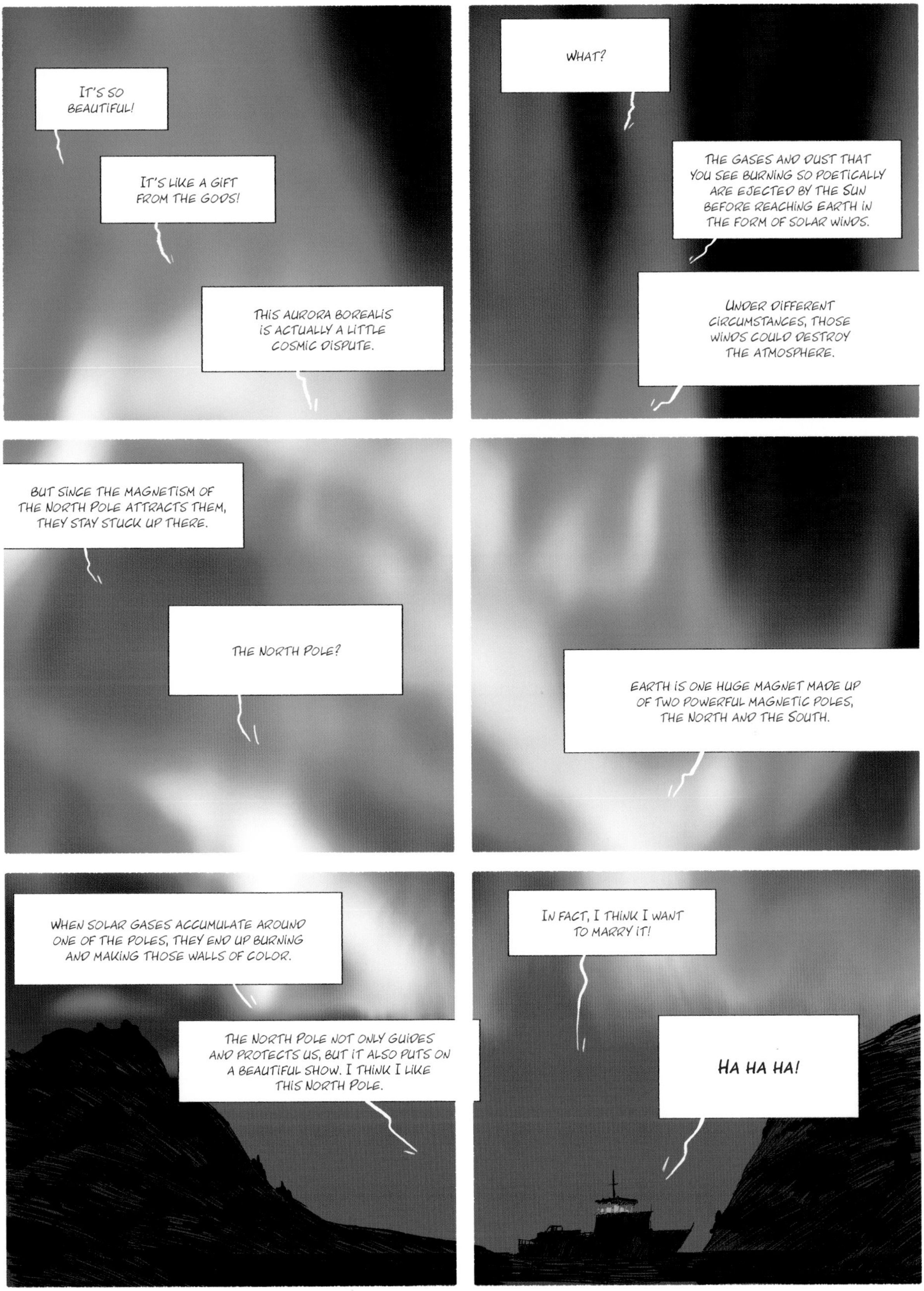
IT'S SO BEAUTIFUL!
IT'S LIKE A GIFT FROM THE GODS!
THIS AURORA BOREALIS IS ACTUALLY A LITTLE COSMIC DISPUTE.
WHAT?
THE GASES AND DUST THAT YOU SEE BURNING SO POETICALLY ARE EJECTED BY THE SUN BEFORE REACHING EARTH IN THE FORM OF SOLAR WINDS.
UNDER DIFFERENT CIRCUMSTANCES, THOSE WINDS COULD DESTROY THE ATMOSPHERE.
BUT SINCE THE MAGNETISM OF THE NORTH POLE ATTRACTS THEM, THEY STAY STUCK UP THERE.
THE NORTH POLE?
EARTH IS ONE HUGE MAGNET MADE UP OF TWO POWERFUL MAGNETIC POLES, THE NORTH AND THE SOUTH.
WHEN SOLAR GASES ACCUMULATE AROUND ONE OF THE POLES, THEY END UP BURNING AND MAKING THOSE WALLS OF COLOR.
THE NORTH POLE NOT ONLY GUIDES AND PROTECTS US, BUT IT ALSO PUTS ON A BEAUTIFUL SHOW. I THINK I LIKE THIS NORTH POLE.
IN FACT, I THINK I WANT TO MARRY IT!
HA HA HA!

IT'S A GOOD OMEN. I'M POSITIVE IT'S GOING TO BE A GIRL.

WE'LL CALL HER AURORA.

LOOK, IT'S POLARIS! WE JUST WENT SLIGHTLY OFF COURSE TO THE NORTH, ACTUALLY. WE'LL BE THERE SOON.

YOU SEE? YOU ARE A REAL CAPTAIN!

YOU'RE WRONG!

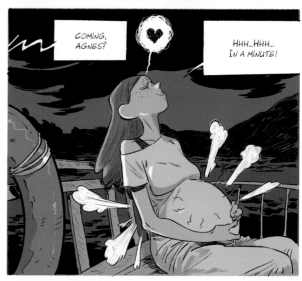

COMING, AGNES?

HHH...HHH... IN A MINUTE!

ANOTHER CONTRACTION?!

HHH...HHH... YOU SURE ARE ANXIOUS TO SEE THE WORLD!

CAN'T BLAME HER FOR THAT.

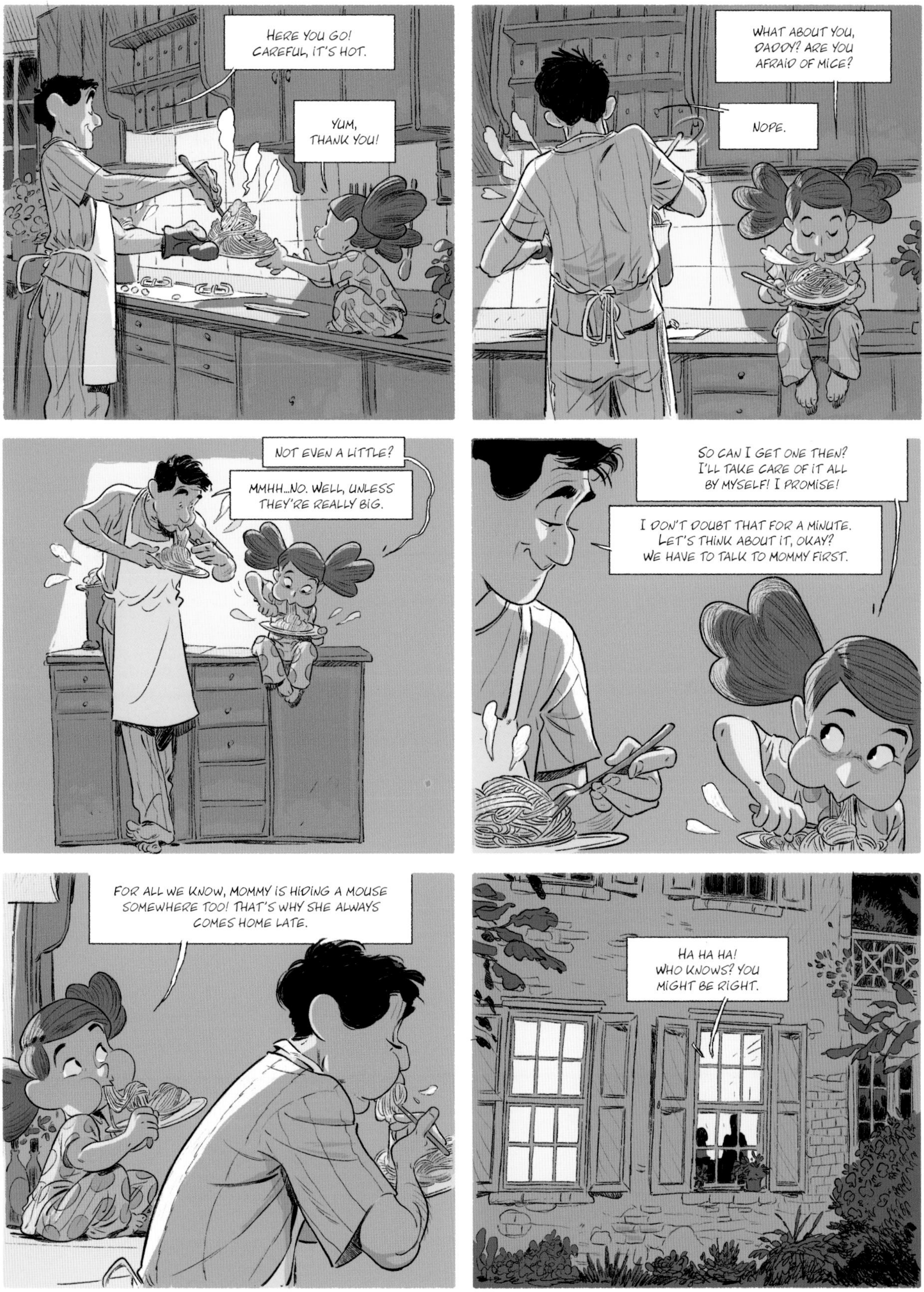
HERE YOU GO! CAREFUL, IT'S HOT.
YUM, THANK YOU!
WHAT ABOUT YOU, DADDY? ARE YOU AFRAID OF MICE?
NOPE.
NOT EVEN A LITTLE?
MMHH...NO. WELL, UNLESS THEY'RE REALLY BIG.
SO CAN I GET ONE THEN? I'LL TAKE CARE OF IT ALL BY MYSELF! I PROMISE!
I DON'T DOUBT THAT FOR A MINUTE. LET'S THINK ABOUT IT, OKAY? WE HAVE TO TALK TO MOMMY FIRST.
FOR ALL WE KNOW, MOMMY IS HIDING A MOUSE SOMEWHERE TOO! THAT'S WHY SHE ALWAYS COMES HOME LATE.
HA HA HA! WHO KNOWS? YOU MIGHT BE RIGHT.

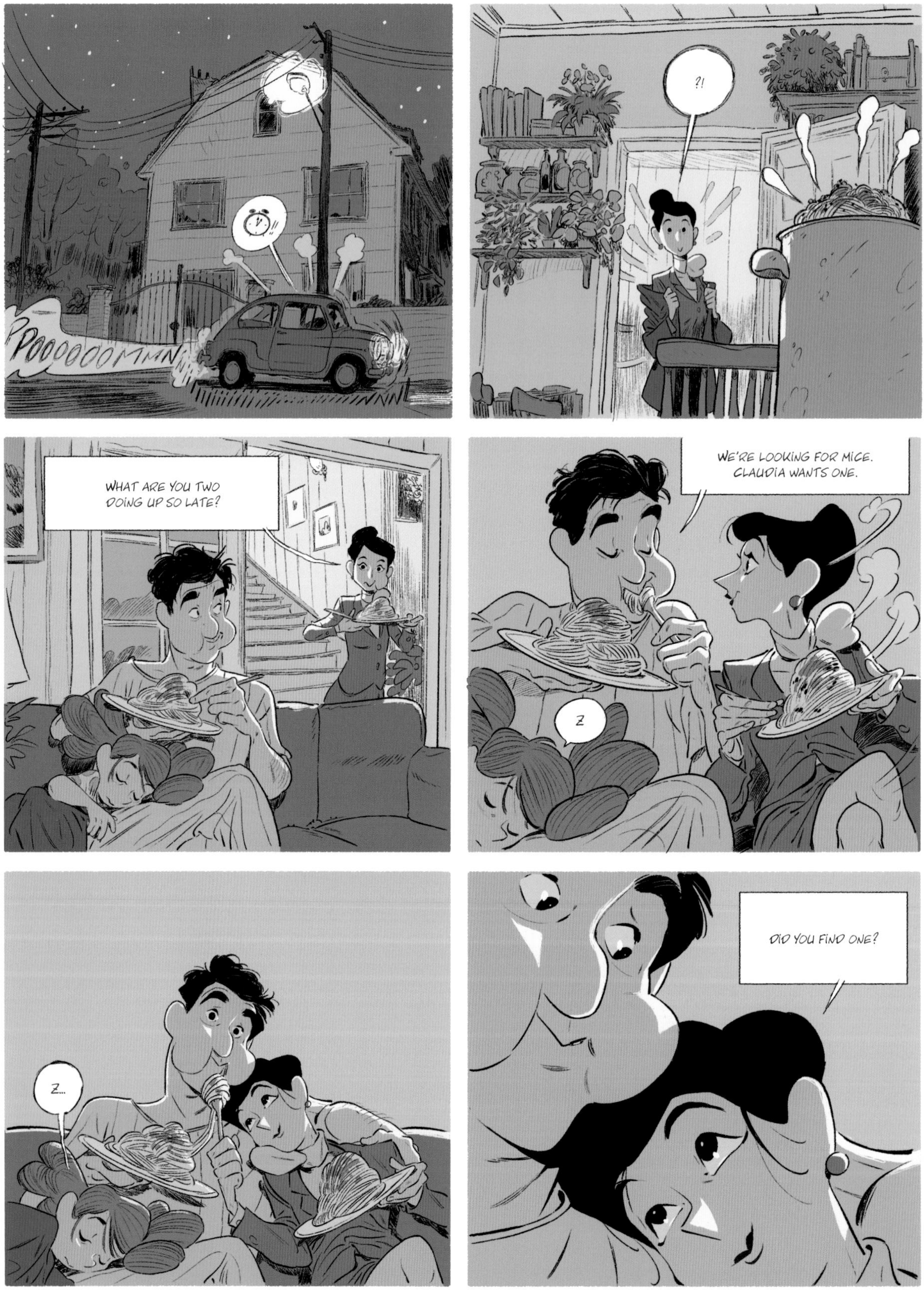
POOOOOOMMN
!!
?!
WHAT ARE YOU TWO DOING UP SO LATE?
WE'RE LOOKING FOR MICE. CLAUDIA WANTS ONE.
Z
Z...
DID YOU FIND ONE?

CHAPTER
7

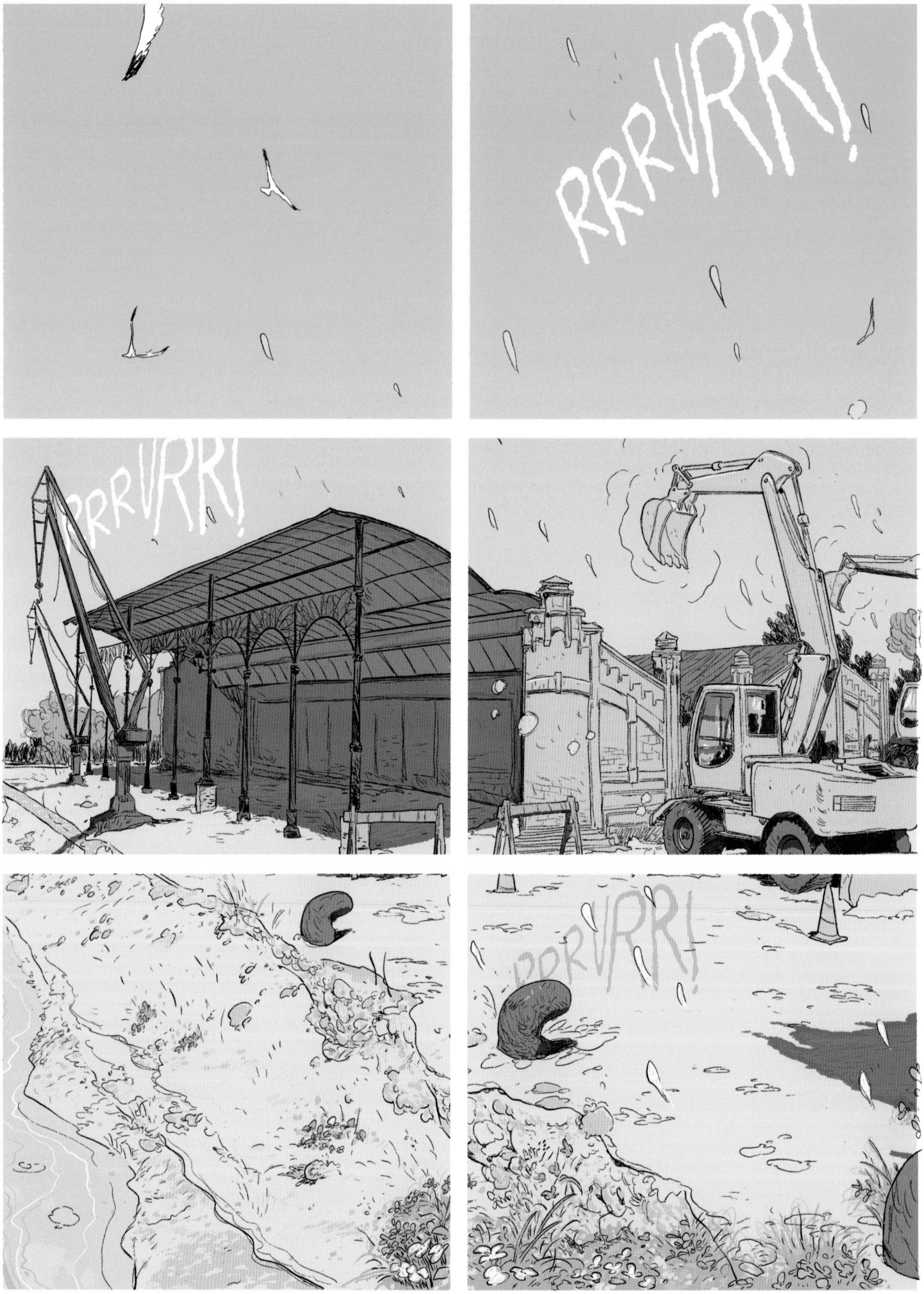
RRRVRR!
RRRVRR!
RRRVRR!

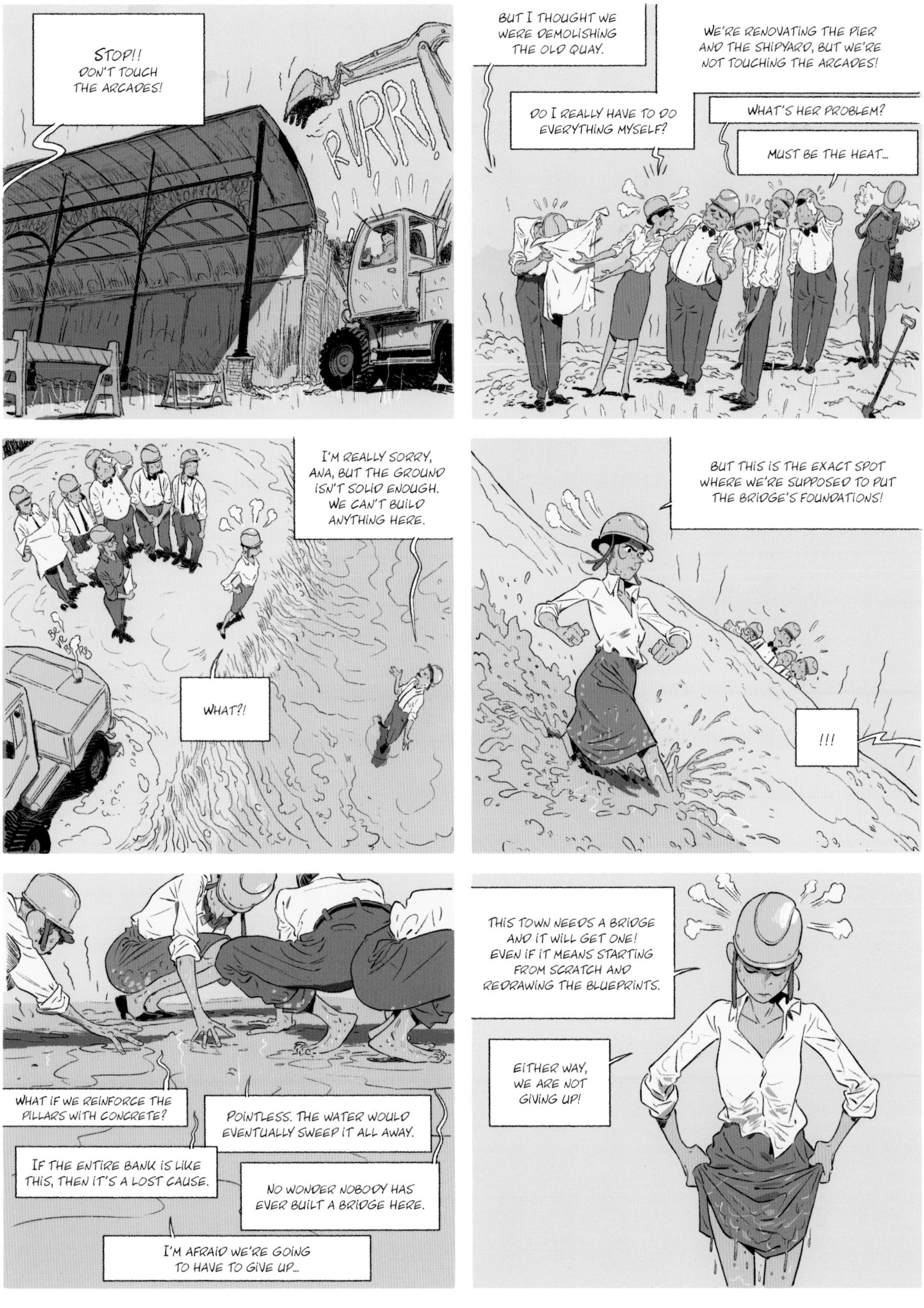

STOP!! DON'T TOUCH THE ARCADES!
RVRR!
BUT I THOUGHT WE WERE DEMOLISHING THE OLD QUAY.
WE'RE RENOVATING THE PIER AND THE SHIPYARD, BUT WE'RE NOT TOUCHING THE ARCADES!
DO I REALLY HAVE TO DO EVERYTHING MYSELF?
WHAT'S HER PROBLEM?
MUST BE THE HEAT...
I'M REALLY SORRY, ANA, BUT THE GROUND ISN'T SOLID ENOUGH. WE CAN'T BUILD ANYTHING HERE.
WHAT?!
BUT THIS IS THE EXACT SPOT WHERE WE'RE SUPPOSED TO PUT THE BRIDGE'S FOUNDATIONS!
!!!
WHAT IF WE REINFORCE THE PILLARS WITH CONCRETE?
POINTLESS. THE WATER WOULD EVENTUALLY SWEEP IT ALL AWAY.
IF THE ENTIRE BANK IS LIKE THIS, THEN IT'S A LOST CAUSE.
NO WONDER NOBODY HAS EVER BUILT A BRIDGE HERE.
I'M AFRAID WE'RE GOING TO HAVE TO GIVE UP...
THIS TOWN NEEDS A BRIDGE AND IT WILL GET ONE! EVEN IF IT MEANS STARTING FROM SCRATCH AND REDRAWING THE BLUEPRINTS.
EITHER WAY, WE ARE NOT GIVING UP!

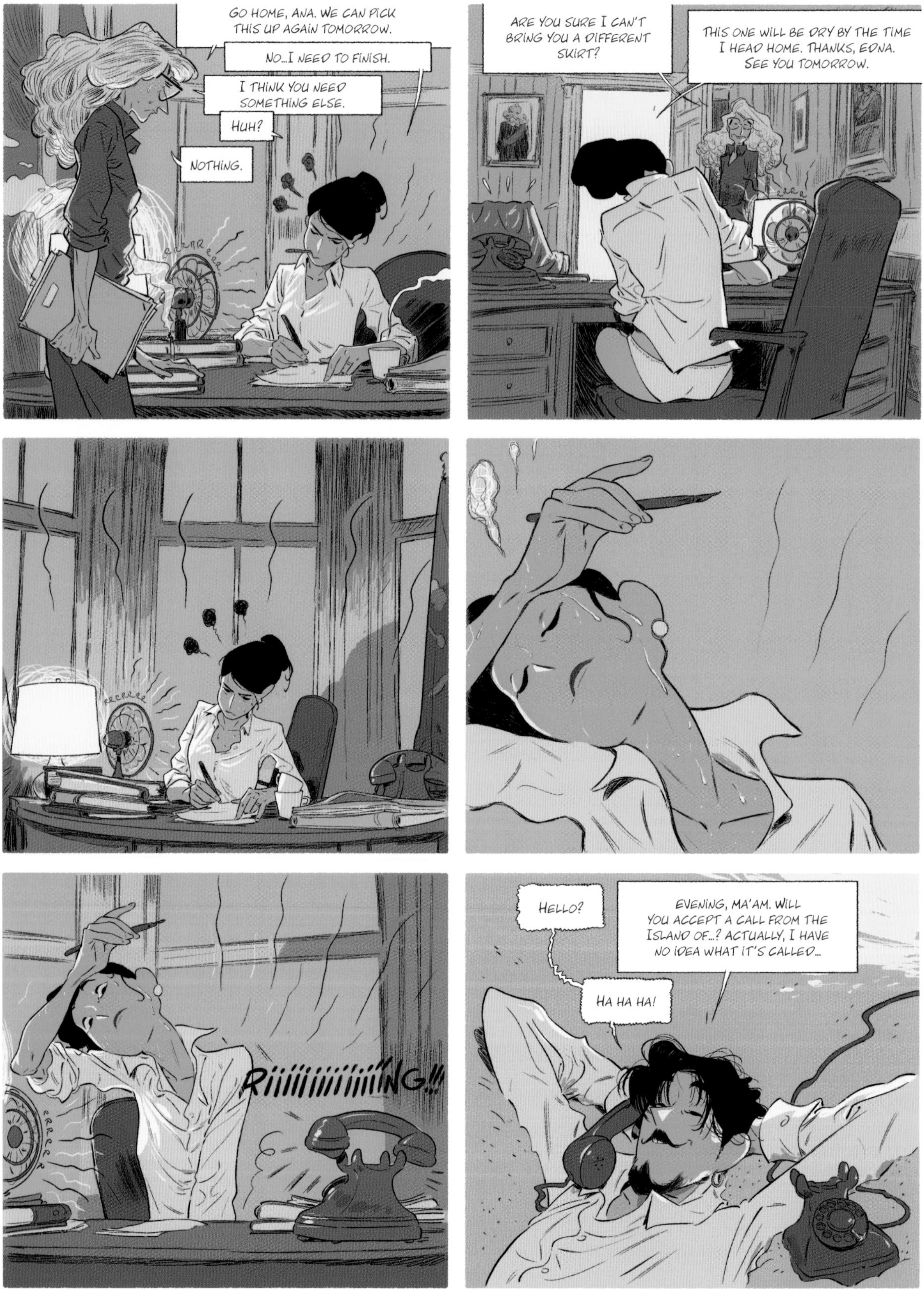
GO HOME, ANA. WE CAN PICK THIS UP AGAIN TOMORROW.
NO...I NEED TO FINISH.
I THINK YOU NEED SOMETHING ELSE.
HUH?
NOTHING.
RRRRR
ARE YOU SURE I CAN'T BRING YOU A DIFFERENT SKIRT?
THIS ONE WILL BE DRY BY THE TIME I HEAD HOME. THANKS, EDNA. SEE YOU TOMORROW.
RRRRRRR
RIIIIIIIIIIIIING!!!
HELLO?
EVENING, MA'AM. WILL YOU ACCEPT A CALL FROM THE ISLAND OF...? ACTUALLY, I HAVE NO IDEA WHAT IT'S CALLED...
HA HA HA!

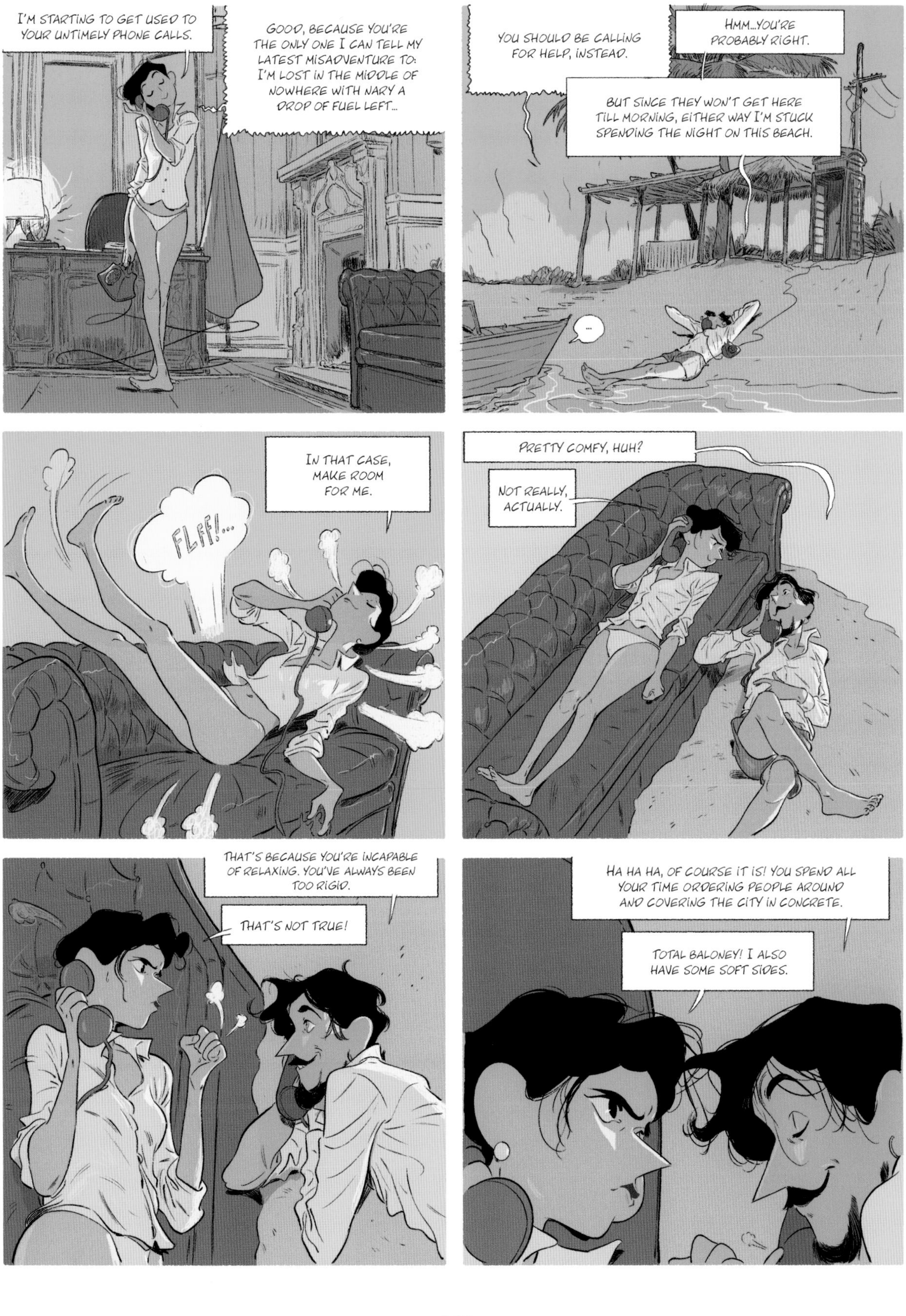
I'M STARTING TO GET USED TO YOUR UNTIMELY PHONE CALLS.
GOOD, BECAUSE YOU'RE THE ONLY ONE I CAN TELL MY LATEST MISADVENTURE TO: I'M LOST IN THE MIDDLE OF NOWHERE WITH NARY A DROP OF FUEL LEFT...
YOU SHOULD BE CALLING FOR HELP, INSTEAD.
HMM...YOU'RE PROBABLY RIGHT.
BUT SINCE THEY WON'T GET HERE TILL MORNING, EITHER WAY I'M STUCK SPENDING THE NIGHT ON THIS BEACH.
...
IN THAT CASE, MAKE ROOM FOR ME.
FLFF!...
PRETTY COMFY, HUH?
NOT REALLY, ACTUALLY.
THAT'S BECAUSE YOU'RE INCAPABLE OF RELAXING. YOU'VE ALWAYS BEEN TOO RIGID.
THAT'S NOT TRUE!
HA HA HA, OF COURSE IT IS! YOU SPEND ALL YOUR TIME ORDERING PEOPLE AROUND AND COVERING THE CITY IN CONCRETE.
TOTAL BALONEY! I ALSO HAVE SOME SOFT SIDES.

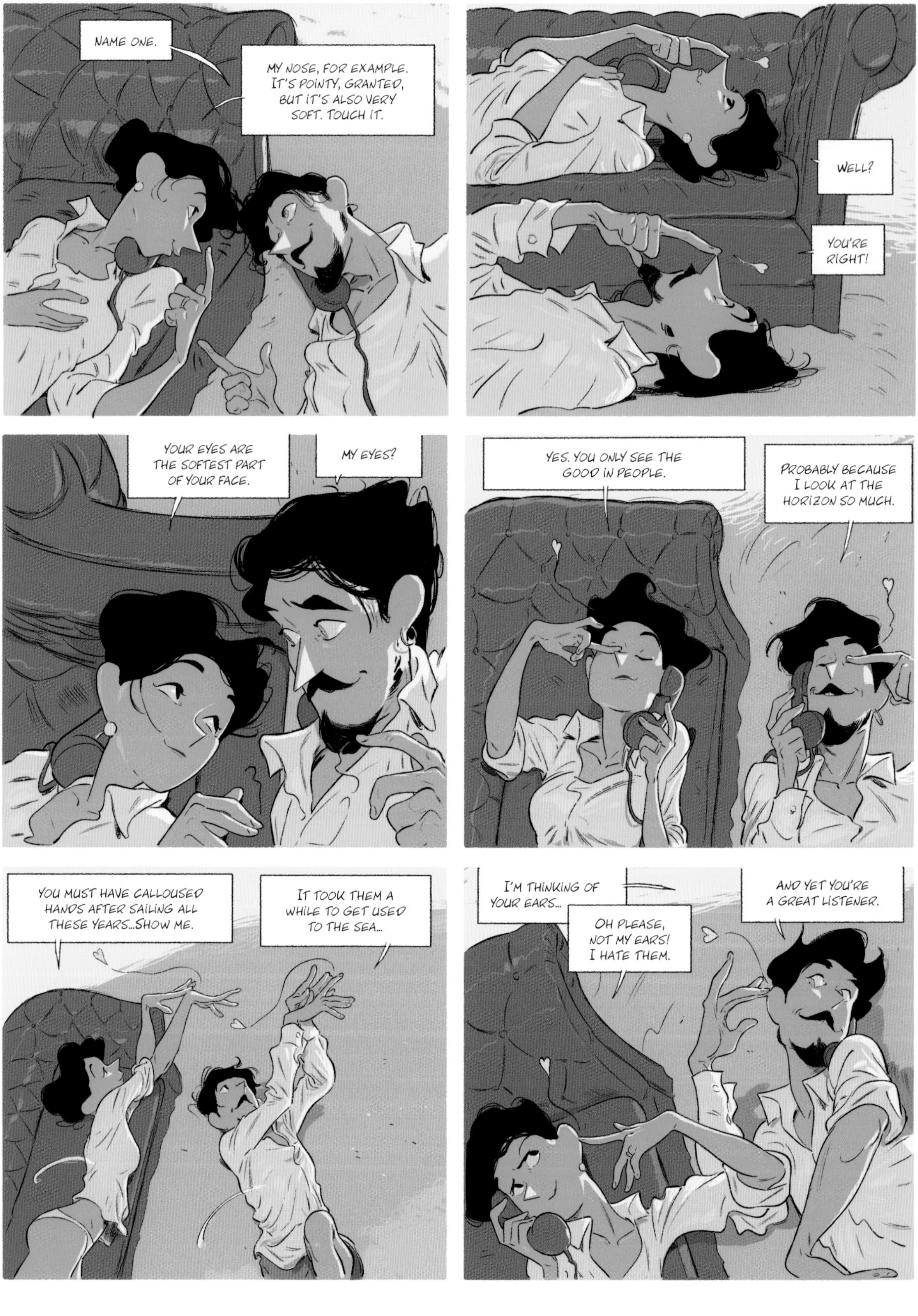
NAME ONE.
MY NOSE, FOR EXAMPLE. IT'S POINTY, GRANTED, BUT IT'S ALSO VERY SOFT. TOUCH IT.
WELL?
YOU'RE RIGHT!
YOUR EYES ARE THE SOFTEST PART OF YOUR FACE.
MY EYES?
YES. YOU ONLY SEE THE GOOD IN PEOPLE.
PROBABLY BECAUSE I LOOK AT THE HORIZON SO MUCH.
YOU MUST HAVE CALLOUSED HANDS AFTER SAILING ALL THESE YEARS...SHOW ME.
IT TOOK THEM A WHILE TO GET USED TO THE SEA...
I'M THINKING OF YOUR EARS...
OH PLEASE, NOT MY EARS! I HATE THEM.
AND YET YOU'RE A GREAT LISTENER.

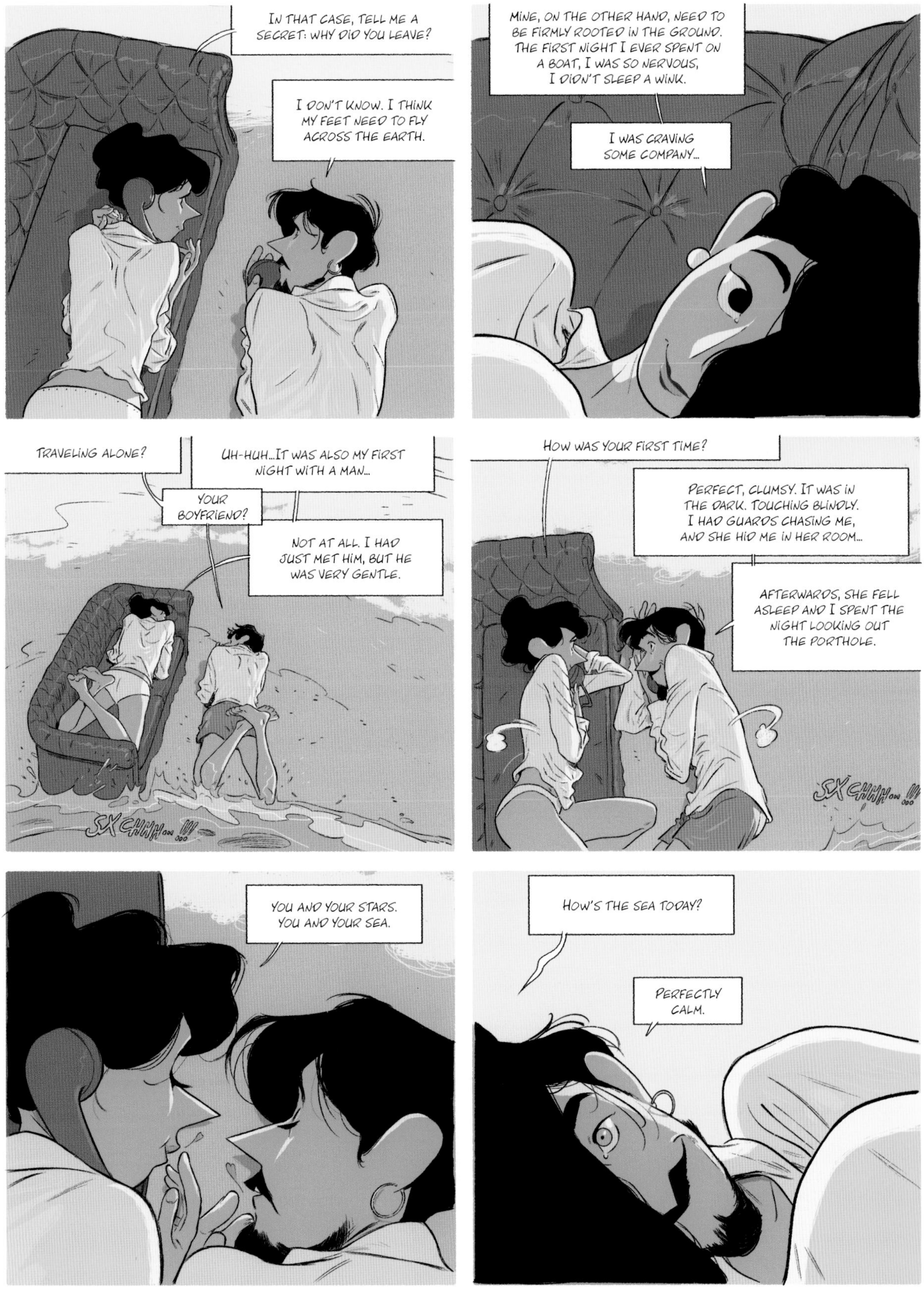
IN THAT CASE, TELL ME A SECRET: WHY DID YOU LEAVE?
I DON'T KNOW. I THINK MY FEET NEED TO FLY ACROSS THE EARTH.
MINE, ON THE OTHER HAND, NEED TO BE FIRMLY ROOTED IN THE GROUND. THE FIRST NIGHT I EVER SPENT ON A BOAT, I WAS SO NERVOUS, I DIDN'T SLEEP A WINK.
I WAS CRAVING SOME COMPANY...
TRAVELING ALONE?
UH-HUH...IT WAS ALSO MY FIRST NIGHT WITH A MAN...
YOUR BOYFRIEND?
NOT AT ALL. I HAD JUST MET HIM, BUT HE WAS VERY GENTLE.
SXCHHH...!!!
HOW WAS YOUR FIRST TIME?
PERFECT, CLUMSY. IT WAS IN THE DARK. TOUCHING BLINDLY. I HAD GUARDS CHASING ME, AND SHE HID ME IN HER ROOM...
AFTERWARDS, SHE FELL ASLEEP AND I SPENT THE NIGHT LOOKING OUT THE PORTHOLE.
SXCHHH...!!!
YOU AND YOUR STARS. YOU AND YOUR SEA.
HOW'S THE SEA TODAY?
PERFECTLY CALM.

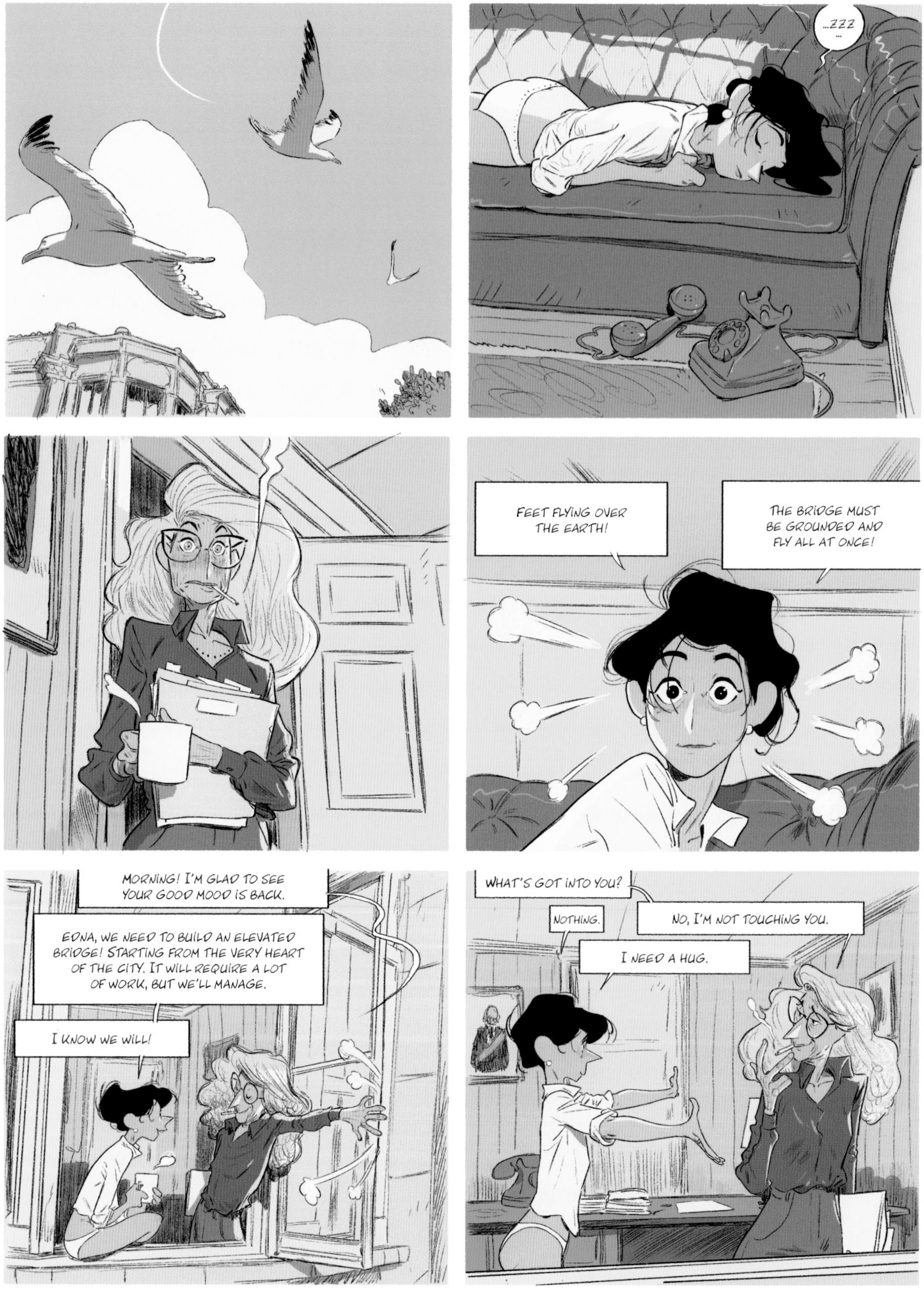
...zzz
...
FEET FLYING OVER THE EARTH!
THE BRIDGE MUST BE GROUNDED AND FLY ALL AT ONCE!
MORNING! I'M GLAD TO SEE YOUR GOOD MOOD IS BACK.
EDNA, WE NEED TO BUILD AN ELEVATED BRIDGE! STARTING FROM THE VERY HEART OF THE CITY. IT WILL REQUIRE A LOT OF WORK, BUT WE'LL MANAGE.
I KNOW WE WILL!
WHAT'S GOT INTO YOU?
NOTHING.
I NEED A HUG.
NO, I'M NOT TOUCHING YOU.

CHAPTER
6

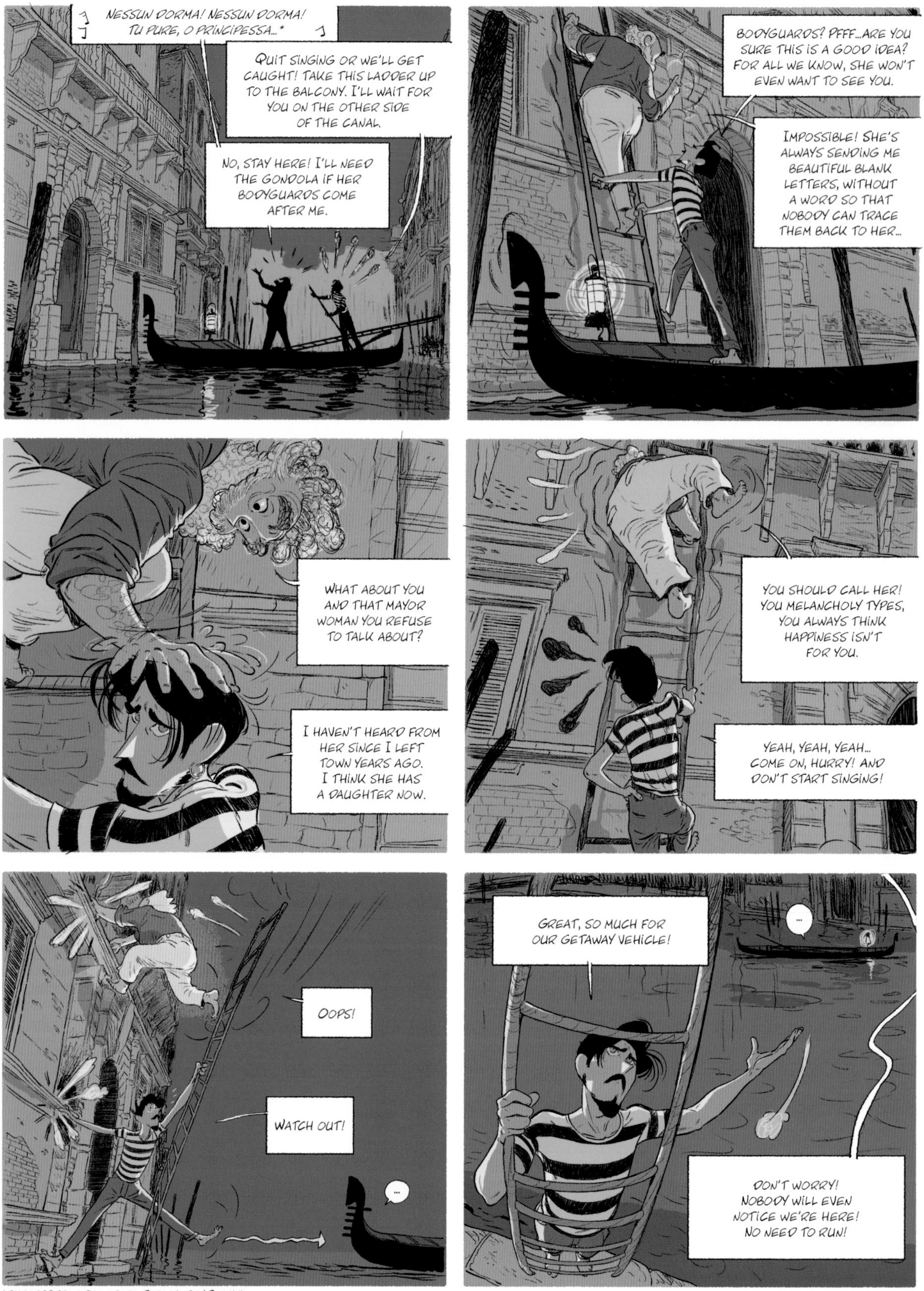
NESSUN DORMA! NESSUN DORMA! TU PURE, O PRINCIPESSA...*
QUIT SINGING OR WE'LL GET CAUGHT! TAKE THIS LADDER UP TO THE BALCONY. I'LL WAIT FOR YOU ON THE OTHER SIDE OF THE CANAL.
NO, STAY HERE! I'LL NEED THE GONDOLA IF HER BODYGUARDS COME AFTER ME.
BODYGUARDS? PFFF...ARE YOU SURE THIS IS A GOOD IDEA? FOR ALL WE KNOW, SHE WON'T EVEN WANT TO SEE YOU.
IMPOSSIBLE! SHE'S ALWAYS SENDING ME BEAUTIFUL BLANK LETTERS, WITHOUT A WORD SO THAT NOBODY CAN TRACE THEM BACK TO HER...
WHAT ABOUT YOU AND THAT MAYOR WOMAN YOU REFUSE TO TALK ABOUT?
I HAVEN'T HEARD FROM HER SINCE I LEFT TOWN YEARS AGO. I THINK SHE HAS A DAUGHTER NOW.
YOU SHOULD CALL HER! YOU MELANCHOLY TYPES, YOU ALWAYS THINK HAPPINESS ISN'T FOR YOU.
YEAH, YEAH, YEAH... COME ON, HURRY! AND DON'T START SINGING!
OOPS!
WATCH OUT!
...
GREAT, SO MUCH FOR OUR GETAWAY VEHICLE!
...
DON'T WORRY! NOBODY WILL EVEN NOTICE WE'RE HERE! NO NEED TO RUN!

*EXCERPT FROM THE OPERA TURANDOT BY PUCCINI.

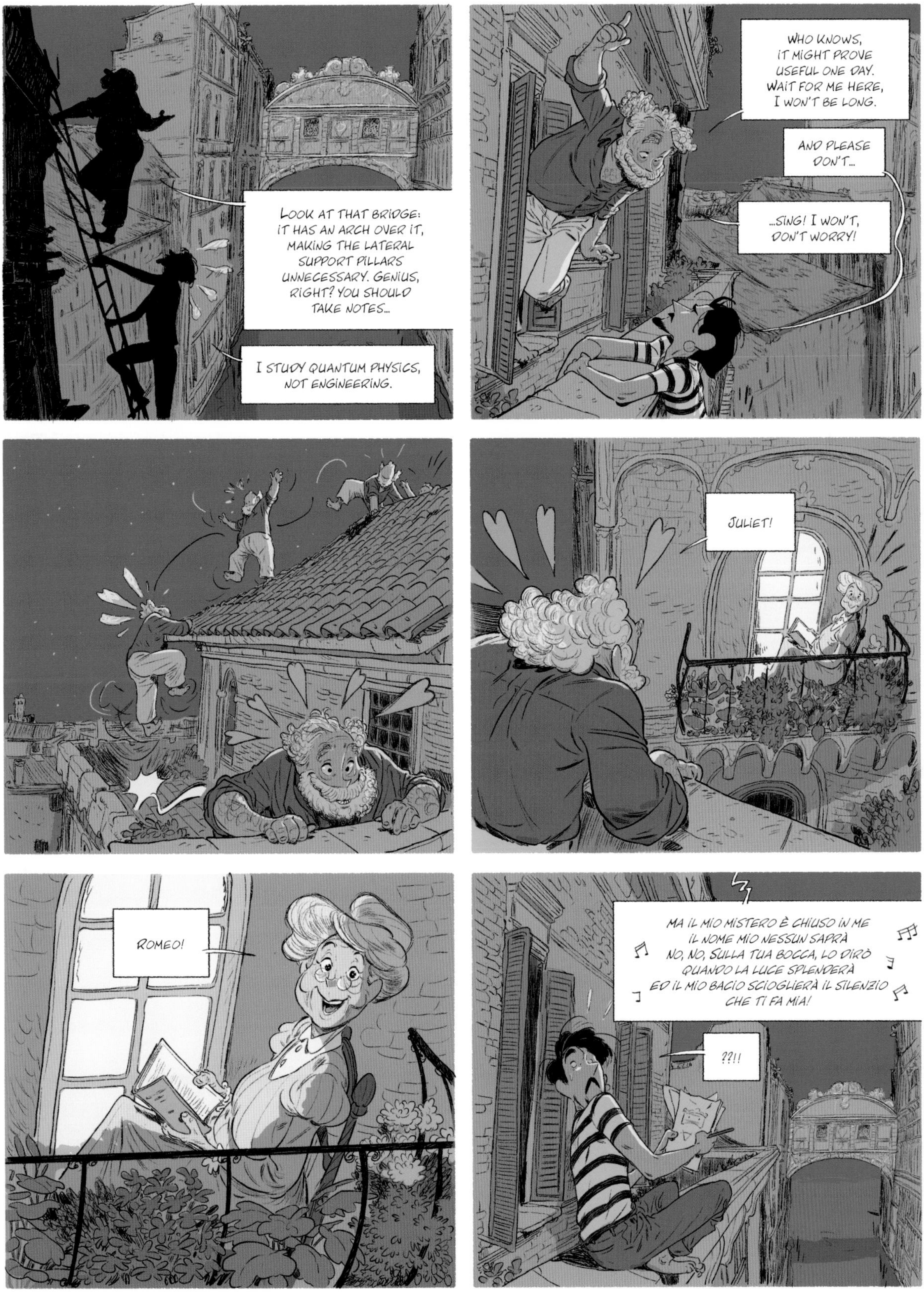
LOOK AT THAT BRIDGE: IT HAS AN ARCH OVER IT, MAKING THE LATERAL SUPPORT PILLARS UNNECESSARY. GENIUS, RIGHT? YOU SHOULD TAKE NOTES...
I STUDY QUANTUM PHYSICS, NOT ENGINEERING.
WHO KNOWS, IT MIGHT PROVE USEFUL ONE DAY. WAIT FOR ME HERE, I WON'T BE LONG.
AND PLEASE DON'T...
...SING! I WON'T, DON'T WORRY!
JULIET!
ROMEO!
MA IL MIO MISTERO È CHIUSO IN ME
IL NOME MIO NESSUN SAPRÀ
NO, NO, SULLA TUA BOCCA, LO DIRÒ
QUANDO LA LUCE SPLENDERÀ
ED IL MIO BACIO SCIOGLIERÀ IL SILENZIO
CHE TI FA MIA!
??!!

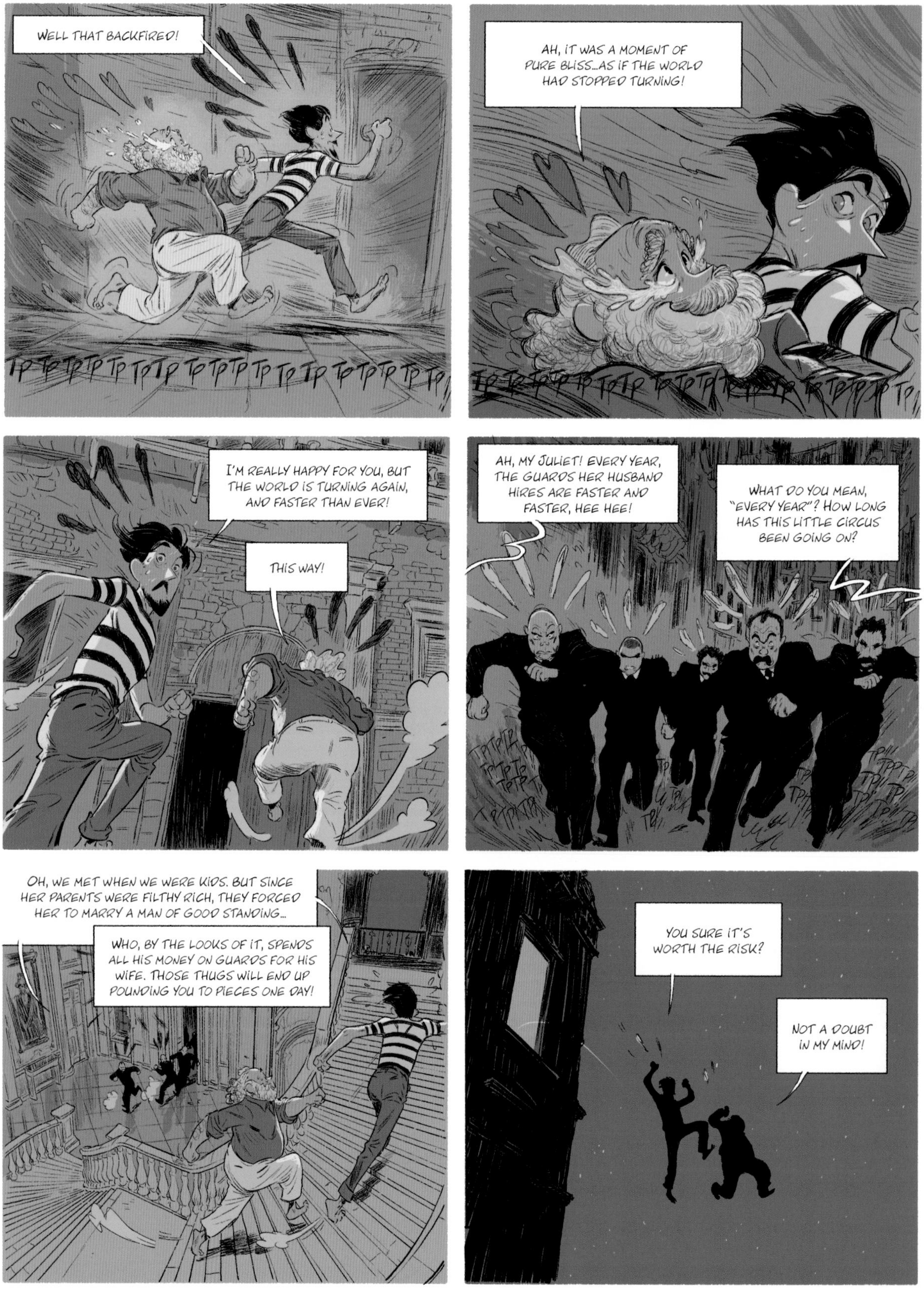
WELL THAT BACKFIRED!
AH, IT WAS A MOMENT OF PURE BLISS...AS IF THE WORLD HAD STOPPED TURNING!
I'M REALLY HAPPY FOR YOU, BUT THE WORLD IS TURNING AGAIN, AND FASTER THAN EVER!
THIS WAY!
AH, MY JULIET! EVERY YEAR, THE GUARDS HER HUSBAND HIRES ARE FASTER AND FASTER, HEE HEE!
WHAT DO YOU MEAN, "EVERY YEAR"? HOW LONG HAS THIS LITTLE CIRCUS BEEN GOING ON?
OH, WE MET WHEN WE WERE KIDS. BUT SINCE HER PARENTS WERE FILTHY RICH, THEY FORCED HER TO MARRY A MAN OF GOOD STANDING...
WHO, BY THE LOOKS OF IT, SPENDS ALL HIS MONEY ON GUARDS FOR HIS WIFE. THOSE THUGS WILL END UP POUNDING YOU TO PIECES ONE DAY!
YOU SURE IT'S WORTH THE RISK?
NOT A DOUBT IN MY MIND!

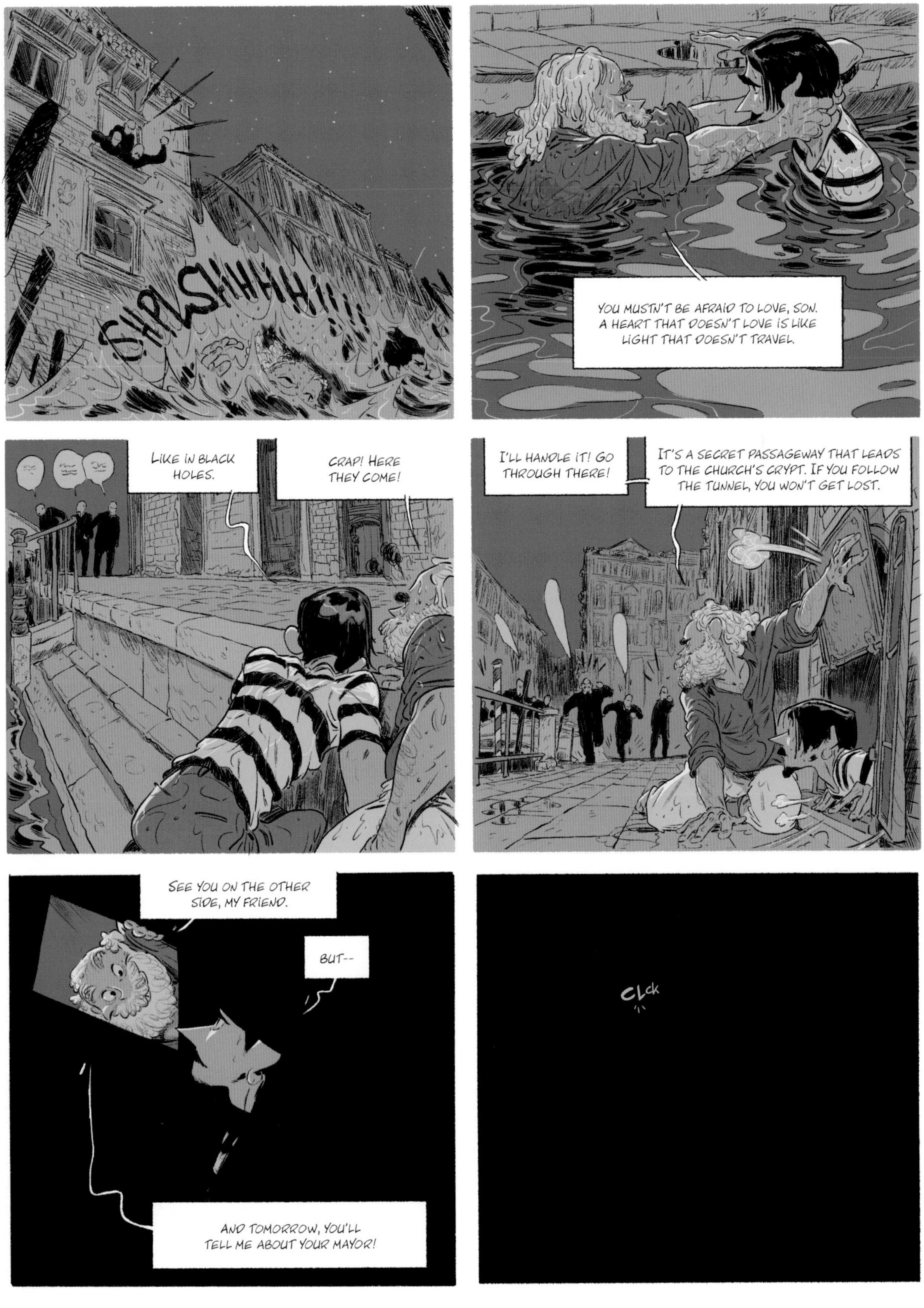
SHPLASHHHHH!!!!
YOU MUSTN'T BE AFRAID TO LOVE, SON. A HEART THAT DOESN'T LOVE IS LIKE LIGHT THAT DOESN'T TRAVEL.
LIKE IN BLACK HOLES.
CRAP! HERE THEY COME!
I'LL HANDLE IT! GO THROUGH THERE!
IT'S A SECRET PASSAGEWAY THAT LEADS TO THE CHURCH'S CRYPT. IF YOU FOLLOW THE TUNNEL, YOU WON'T GET LOST.
SEE YOU ON THE OTHER SIDE, MY FRIEND.
BUT--
AND TOMORROW, YOU'LL TELL ME ABOUT YOUR MAYOR!
CLck

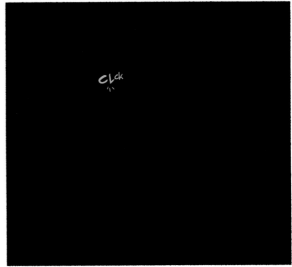

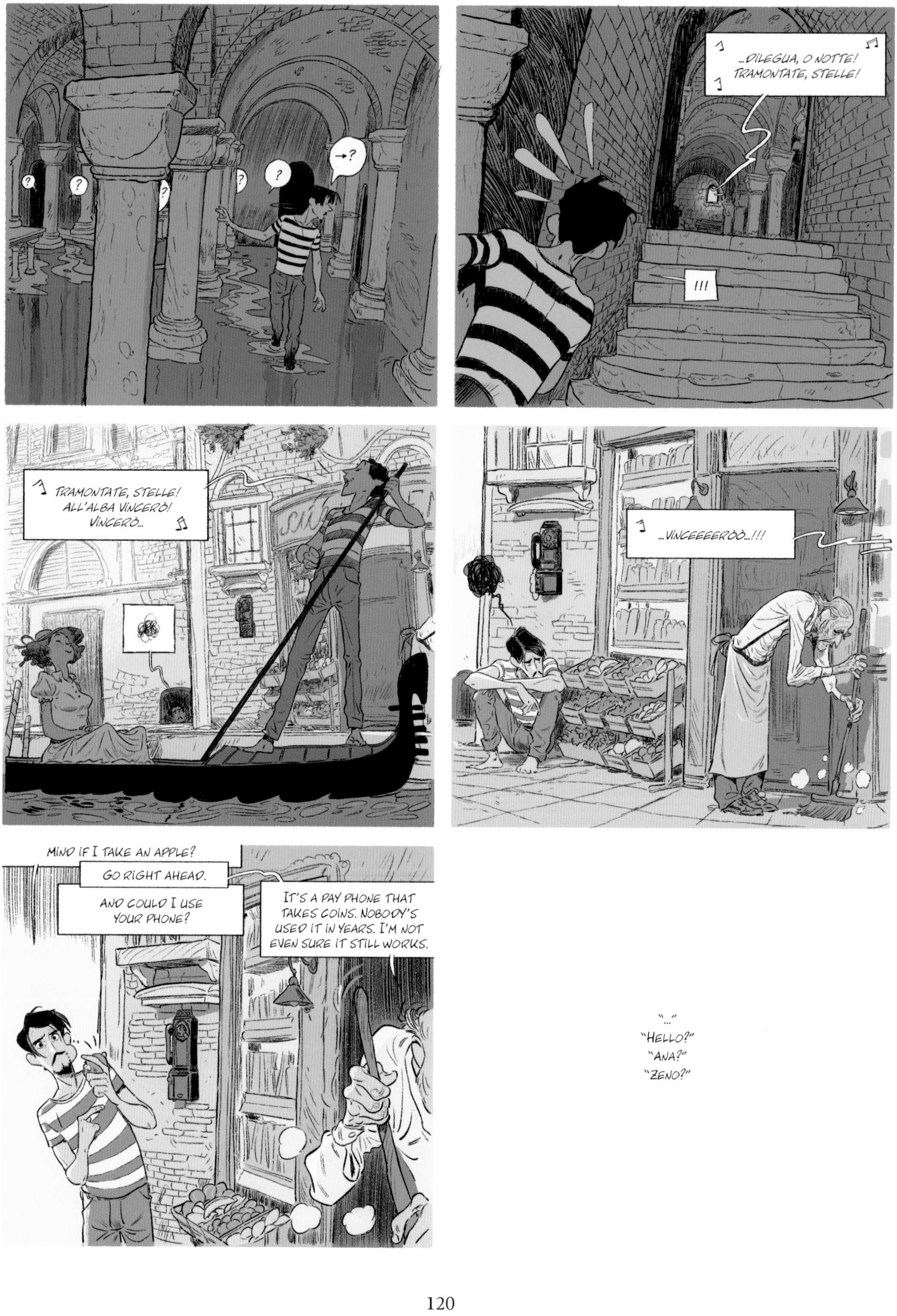
?
?
?
?
?
→?
...DILEGUA, O NOTTE! TRAMONTATE, STELLE!
!!!
TRAMONTATE, STELLE! ALL'ALBA VINCERÒ! VINCERÒ...
...VINCEEEERÒÒ...!!!
MIND IF I TAKE AN APPLE?
GO RIGHT AHEAD.
AND COULD I USE YOUR PHONE?
IT'S A PAY PHONE THAT TAKES COINS. NOBODY'S USED IT IN YEARS. I'M NOT EVEN SURE IT STILL WORKS.

"..."
"HELLO?"
"ANA?"
"ZENO?"

CHAPTER
5

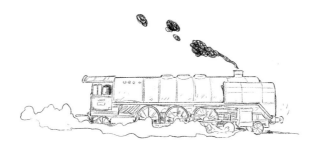

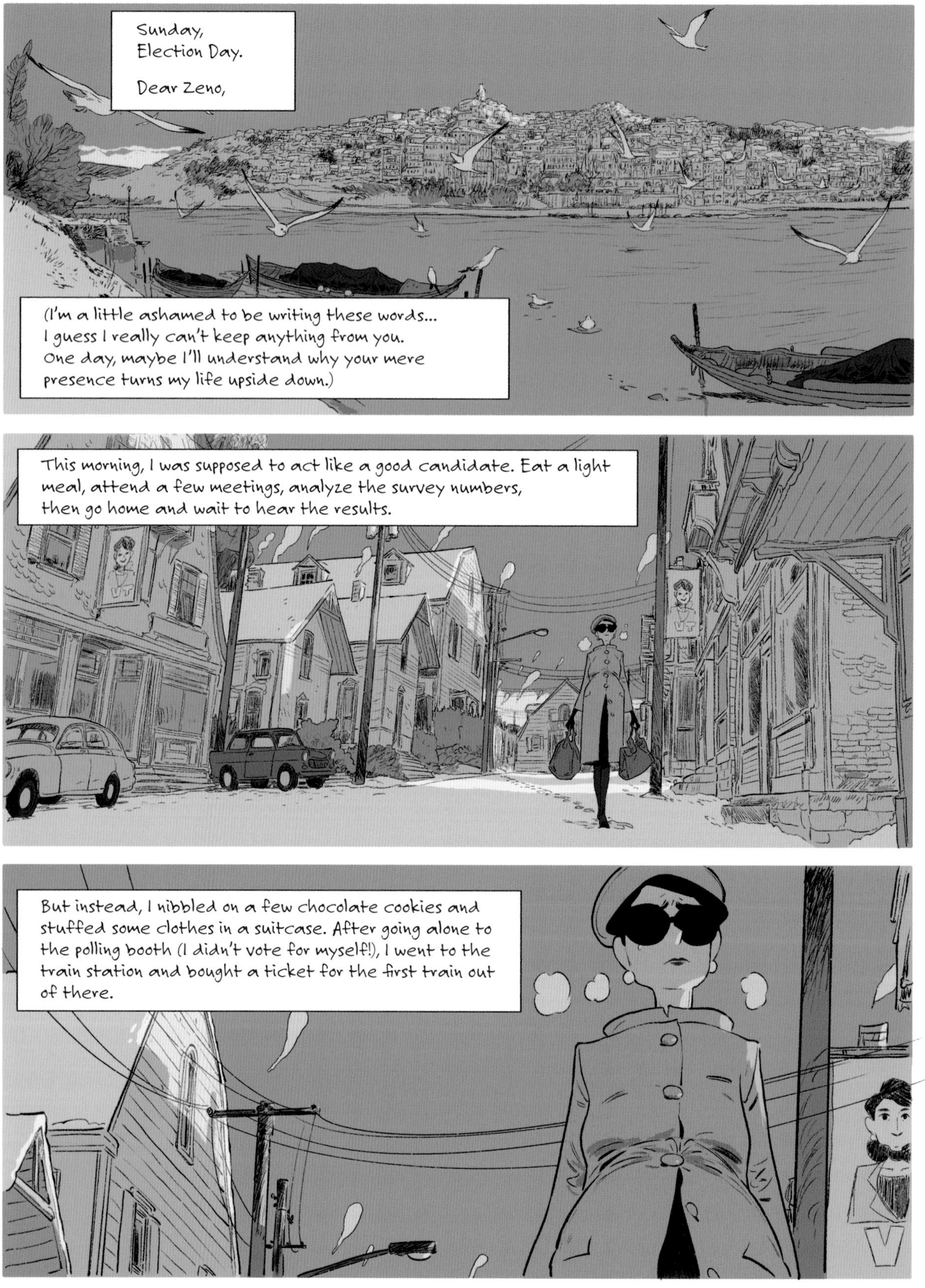
Sunday,
Election Day.
Dear Zeno,
(I'm a little ashamed to be writing these words... I guess I really can't keep anything from you. One day, maybe I'll understand why your mere presence turns my life upside down.)
This morning, I was supposed to act like a good candidate. Eat a light meal, attend a few meetings, analyze the survey numbers, then go home and wait to hear the results.
But instead, I nibbled on a few chocolate cookies and stuffed some clothes in a suitcase. After going alone to the polling booth (I didn't vote for myself!), I went to the train station and bought a ticket for the first train out of there.

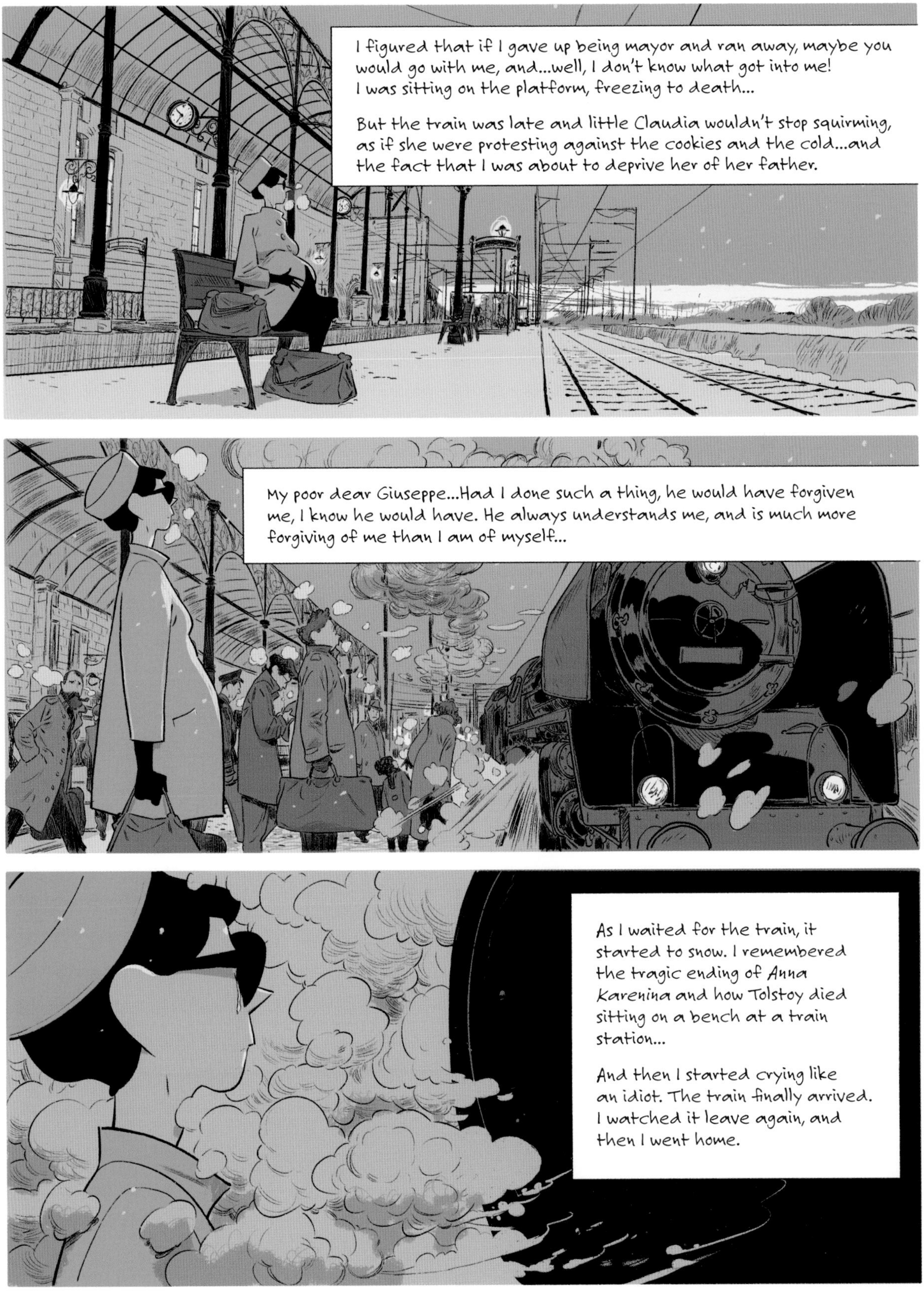
I figured that if I gave up being mayor and ran away, maybe you would go with me, and...well, I don't know what got into me! I was sitting on the platform, freezing to death...
But the train was late and little Claudia wouldn't stop squirming, as if she were protesting against the cookies and the cold...and the fact that I was about to deprive her of her father.
My poor dear Giuseppe...Had I done such a thing, he would have forgiven me, I know he would have. He always understands me, and is much more forgiving of me than I am of myself...
As I waited for the train, it started to snow. I remembered the tragic ending of *Anna Karenina* and how Tolstoy died sitting on a bench at a train station...
And then I started crying like an idiot. The train finally arrived. I watched it leave again, and then I went home.

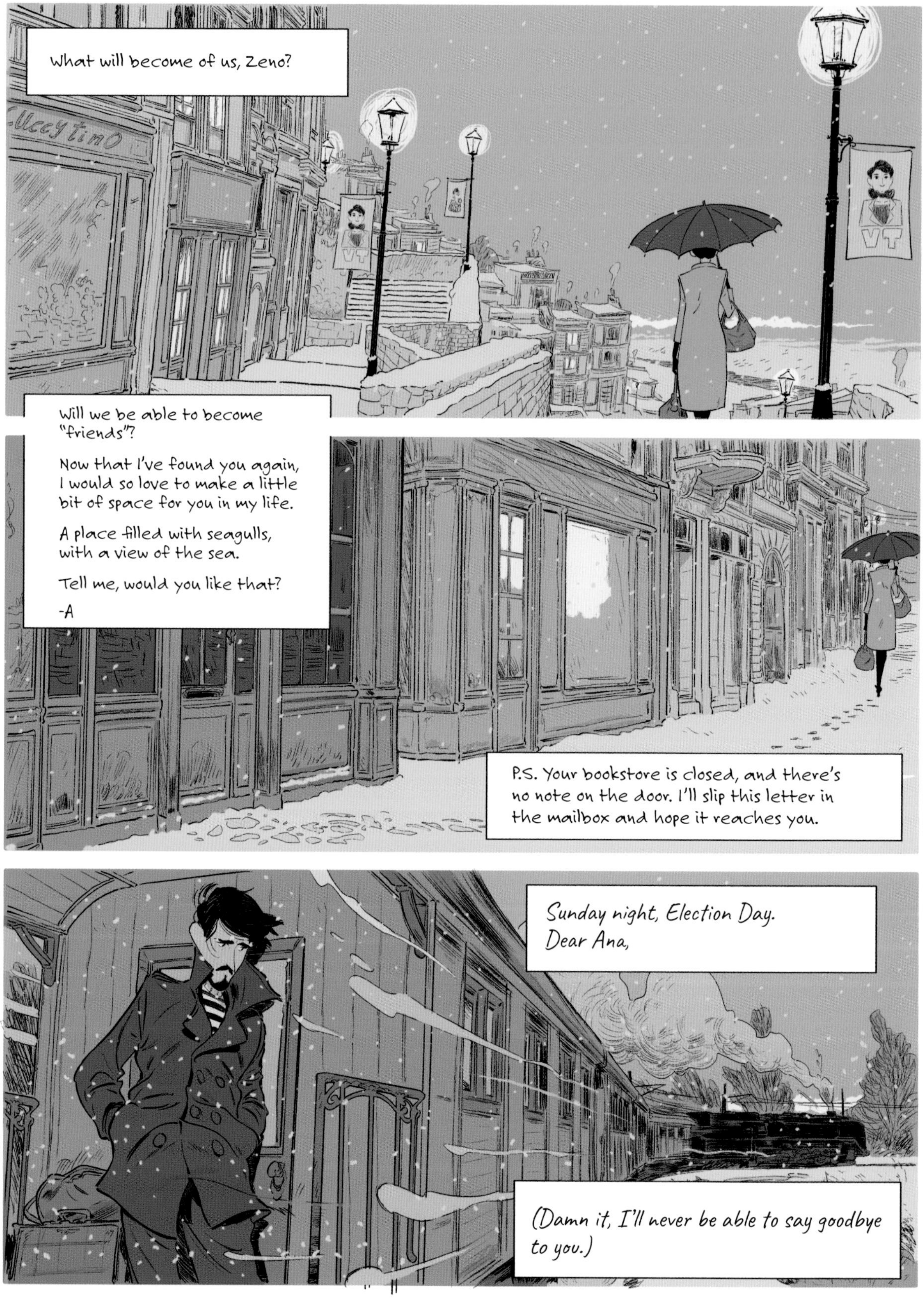
What will become of us, Zeno?
Will we be able to become "friends"?
Now that I've found you again, I would so love to make a little bit of space for you in my life.
A place filled with seagulls, with a view of the sea.
Tell me, would you like that?
-A
P.S. Your bookstore is closed, and there's no note on the door. I'll slip this letter in the mailbox and hope it reaches you.
Sunday night, Election Day.
Dear Ana,
(Damn it, I'll never be able to say goodbye to you.)

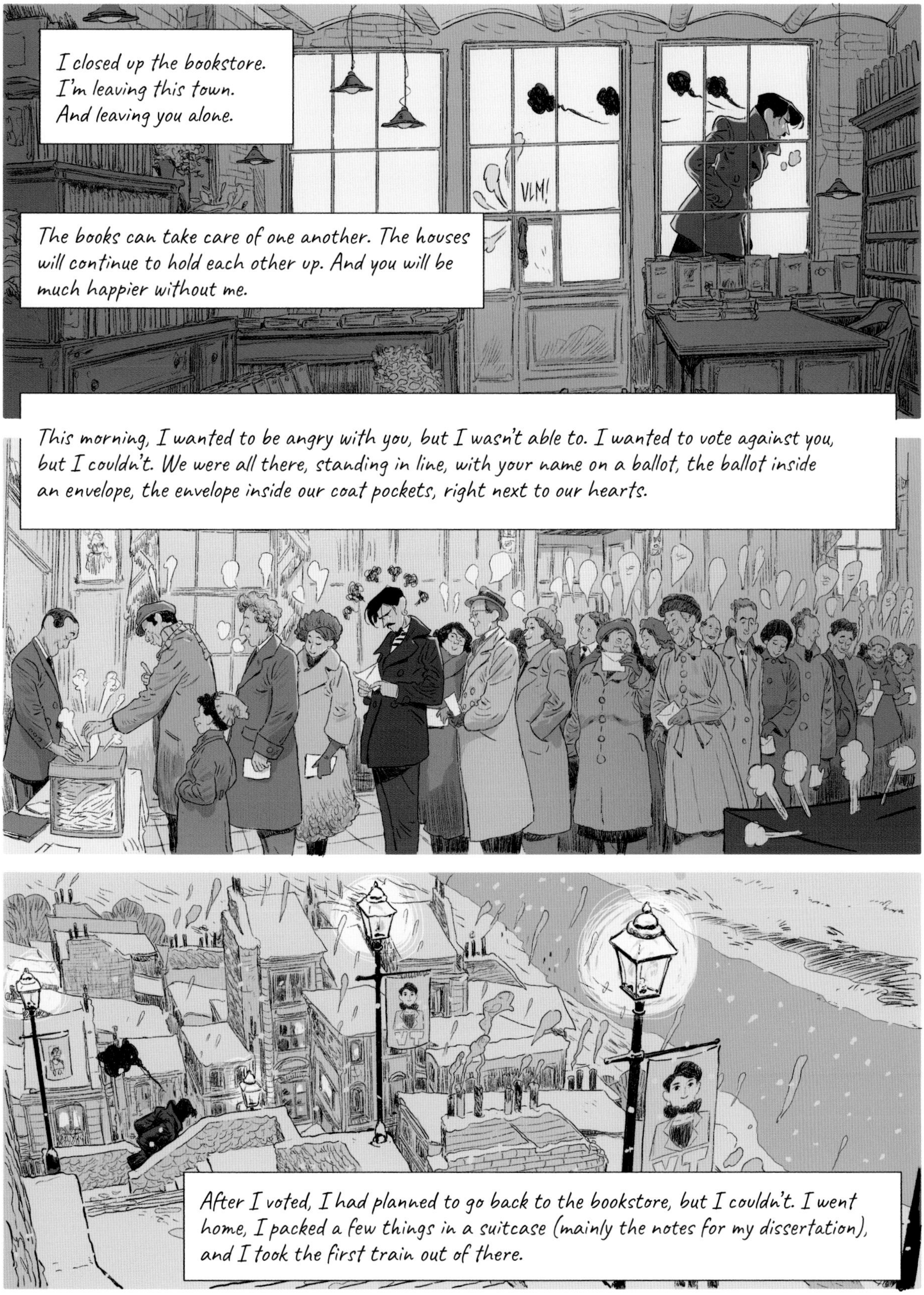
I closed up the bookstore.
I'm leaving this town.
And leaving you alone.
VLM!
The books can take care of one another. The houses will continue to hold each other up. And you will be much happier without me.
This morning, I wanted to be angry with you, but I wasn't able to. I wanted to vote against you, but I couldn't. We were all there, standing in line, with your name on a ballot, the ballot inside an envelope, the envelope inside our coat pockets, right next to our hearts.
After I voted, I had planned to go back to the bookstore, but I couldn't. I went home, I packed a few things in a suitcase (mainly the notes for my dissertation), and I took the first train out of there.

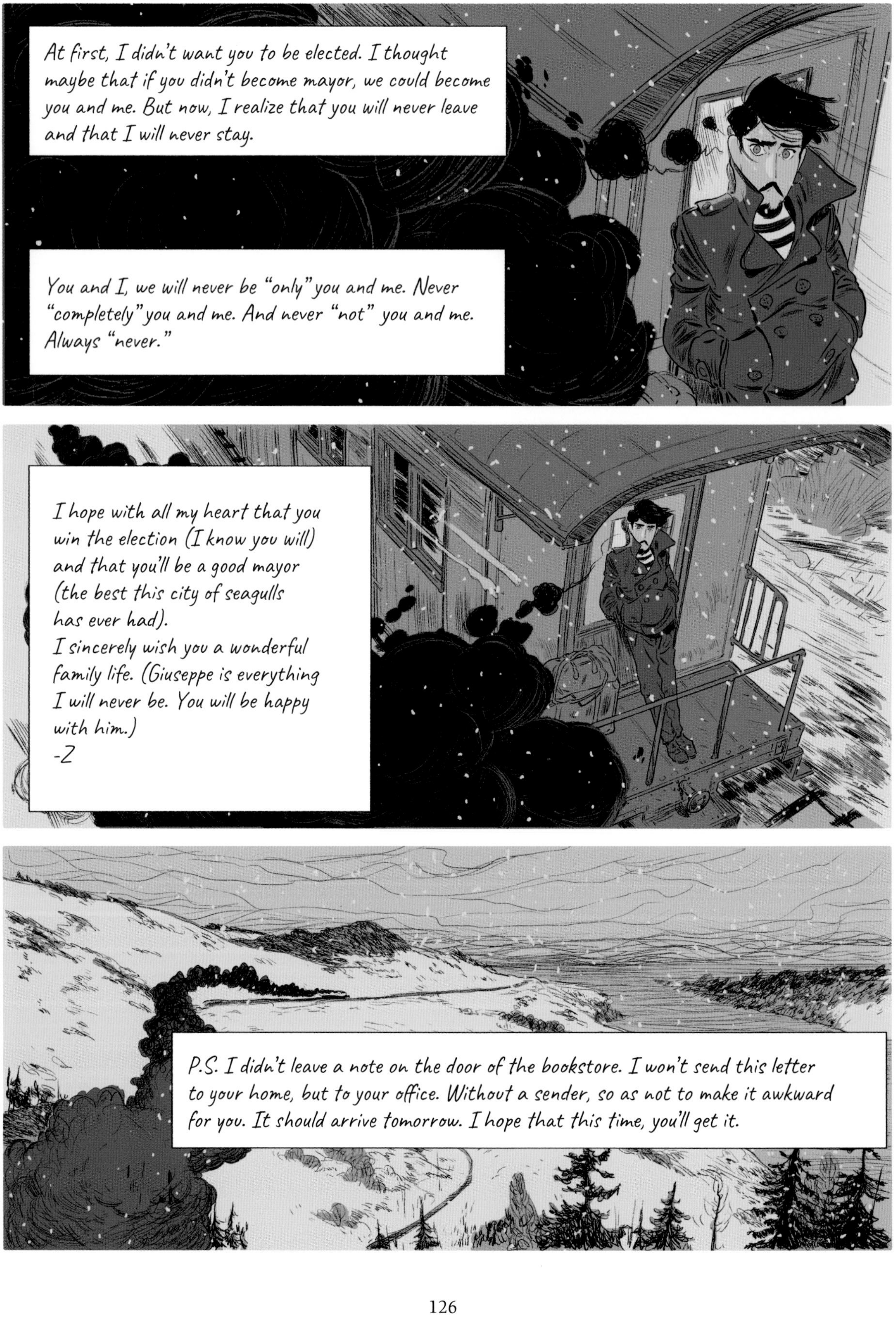
At first, I didn't want you to be elected. I thought maybe that if you didn't become mayor, we could become you and me. But now, I realize that you will never leave and that I will never stay.
You and I, we will never be "only" you and me. Never "completely" you and me. And never "not" you and me. Always "never."
I hope with all my heart that you win the election (I know you will) and that you'll be a good mayor (the best this city of seagulls has ever had).
I sincerely wish you a wonderful family life. (Giuseppe is everything I will never be. You will be happy with him.)
-Z
P.S. I didn't leave a note on the door of the bookstore. I won't send this letter to your home, but to your office. Without a sender, so as not to make it awkward for you. It should arrive tomorrow. I hope that this time, you'll get it.

CHAPTER
4

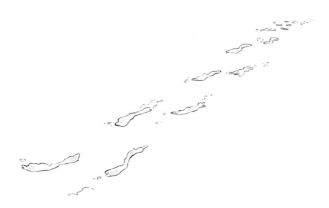

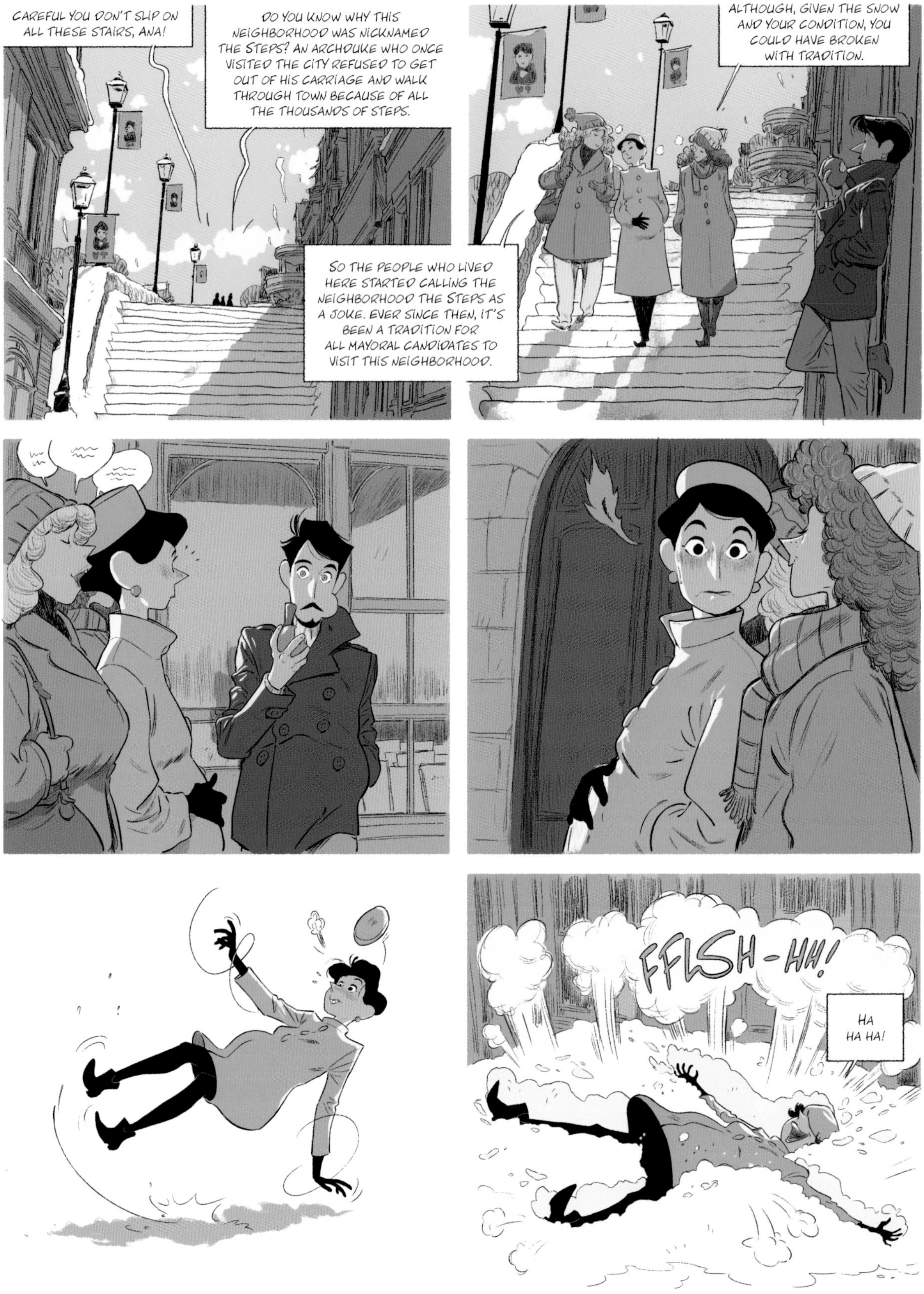

CAREFUL YOU DON'T SLIP ON ALL THESE STAIRS, ANA!
DO YOU KNOW WHY THIS NEIGHBORHOOD WAS NICKNAMED THE STEPS? AN ARCHDUKE WHO ONCE VISITED THE CITY REFUSED TO GET OUT OF HIS CARRIAGE AND WALK THROUGH TOWN BECAUSE OF ALL THE THOUSANDS OF STEPS.
SO THE PEOPLE WHO LIVED HERE STARTED CALLING THE NEIGHBORHOOD THE STEPS AS A JOKE. EVER SINCE THEN, IT'S BEEN A TRADITION FOR ALL MAYORAL CANDIDATES TO VISIT THIS NEIGHBORHOOD.
ALTHOUGH, GIVEN THE SNOW AND YOUR CONDITION, YOU COULD HAVE BROKEN WITH TRADITION.
FFLSH-HH!
HA HA HA!

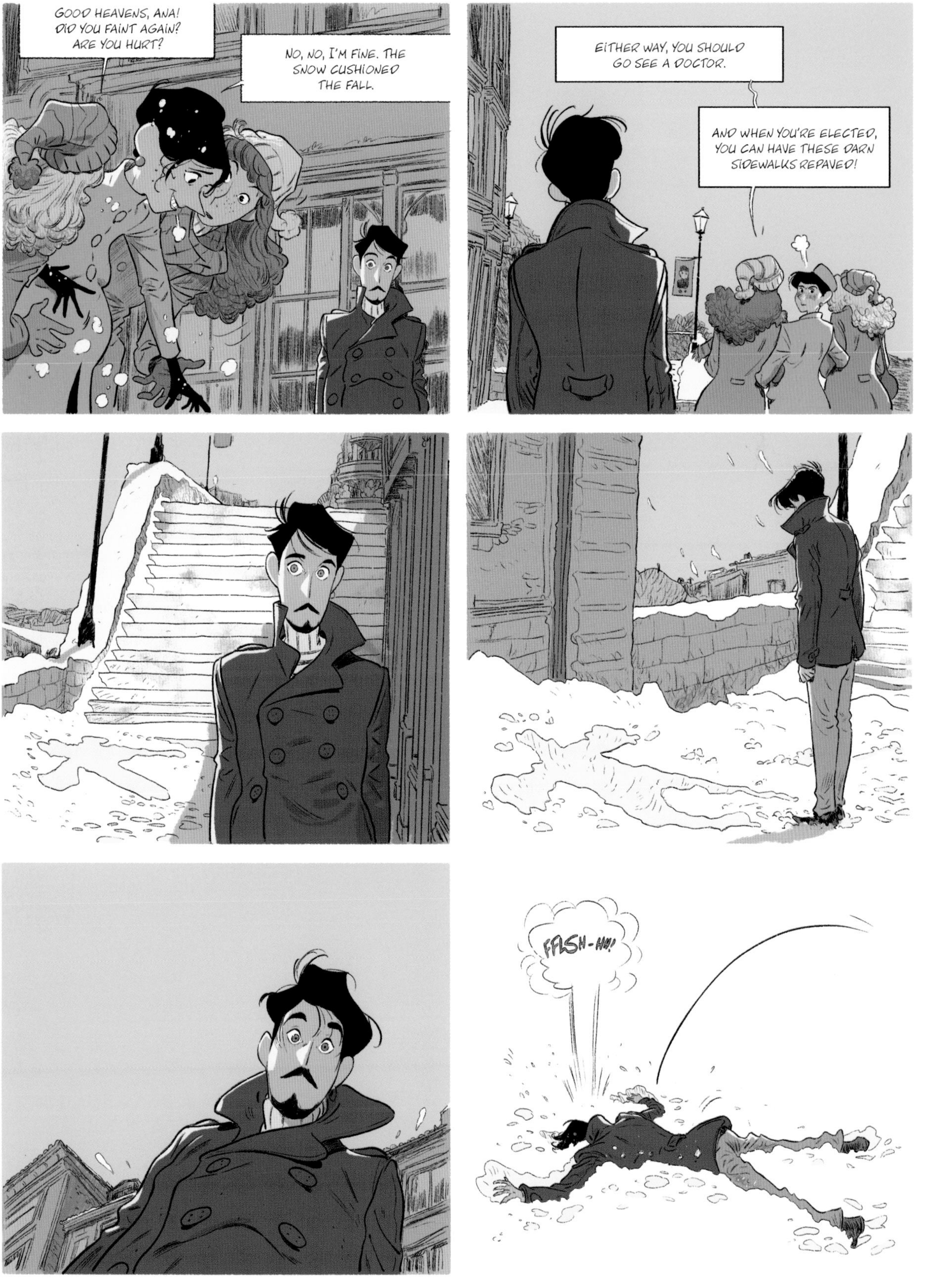
GOOD HEAVENS, ANA! DID YOU FAINT AGAIN? ARE YOU HURT?
NO, NO, I'M FINE. THE SNOW CUSHIONED THE FALL.
EITHER WAY, YOU SHOULD GO SEE A DOCTOR.
AND WHEN YOU'RE ELECTED, YOU CAN HAVE THESE DARN SIDEWALKS REPAVED!
FFLSH-HH!

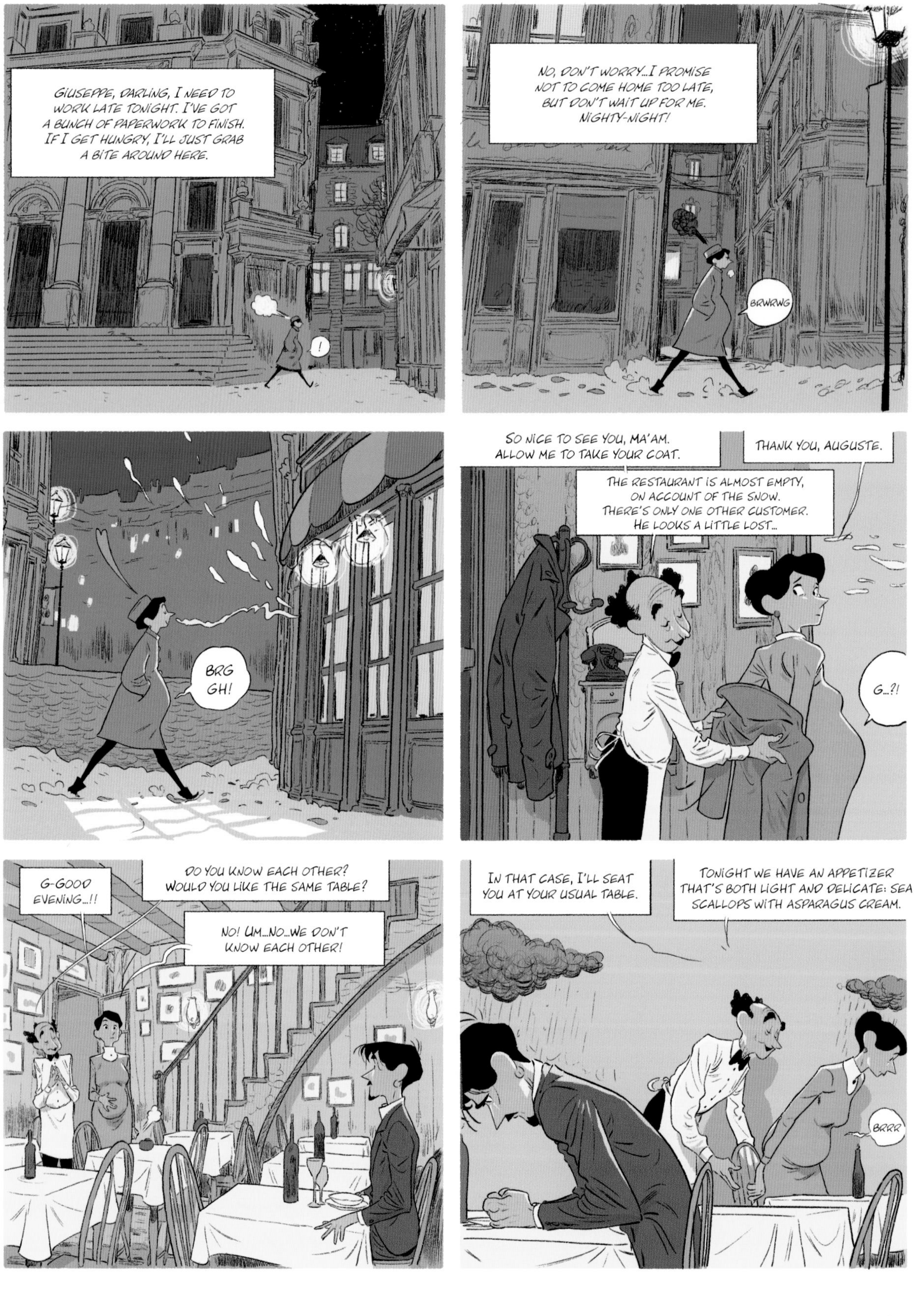
GIUSEPPE, DARLING, I NEED TO WORK LATE TONIGHT. I'VE GOT A BUNCH OF PAPERWORK TO FINISH. IF I GET HUNGRY, I'LL JUST GRAB A BITE AROUND HERE.
!
NO, DON'T WORRY...I PROMISE NOT TO COME HOME TOO LATE, BUT DON'T WAIT UP FOR ME. NIGHTY-NIGHT!
BRWRWG
BRG GH!
SO NICE TO SEE YOU, MA'AM. ALLOW ME TO TAKE YOUR COAT.
THANK YOU, AUGUSTE.
THE RESTAURANT IS ALMOST EMPTY, ON ACCOUNT OF THE SNOW. THERE'S ONLY ONE OTHER CUSTOMER. HE LOOKS A LITTLE LOST...
G...?!
G-GOOD EVENING...!!
DO YOU KNOW EACH OTHER? WOULD YOU LIKE THE SAME TABLE?
NO! UM...NO...WE DON'T KNOW EACH OTHER!
IN THAT CASE, I'LL SEAT YOU AT YOUR USUAL TABLE.
TONIGHT WE HAVE AN APPETIZER THAT'S BOTH LIGHT AND DELICATE: SEA SCALLOPS WITH ASPARAGUS CREAM.
BRRR

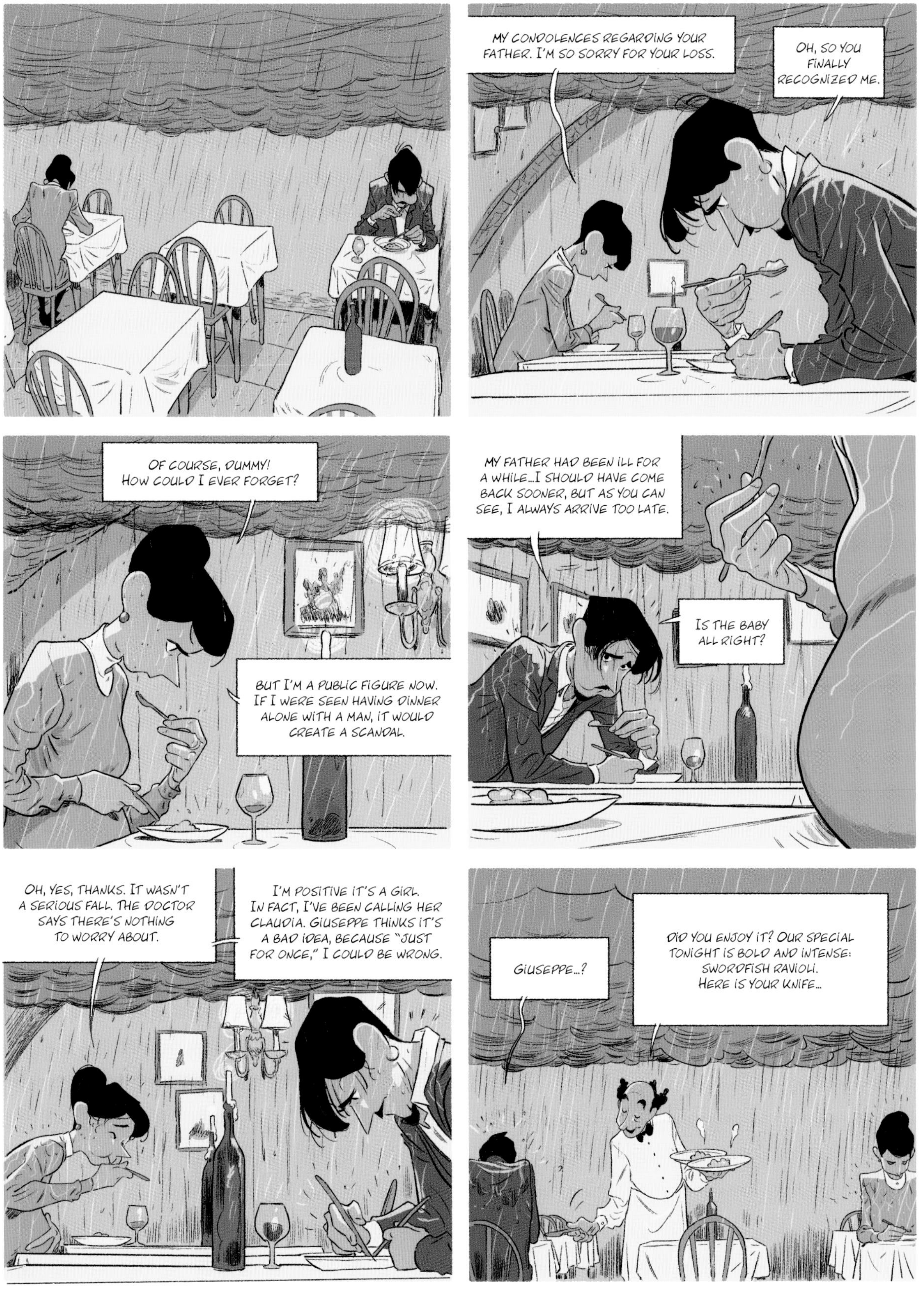
MY CONDOLENCES REGARDING YOUR FATHER. I'M SO SORRY FOR YOUR LOSS.
OH, SO YOU FINALLY RECOGNIZED ME.
OF COURSE, DUMMY! HOW COULD I EVER FORGET?
BUT I'M A PUBLIC FIGURE NOW. IF I WERE SEEN HAVING DINNER ALONE WITH A MAN, IT WOULD CREATE A SCANDAL.
MY FATHER HAD BEEN ILL FOR A WHILE...I SHOULD HAVE COME BACK SOONER, BUT AS YOU CAN SEE, I ALWAYS ARRIVE TOO LATE.
IS THE BABY ALL RIGHT?
OH, YES, THANKS. IT WASN'T A SERIOUS FALL. THE DOCTOR SAYS THERE'S NOTHING TO WORRY ABOUT.
I'M POSITIVE IT'S A GIRL. IN FACT, I'VE BEEN CALLING HER CLAUDIA. GIUSEPPE THINKS IT'S A BAD IDEA, BECAUSE "JUST FOR ONCE," I COULD BE WRONG.
GIUSEPPE...?
DID YOU ENJOY IT? OUR SPECIAL TONIGHT IS BOLD AND INTENSE: SWORDFISH RAVIOLI. HERE IS YOUR KNIFE...

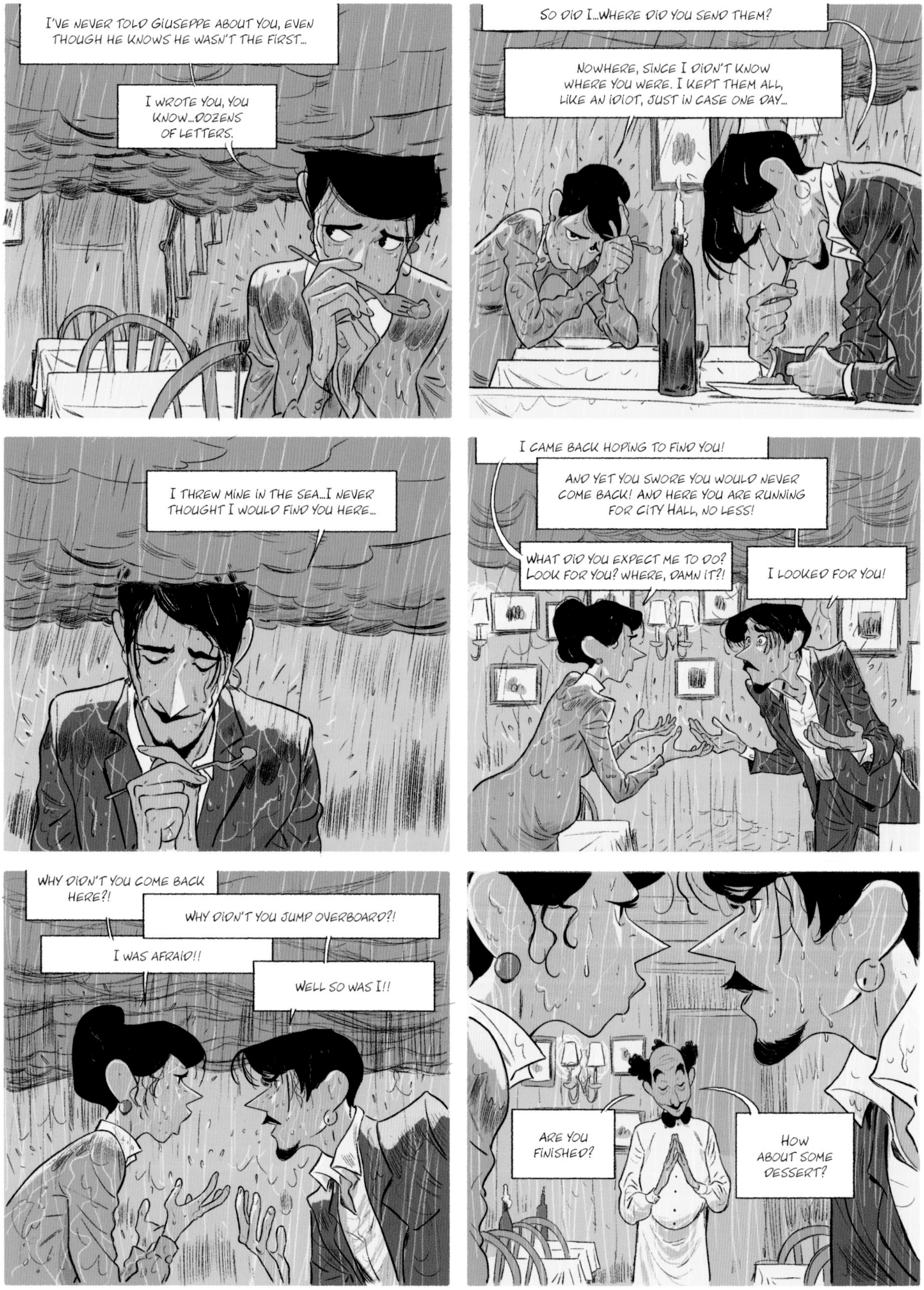
I'VE NEVER TOLD GIUSEPPE ABOUT YOU, EVEN THOUGH HE KNOWS HE WASN'T THE FIRST...
I WROTE YOU, YOU KNOW...DOZENS OF LETTERS.
SO DID I...WHERE DID YOU SEND THEM?
NOWHERE, SINCE I DIDN'T KNOW WHERE YOU WERE. I KEPT THEM ALL, LIKE AN IDIOT, JUST IN CASE ONE DAY...
I THREW MINE IN THE SEA...I NEVER THOUGHT I WOULD FIND YOU HERE...
I CAME BACK HOPING TO FIND YOU!
AND YET YOU SWORE YOU WOULD NEVER COME BACK! AND HERE YOU ARE RUNNING FOR CITY HALL, NO LESS!
WHAT DID YOU EXPECT ME TO DO? LOOK FOR YOU? WHERE, DAMN IT?!
I LOOKED FOR YOU!
WHY DIDN'T YOU COME BACK HERE?!
WHY DIDN'T YOU JUMP OVERBOARD?!
I WAS AFRAID!!
WELL SO WAS I!!
ARE YOU FINISHED?
HOW ABOUT SOME DESSERT?

CHAPTER
3

I DON'T WANT TO GO. I HATE FUNERALS.

OF COURSE YOU WANT TO GO. DANTE WAS YOUR FRIEND. NOW GET YOUR BUTT OUT OF THAT HORRIBLE ARMCHAIR, WE'RE LATE.

ANA, WHEN YOU TAKE OVER THIS OFFICE, YOU'LL HAVE TO FIND YOURSELF A NEW SOFA, BECAUSE I INTEND TO TAKE THESE CHAIRS WITH ME. I'VE GROWN ATTACHED TO THEM OVER THE YEARS.

I HAVE TO BE ELECTED FIRST, MR. XAVIER.

YOU WILL, NO QUESTION ABOUT IT! YOU WILL BE THE MAYOR OF THIS CITY FOR AS LONG AS YOU WANT.

MY DEAR ANA, XAVIER HAS TOLD ME SO MUCH ABOUT YOU. TWO DIPLOMAS, A SEAT AS MEMBER OF PARLIAMENT...

THIS GIRL IS A RARE FIND! SHE'S DESTINED TO ACHIEVE GREAT THINGS!

SO YOUNG AND ALREADY SO BRILLIANT! WHAT'S YOUR SECRET?

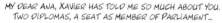

I'VE NEVER BEEN VERY GOOD AT BEING IDLE.

I'LL TELL YOU HER SECRET: SHE SPENDS ALL HER NIGHTS WORKING!

I'M NOT VERY GOOD AT GETTING SLEEP, EITHER.

XAVIER USED TO SPEND LONG NIGHTS AT THE OFFICE TOO. BUT OVER TIME, HE GREW LAZY. NOWADAYS, HE GOES TO BED WITH THE CHICKENS.

LAZY, ME?!

AND ON THE NIGHTS HE STAYED LATE AT WORK, IT WAS WITH A DIFFERENT KIND OF CHICK....

THAT'S NOT TRUE!

OF COURSE IT IS! WHAT WAS THE NAME OF THAT CHICK WHO OWNED THE BAR AND GRILL?

I HAVE NO IDEA WHAT YOU'RE TALKING ABOUT...

134

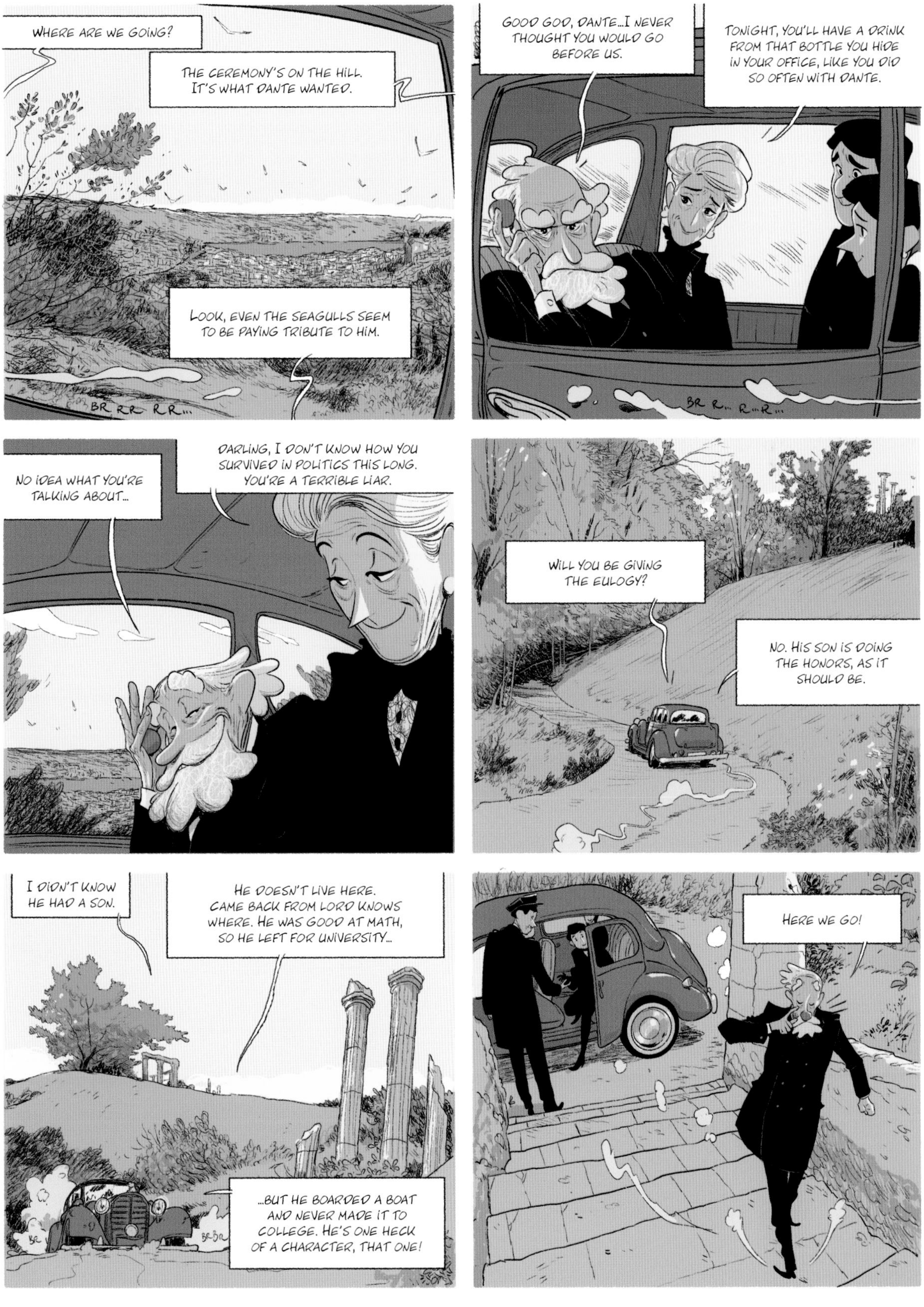
WHERE ARE WE GOING?
THE CEREMONY'S ON THE HILL. IT'S WHAT DANTE WANTED.
LOOK, EVEN THE SEAGULLS SEEM TO BE PAYING TRIBUTE TO HIM.
BR RR RR...
GOOD GOD, DANTE... I NEVER THOUGHT YOU WOULD GO BEFORE US.
TONIGHT, YOU'LL HAVE A DRINK FROM THAT BOTTLE YOU HIDE IN YOUR OFFICE, LIKE YOU DID SO OFTEN WITH DANTE.
BR R... R...R...
NO IDEA WHAT YOU'RE TALKING ABOUT...
DARLING, I DON'T KNOW HOW YOU SURVIVED IN POLITICS THIS LONG. YOU'RE A TERRIBLE LIAR.
WILL YOU BE GIVING THE EULOGY?
NO. HIS SON IS DOING THE HONORS, AS IT SHOULD BE.
I DIDN'T KNOW HE HAD A SON.
HE DOESN'T LIVE HERE. CAME BACK FROM LORD KNOWS WHERE. HE WAS GOOD AT MATH, SO HE LEFT FOR UNIVERSITY...
...BUT HE BOARDED A BOAT AND NEVER MADE IT TO COLLEGE. HE'S ONE HECK OF A CHARACTER, THAT ONE!
BR
BR BR
HERE WE GO!

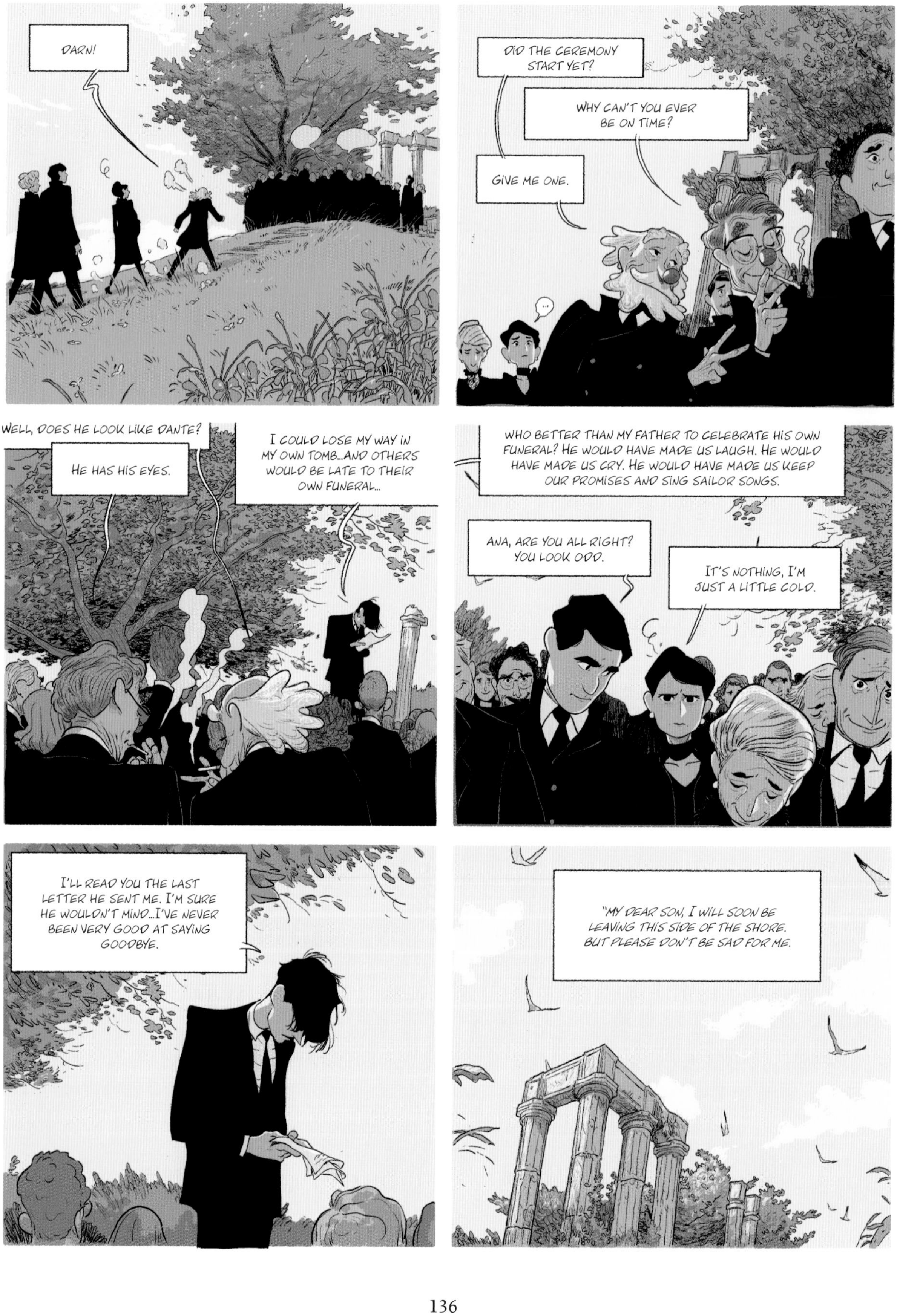
DARN!
DID THE CEREMONY START YET?
WHY CAN'T YOU EVER BE ON TIME?
GIVE ME ONE.
...
WELL, DOES HE LOOK LIKE DANTE?
HE HAS HIS EYES.
I COULD LOSE MY WAY IN MY OWN TOMB...AND OTHERS WOULD BE LATE TO THEIR OWN FUNERAL...
WHO BETTER THAN MY FATHER TO CELEBRATE HIS OWN FUNERAL? HE WOULD HAVE MADE US LAUGH. HE WOULD HAVE MADE US CRY. HE WOULD HAVE MADE US KEEP OUR PROMISES AND SING SAILOR SONGS.
ANA, ARE YOU ALL RIGHT? YOU LOOK ODD.
IT'S NOTHING, I'M JUST A LITTLE COLD.
I'LL READ YOU THE LAST LETTER HE SENT ME. I'M SURE HE WOULDN'T MIND...I'VE NEVER BEEN VERY GOOD AT SAYING GOODBYE.
"MY DEAR SON, I WILL SOON BE LEAVING THIS SIDE OF THE SHORE. BUT PLEASE DON'T BE SAD FOR ME.

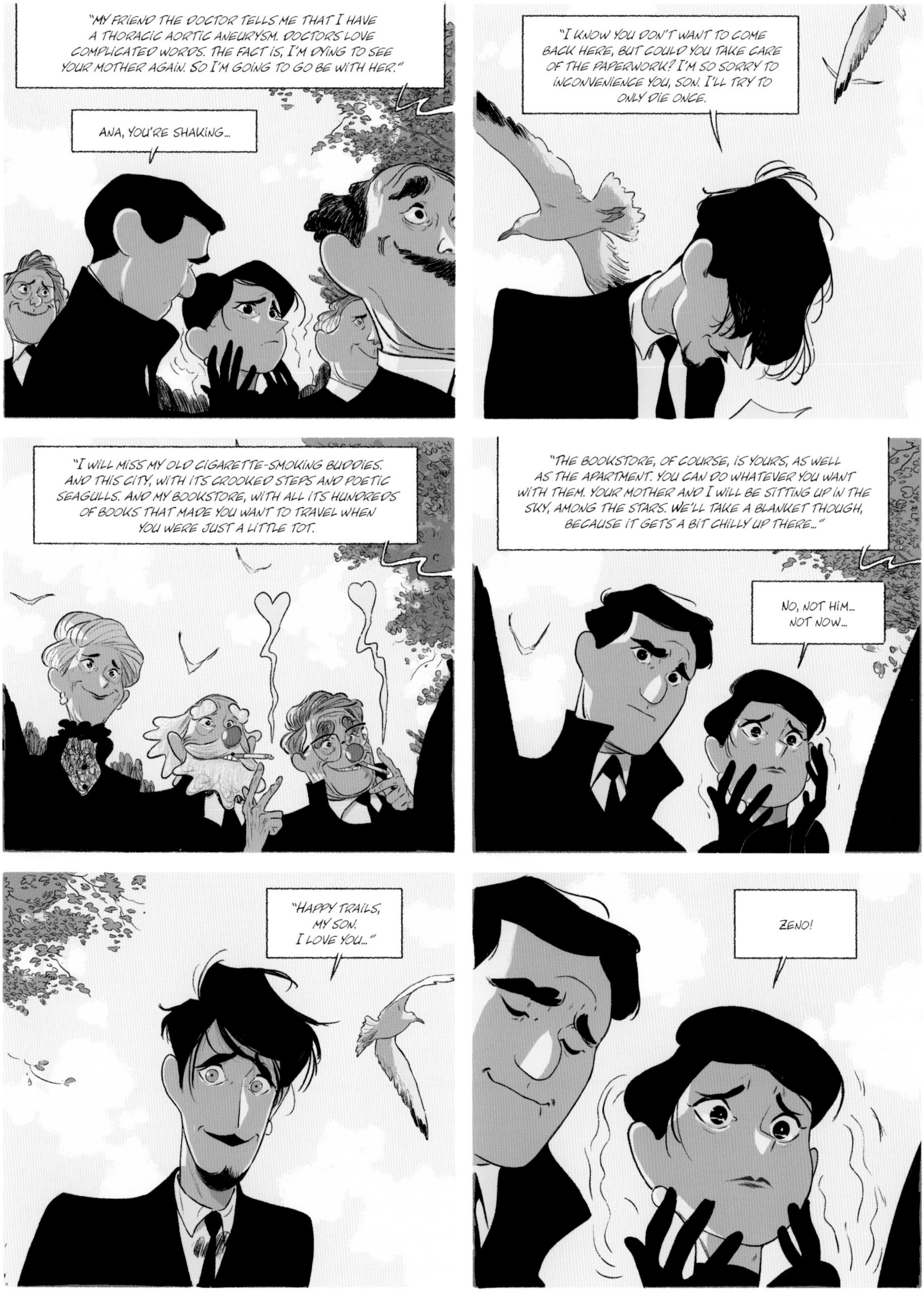
"MY FRIEND THE DOCTOR TELLS ME THAT I HAVE A THORACIC AORTIC ANEURYSM. DOCTORS LOVE COMPLICATED WORDS. THE FACT IS, I'M DYING TO SEE YOUR MOTHER AGAIN. SO I'M GOING TO GO BE WITH HER."
ANA, YOU'RE SHAKING...
"I KNOW YOU DON'T WANT TO COME BACK HERE, BUT COULD YOU TAKE CARE OF THE PAPERWORK? I'M SO SORRY TO INCONVENIENCE YOU, SON. I'LL TRY TO ONLY DIE ONCE.
"I WILL MISS MY OLD CIGARETTE-SMOKING BUDDIES. AND THIS CITY, WITH ITS CROOKED STEPS AND POETIC SEAGULLS. AND MY BOOKSTORE, WITH ALL ITS HUNDREDS OF BOOKS THAT MADE YOU WANT TO TRAVEL WHEN YOU WERE JUST A LITTLE TOT.
"THE BOOKSTORE, OF COURSE, IS YOURS, AS WELL AS THE APARTMENT. YOU CAN DO WHATEVER YOU WANT WITH THEM. YOUR MOTHER AND I WILL BE SITTING UP IN THE SKY, AMONG THE STARS. WE'LL TAKE A BLANKET THOUGH, BECAUSE IT GETS A BIT CHILLY UP THERE..."
NO, NOT HIM... NOT NOW...
"HAPPY TRAILS, MY SON. I LOVE YOU..."
ZENO!

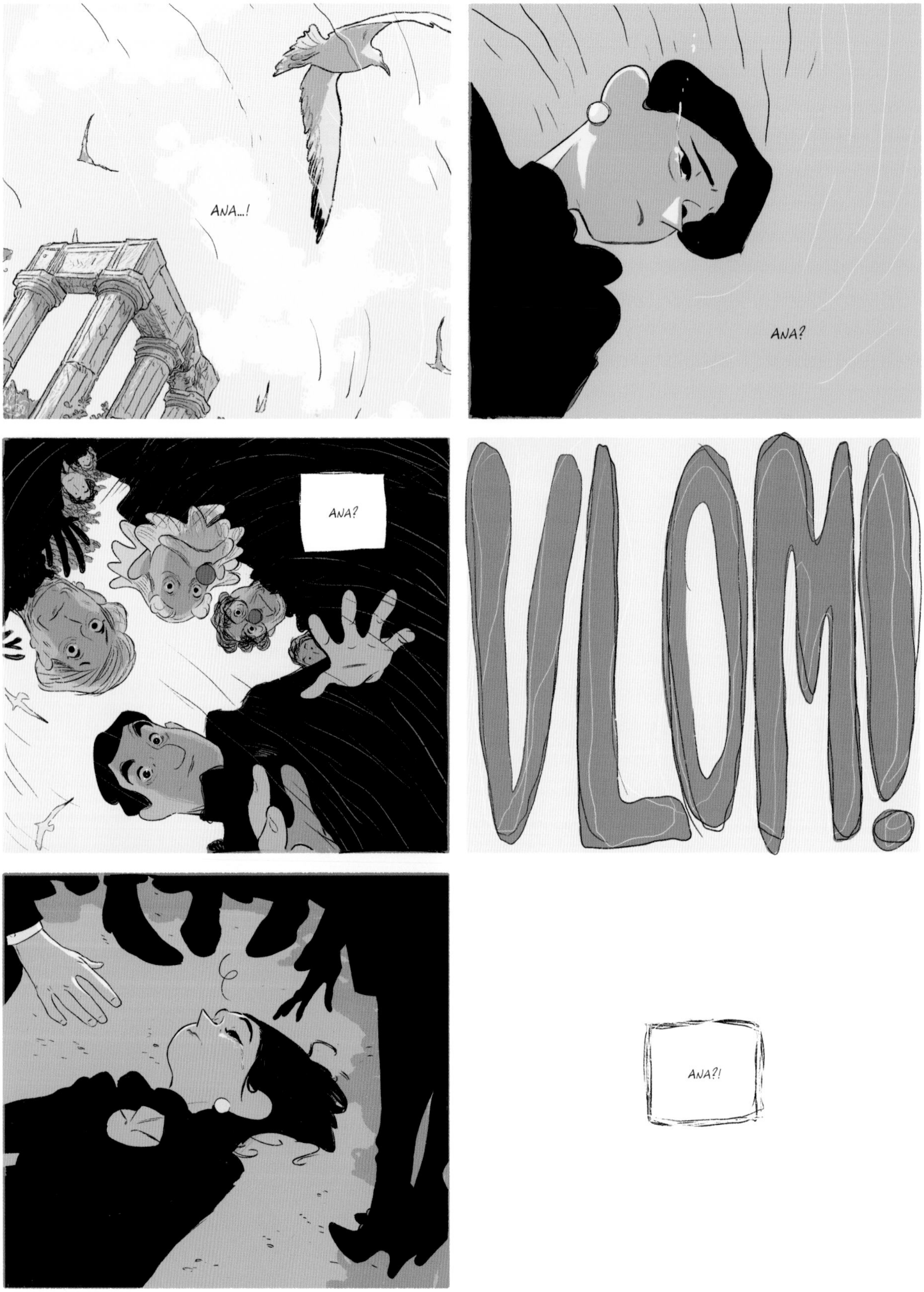
ANA...!
ANA?
ANA?
VLOM!
ANA?!

CHAPTER
2

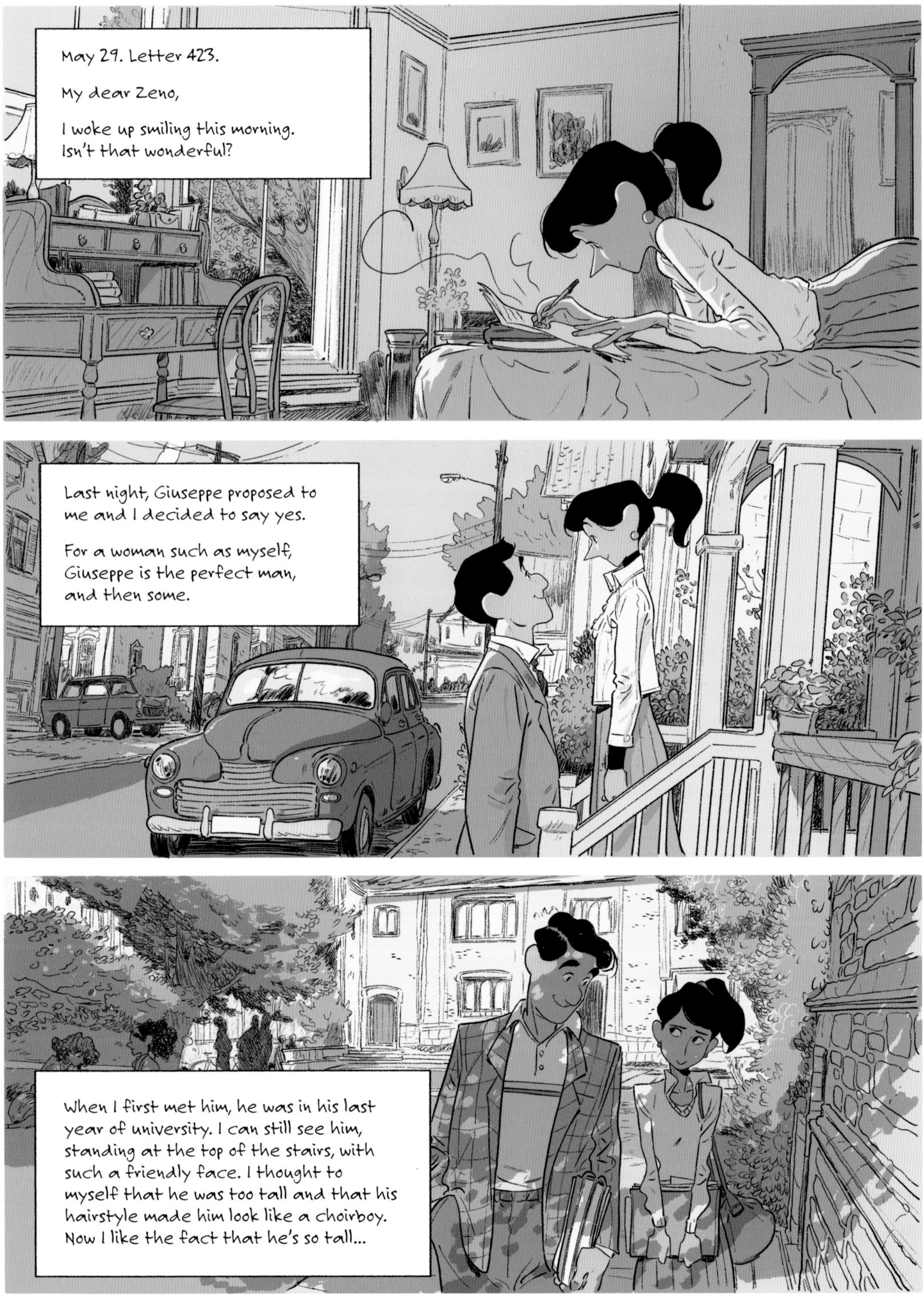
May 29. Letter 423.
My dear Zeno,
I woke up smiling this morning. Isn't that wonderful?
Last night, Giuseppe proposed to me and I decided to say yes.
For a woman such as myself, Giuseppe is the perfect man, and then some.
When I first met him, he was in his last year of university. I can still see him, standing at the top of the stairs, with such a friendly face. I thought to myself that he was too tall and that his hairstyle made him look like a choirboy. Now I like the fact that he's so tall...

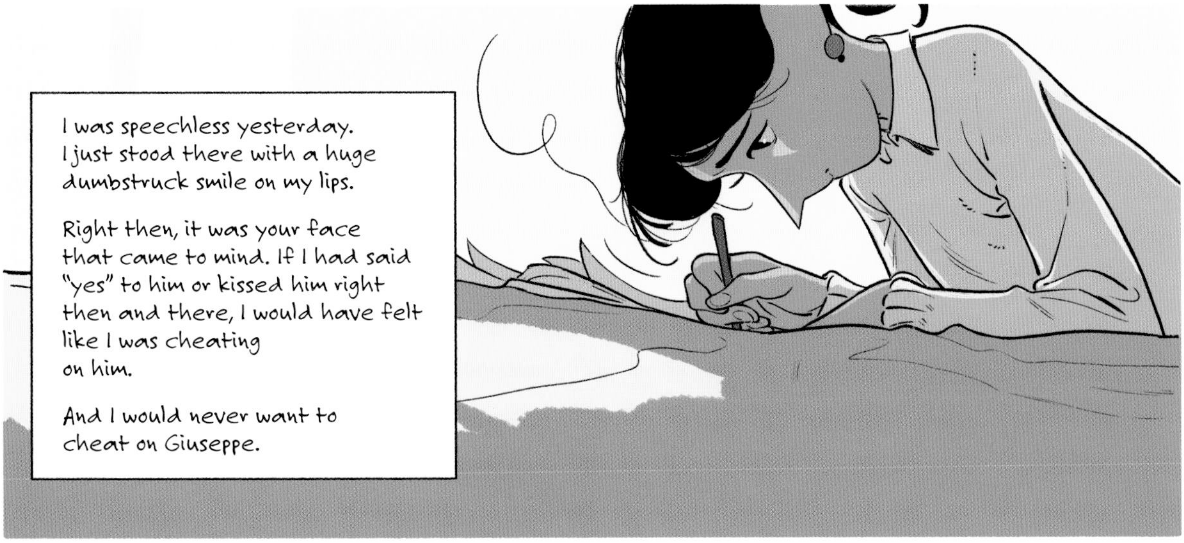
I was speechless yesterday. I just stood there with a huge dumbstruck smile on my lips.
Right then, it was your face that came to mind. If I had said "yes" to him or kissed him right then and there, I would have felt like I was cheating on him.
And I would never want to cheat on Giuseppe.

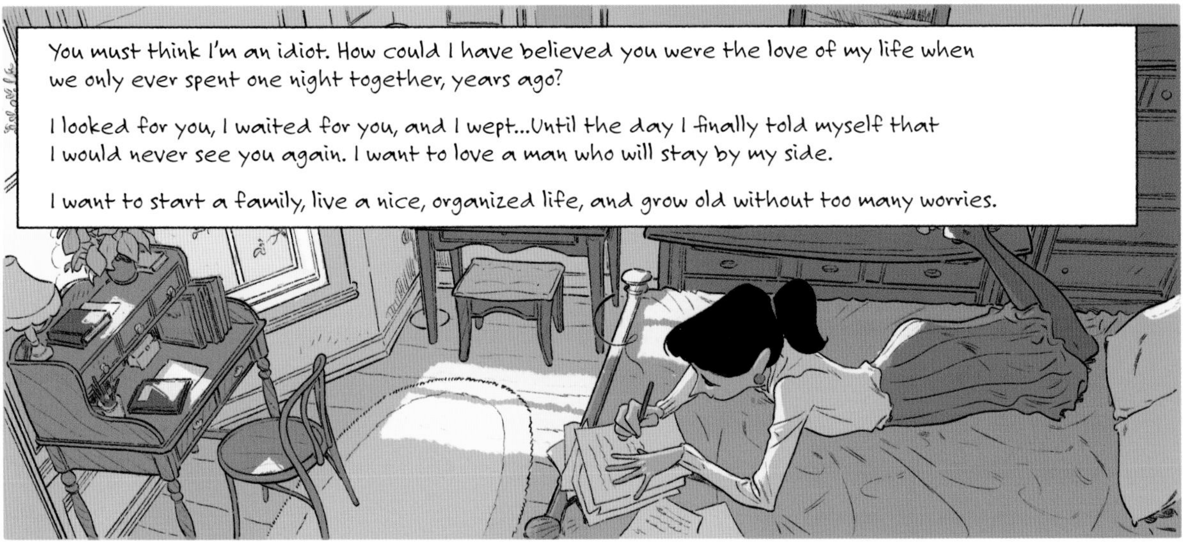
You must think I'm an idiot. How could I have believed you were the love of my life when we only ever spent one night together, years ago?
I looked for you, I waited for you, and I wept...Until the day I finally told myself that I would never see you again. I want to love a man who will stay by my side.
I want to start a family, live a nice, organized life, and grow old without too many worries.

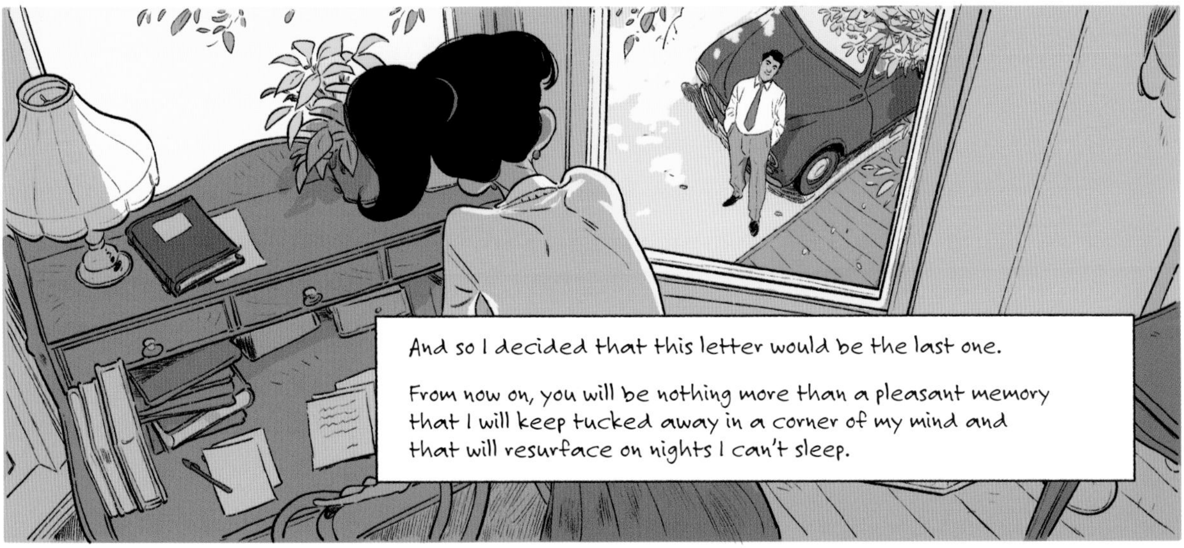
And so I decided that this letter would be the last one.
From now on, you will be nothing more than a pleasant memory that I will keep tucked away in a corner of my mind and that will resurface on nights I can't sleep.

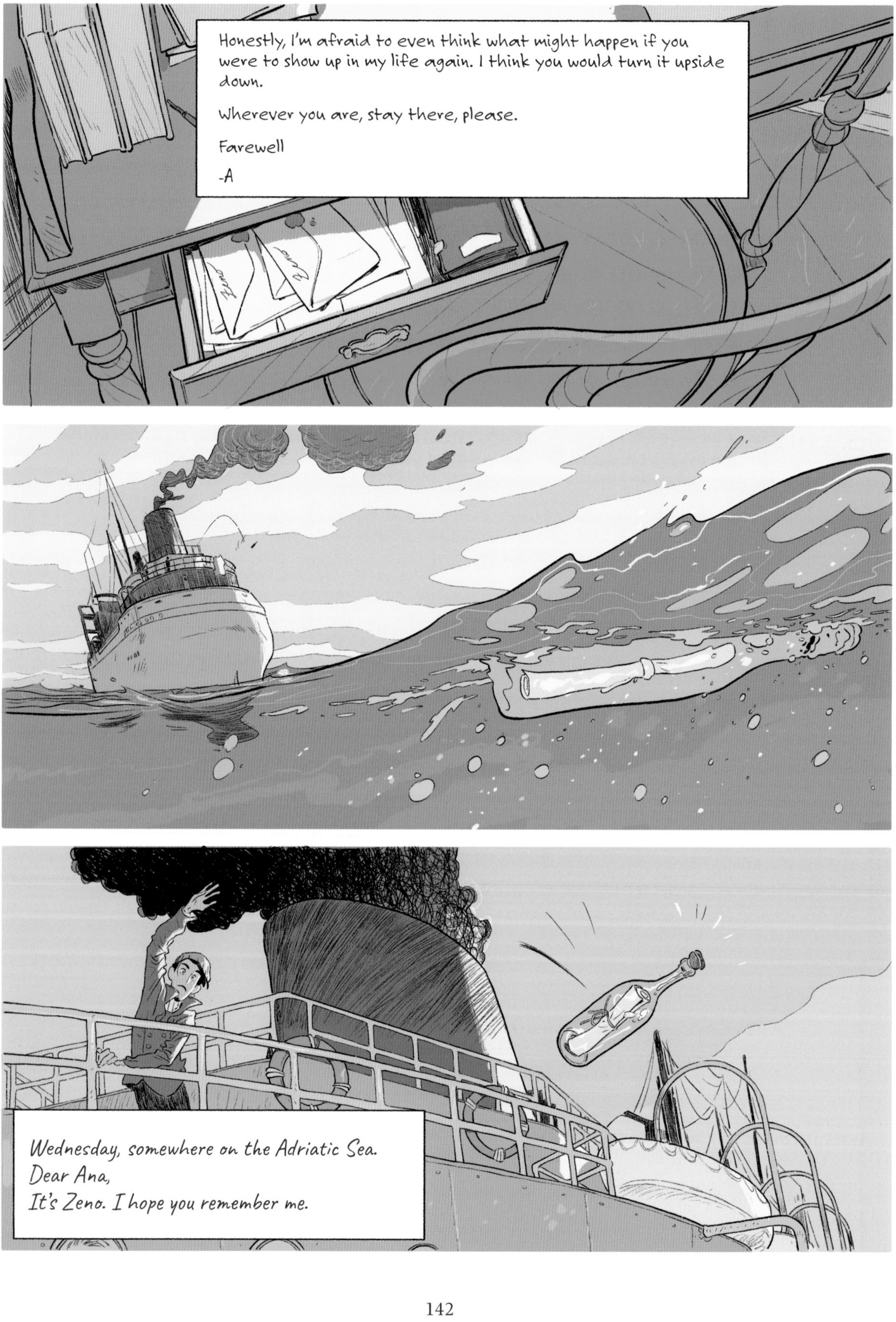
Honestly, I'm afraid to even think what might happen if you were to show up in my life again. I think you would turn it upside down.
Wherever you are, stay there, please.
Farewell
-A
Wednesday, somewhere on the Adriatic Sea.
Dear Ana,
It's Zeno. I hope you remember me.

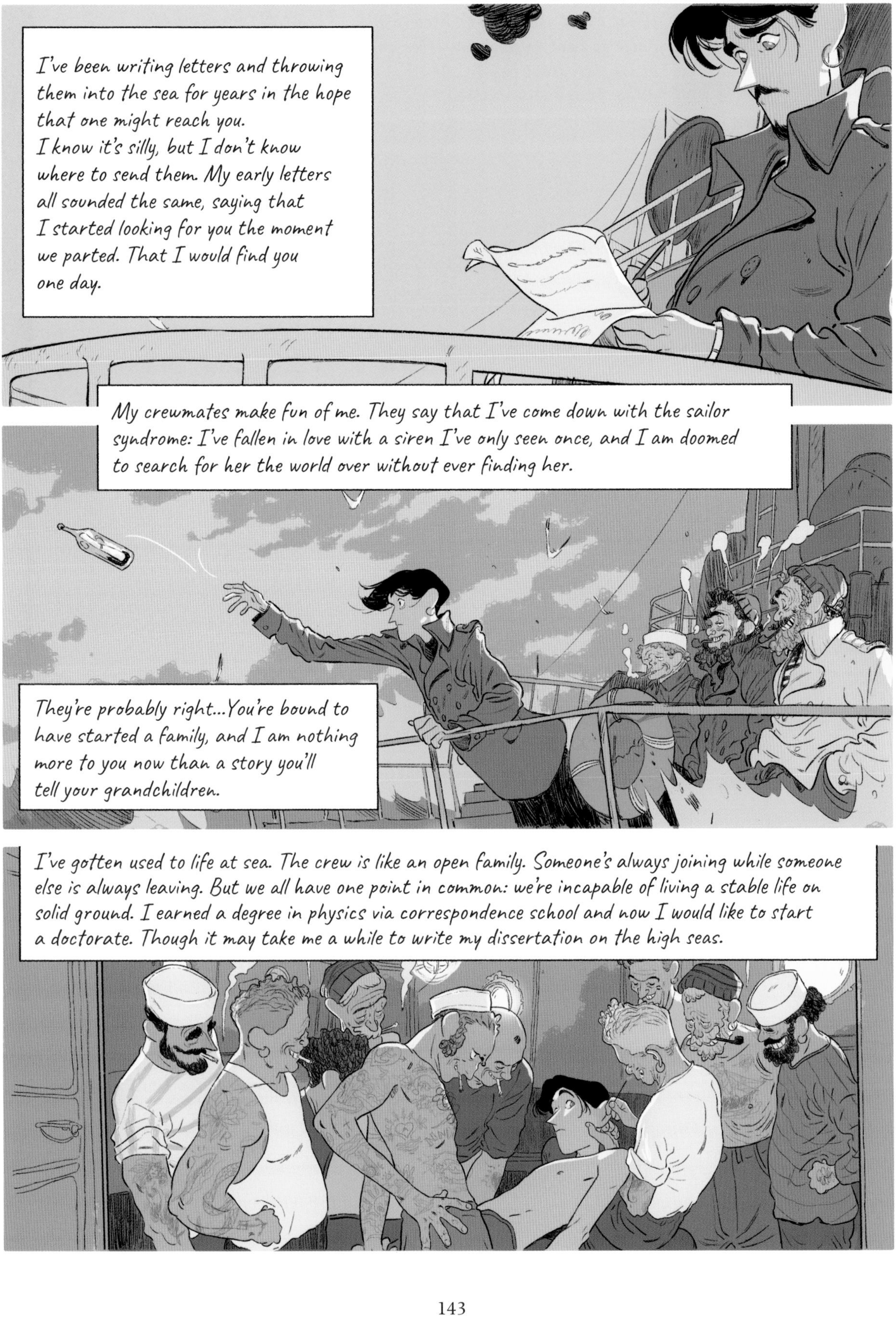
I've been writing letters and throwing them into the sea for years in the hope that one might reach you.
I know it's silly, but I don't know where to send them. My early letters all sounded the same, saying that I started looking for you the moment we parted. That I would find you one day.
My crewmates make fun of me. They say that I've come down with the sailor syndrome: I've fallen in love with a siren I've only seen once, and I am doomed to search for her the world over without ever finding her.
They're probably right...You're bound to have started a family, and I am nothing more to you now than a story you'll tell your grandchildren.
I've gotten used to life at sea. The crew is like an open family. Someone's always joining while someone else is always leaving. But we all have one point in common: we're incapable of living a stable life on solid ground. I earned a degree in physics via correspondence school and now I would like to start a doctorate. Though it may take me a while to write my dissertation on the high seas.

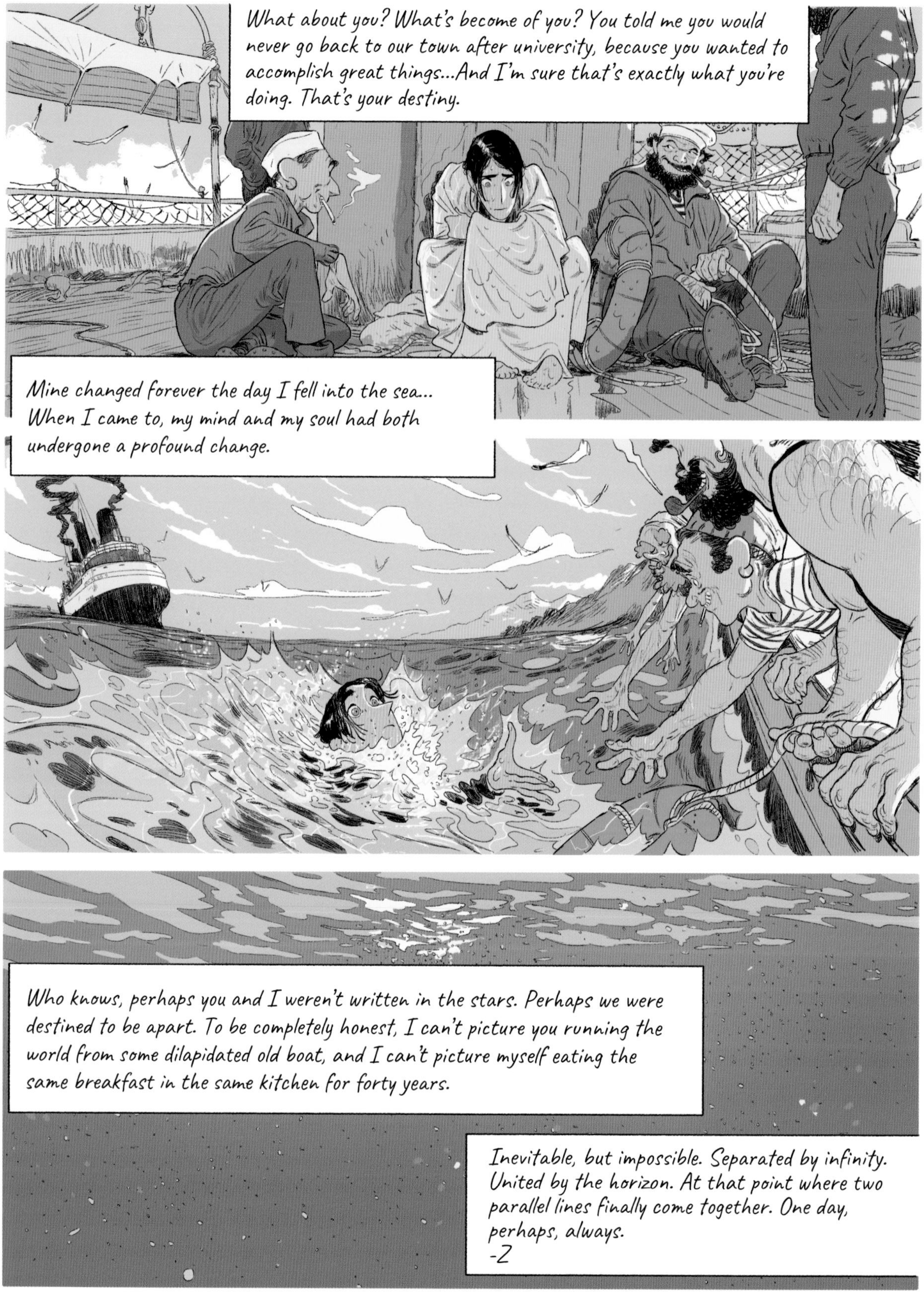
What about you? What's become of you? You told me you would never go back to our town after university, because you wanted to accomplish great things...And I'm sure that's exactly what you're doing. That's your destiny.
Mine changed forever the day I fell into the sea... When I came to, my mind and my soul had both undergone a profound change.
Who knows, perhaps you and I weren't written in the stars. Perhaps we were destined to be apart. To be completely honest, I can't picture you running the world from some dilapidated old boat, and I can't picture myself eating the same breakfast in the same kitchen for forty years.
Inevitable, but impossible. Separated by infinity. United by the horizon. At that point where two parallel lines finally come together. One day, perhaps, always.
-Z

CHAPTER
1

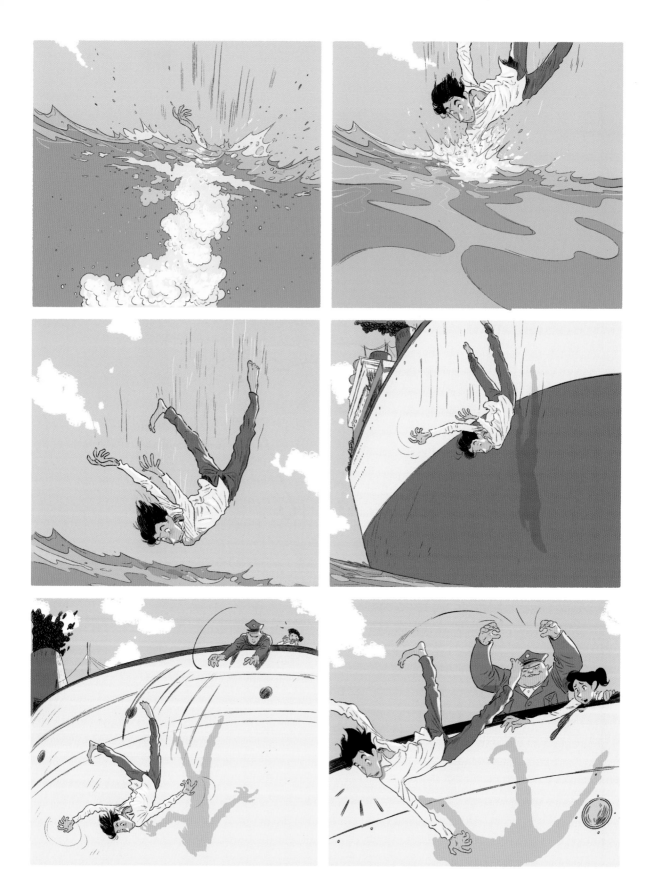

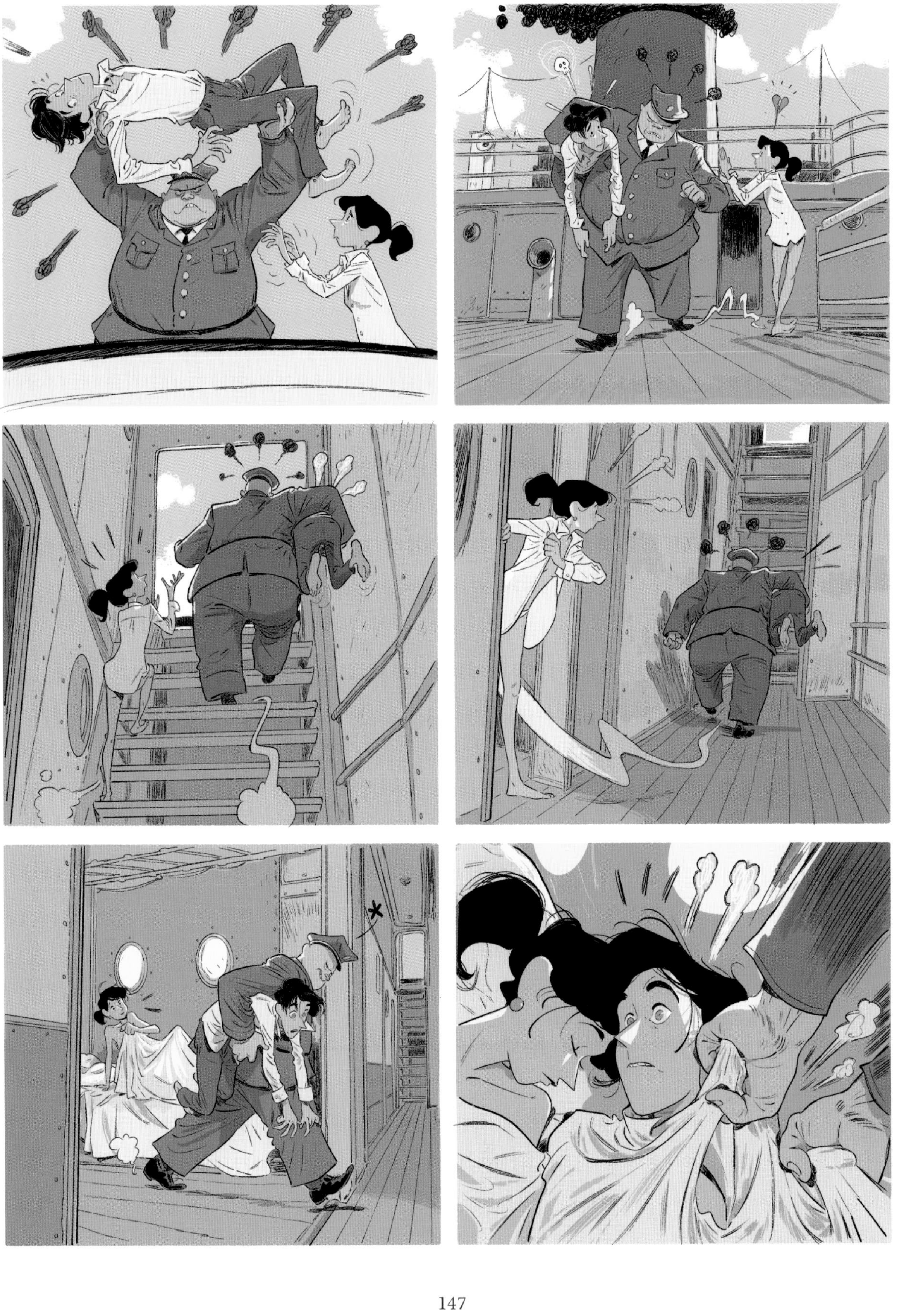

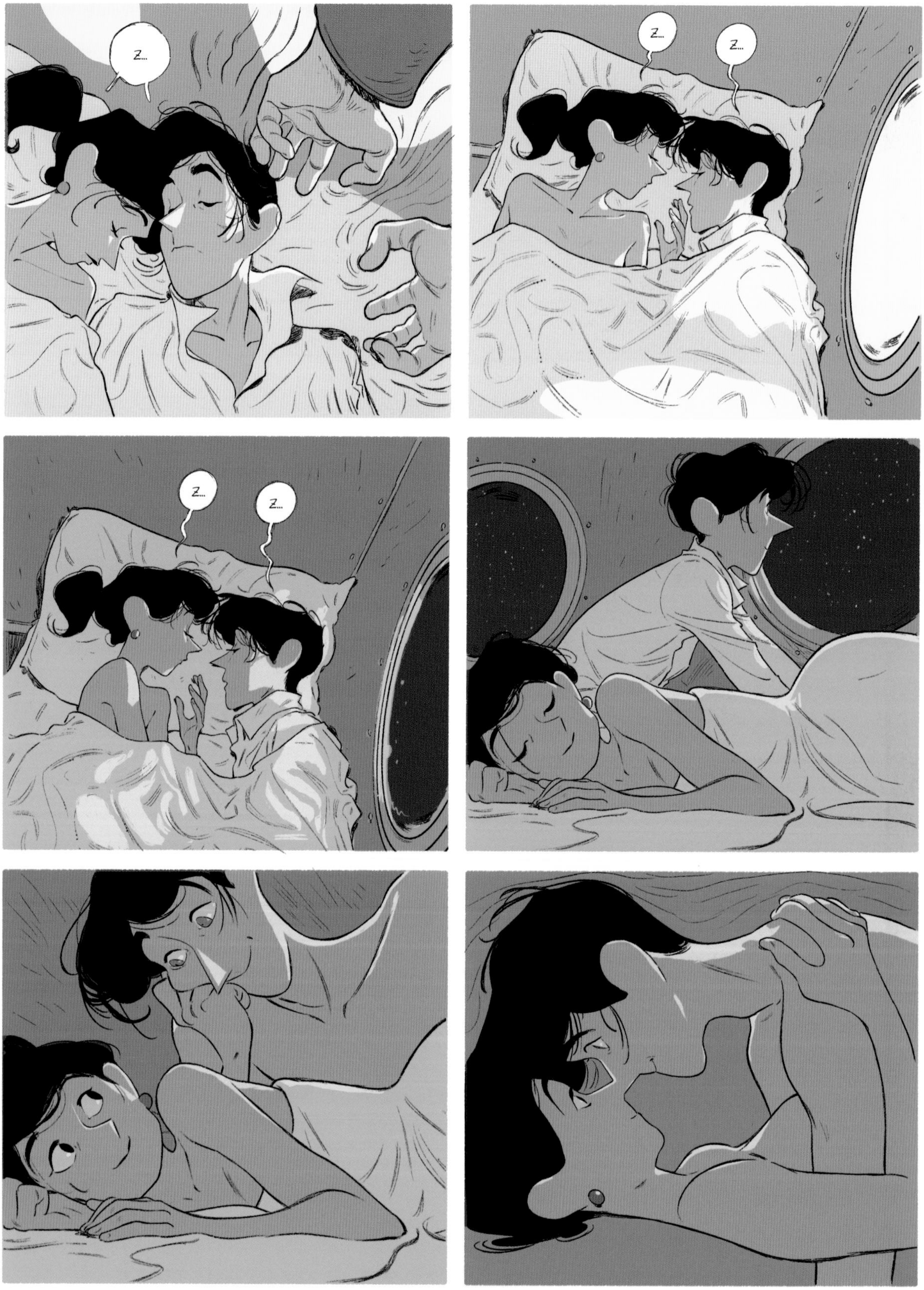
Z...
Z...
Z...
Z...
Z...

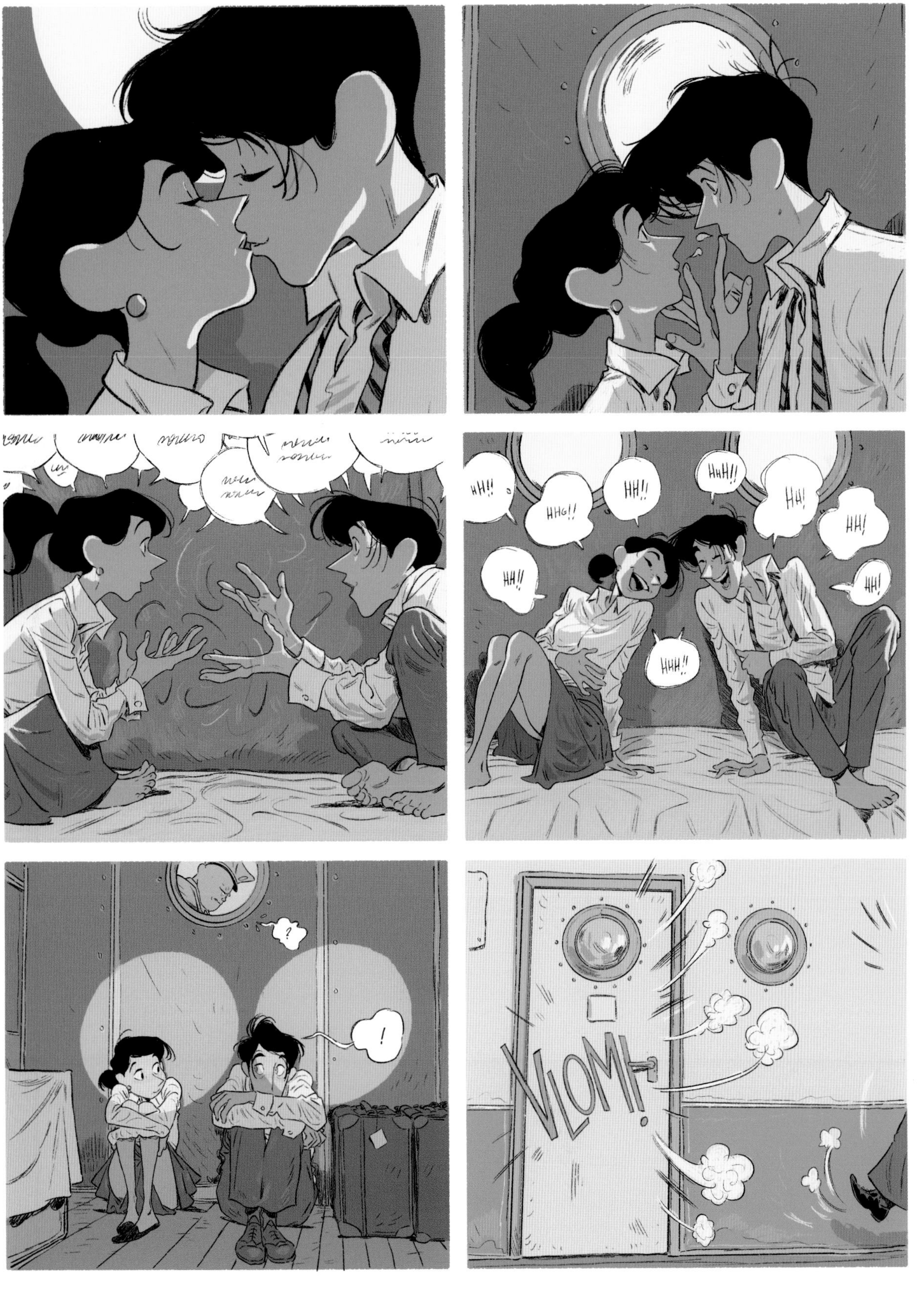
HH!!
HHG!!
HH!!
HHH!!
HH!
HH!
HH!!
HH!
HHH!!
?
!
VLOM!

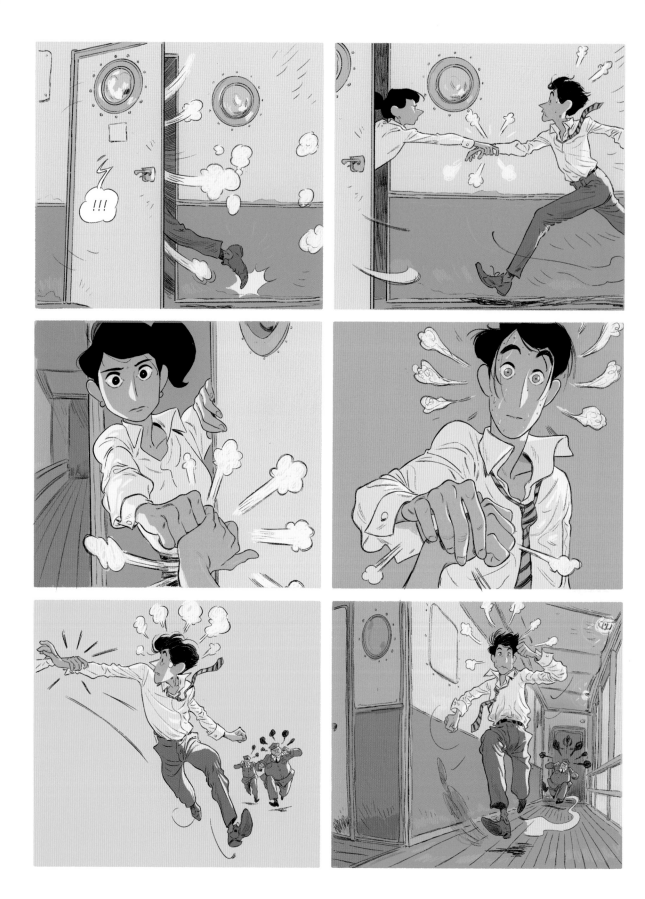

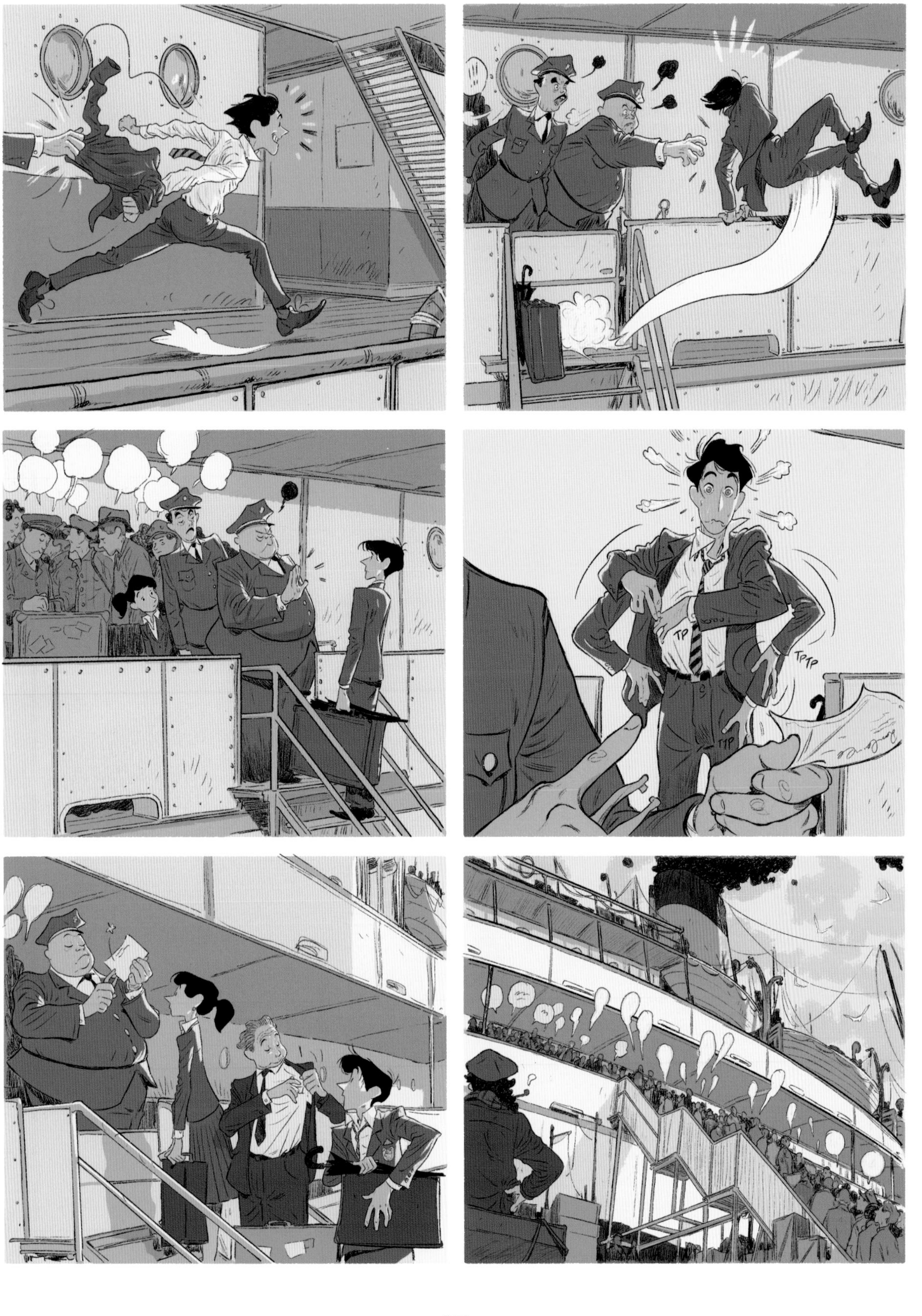
TP
TPTP